CONSCIOUSNESS AND THE SELF

"I never can catch myself at any time without a perception, and never can observe any thing but the perception." These famous words of David Hume, on his inability to perceive the self, set the stage for JeeLoo Liu and John Perry's collection of essays on self-awareness and self-knowledge. This volume connects recent scientific studies on consciousness with the traditional issues about the self explored by Descartes, Locke, and Hume. Experts in the field offer contrasting perspectives on matters such as the relation between consciousness and self-awareness, the notion of personhood, and the epistemic access to one's own thoughts, desires, or attitudes. The volume will be of interest to philosophers, psychologists, neuroscientists, cognitive scientists, and others working on the central topics of consciousness and the self.

JEELOO LIU is Associate Professor of Philosophy at California State University, Fullerton. She is the author of *An Introduction to Chinese Philosophy: From Ancient Philosophy to Chinese Buddhism* (2006).

JOHN PERRY is Emeritus Professor of Philosophy at Stanford University, and Distinguished Professor of Philosophy at the University of California, Riverside. He is the author of *Knowledge, Possibility and Consciousness* (2001), *Identity, Personal Identity and the Self* (2002), and a number of other books.

D1475167

CONSCIOUSNESS AND THE SELF: NEW ESSAYS

JEELOO LIU

and

JOHN PERRY

CAMBRIDGE
UNIVERSITY PRESS

CAMBRIDGE
UNIVERSITY PRESS

University Printing House, Cambridge CB2 8BS, United Kingdom

Published in the United States of America by Cambridge University Press, New York

Cambridge University Press is part of the University of Cambridge.

It furthers the University's mission by disseminating knowledge in the pursuit of education, learning and research at the highest international levels of excellence.

www.cambridge.org
Information on this title: www.cambridge.org/9781107414716

© Cambridge University Press 2012

First published 2012
First paperback edition 2014

A catalogue record for this publication is available from the British Library

Library of Congress Cataloguing in Publication data
Consciousness and the self : new essays / [edited by] JeeLoo Liu, John Perry.
p. cm.
ISBN 978-1-107-00075-9
1. Self-consciousness (Awareness)   I. Liu, JeeLoo.   II. Perry, John, 1943–   III. Title.
BD450.C62677   2011
126–dc23
2011028651

ISBN 978-1-107-00075-9 Hardback
ISBN 978-1-107-41471-6 Paperback

Contents

Acknowledgments

This book emerged from the 39th annual philosophy symposium on the same topic, *Consciousness and the Self*, at California State University, Fullerton, in April 2009. The symposium speakers included Alex Byrne, David Chalmers, Fred Dretske, John Perry, Jesse Prinz, Eric Schwitzgebel, and Sydney Shoemaker. The symposium was a huge success, and all speakers except for Chalmers agreed to put their papers together in a book. On this basis, I invited several other philosophers working on the issue of self-awareness and self-knowledge to join the collection: Owen Flanagan (Duke University), Uriah Kriegel (University of Arizona), Lucy O'Brien (University College London, UK), and David Rosenthal (CUNY Graduate Center). My deepest gratitude goes to all the authors who contributed their newest work written just for this collection. They have all been very supportive of this book project and have taught me a great deal through their talks, writings, and personal communications. Even though David Chalmers is not among the contributing authors, I would like to say that the whole symposium as well as this book would not have materialized if it were not for his brilliant insights and helpful input in the whole process.

I want to thank my colleagues at CSUF Philosophy Department for their support during the symposium. My *Consciousness and the Self* seminar students in Spring 2009 were an amazing bunch. They were undergraduate students who had not studied much analytic philosophy before taking my seminar, but they made a tremendous effort in learning and thinking with me and with the speakers. Several of them served as speakers or commentators at the symposium and their performance was highly impressive. I would like to acknowledge these students for their dedication to learning and their achievements: Brent Boos, Pamela Chui, Kelsey Fernandez, Nathan Lujan, Alis Rabet, Jonathan Stracker, Mimi Vong, and Sandra Woloschuk.

I am deeply indebted to my co-editor, John Perry, who has been a mentor to me ever since we first met in 2002 at the Creighton Club, a long-standing upstate New York philosophical association. Working with him on this book has been a great learning experience for me and I am honored to have had the chance to edit this book with him.

Finally, I would like to thank my beloved husband Michael Cranston, and our wonderful sons, Collin and Dillon, for always being patient with me when I was glued to my computer working away in the evenings.

JEELOO LIU

I am very grateful for the opportunity to help JeeLoo Liu in converting the symposium she organized into a book. I have thoroughly enjoyed our collaboration, and learned a great deal from paying close attention to the papers by the other authors. We both thank Hilary Gaskin and Cambridge University Press for their support.

JOHN PERRY

Contributors

ALEX BYRNE is Professor of Philosophy at Massachusetts Institute of Technology.

FRED DRETSKE is Senior Research Scholar at Duke University and Professor Emeritus of Stanford University.

OWEN FLANAGAN is James B. Duke Professor of Philosophy and Professor of Psychological and Brain Sciences at Duke University.

URIAH KRIEGEL is Associate Professor of Philosophy at the University of Arizona.

JEELOO LIU is Associate Professor of Philosophy at California State University, Fullerton.

LUCY O'BRIEN is Reader at University College London, United Kingdom.

JOHN PERRY is Professor of Philosophy at the University of California, Riverside and Henry W. Stuart Professor of Philosophy (Emeritus) at Stanford University.

JESSE PRINZ is Distinguished Professor of Philosophy at the City University of New York Graduate Center.

DAVID ROSENTHAL is Professor of Philosophy and Coordinator of Interdisciplinary Concentration in Cognitive Science at the City University of New York Graduate Center.

ERIC SCHWITZGEBEL is Professor of Philosophy at the University of California, Riverside.

SYDNEY SHOEMAKER is Professor Emeritus of Philosophy at Cornell University, where he was Susan Linn Sage Professor before retirement.

Introduction

JeeLoo Liu

In our everyday activities, the self is ever-present in the back of our minds. We remember what we did the moment before and we think about what we want to do next; we feel happy and energetic, or bored and tired; we have a sense of our goals when we act; we think about what we would like to eat for dinner and we know what our favorite TV show is. In our interactions with others, we think about how they see us, whether they like us or are impressed by us. We have certain emotions related to this keen awareness of ourselves: we feel embarrassed, remorseful, ashamed, proud, or confident because of things we have done or did not do. We see ourselves as continuous in time: what happened to us in the past affects who we are and what we believe now; we make plans for the future because we believe that the future self will be us and will be affected by our current plan and behavior. Even though we do not have an internal mirror to see ourselves, our every thought seems to revolve around the sense of a self. But what is the self? How is our sense of the self established in the first place?

The title of this book is *Consciousness and the Self*. The main focus of the collected essays is not to establish a metaphysical claim about the existence or the nature of the self, but to investigate the connection between our conscious life and our sense of the self; in other words, the *phenomenological* routes to the self. Whether or not we can establish the existence of a self, we undeniably have a sense of our self in our daily conscious life, in our reflections, sensations, discourses, memories, and our life plans. Phenomenally, I know *what it is like to be me*, and no one else can have my phenomenal awareness of my self. My self and my awareness of myself seem essentially intertwined.

Descartes' famous *cogito, ergo sum* points out the necessary presence of a self in consciousness: The *I* necessarily exists as the subject of thinking. It is a thinking thing embodied in the act of thinking itself. Descartes says, "So after considering everything very thoroughly, I must finally conclude that this proposition, I am, I exist, is necessarily true whenever it is put forward by me or conceived in my mind" (Descartes [1641] 1984, 17). The *I* is essential to consciousness; all thinking requires a thinker. If I reflect on my act of thinking, then I know that there must be an *I* doing the thinking. Descartes' argument can be interpreted as deriving certainty of the second-order self-reflective thought on the first-order thinking. The certainty is only established for *synchronic* unity in thinking – at each single moment of thinking, I know that I exist as the thinker.

John Locke, however, emphasizes the *diachronic* unity of the self in all our conscious moments:

When we see, hear, smell, taste, feel, meditate, or will anything, we know that we do so. Thus it is always as to our present sensations and perceptions: and by this every one is to himself that which he calls self: – it not being considered, in this case, whether the same self be continued in the same or diverse substances. For, since consciousness always accompanies thinking, and it is that which makes every one to be what he calls self, and thereby distinguishes himself from all other thinking things, in this alone consists personal identity, i.e. the sameness of a rational being, and as far as this consciousness can be extended backwards to any past action or thought, so far reaches the identity of that person; it is the same self now it was then; and it is by the same self with this present one that now reflects on it, that that action was done. (Locke [1689] 1975, 335)

In this passage, Locke sums up the connection between consciousness and the self: *consciousness is that which makes up the self* – both the presence of the self in occurrent conscious moments, and the persistence of the self in consciousness extended backwards in time. Self-consciousness is essential to personhood, and personal identity is grounded on one's memories or ownership of past deeds: *I was the one who did this*. The ascription of a past life to oneself is based on the assumption of a self that persists from the past to the present. Such persistence of the self, according to Locke, is sustained in consciousness alone, wherever that consciousness resides – whether in a single immaterial substance, or a succession of immaterial substances, or even, as he was willing to consider, in the brain, a succession of complexes of material substances.

Nevertheless, David Hume raises skepticism about our ability to perceive the self. Hume says,

All [our particular perceptions] are different, and distinguishable, and separable from each other, and may be separately considered, and may exist separately, and have no need of any thing to support their existence. After what manner therefore do they belong to self, and how are they connected with it? For my part, when I enter most intimately into what I call myself, I always stumble on some particular perception or other, of heat or cold, light or shade, love or hatred, pain or pleasure.

I never can catch myself at any time without a perception, and never can observe any thing but the perception. (Hume [1739] 2000, 252)

Hume's skepticism is about our supposedly intimate consciousness of what we call "the self." He holds that for any real idea, there must be a preceding impression from which one derives the idea. However, our impressions are of our constantly changing perceptions, sensations, passions and emotions, and the like. We do not have such an impression of an everlasting self, persisting through all these changing impressions. If we do not have an impression of the self, then we cannot be said to have a clear idea of the self. The mind is like a kind of theater, according to Hume, "where several perceptions successively make their appearance; pass, repass, glide away, and mingle in an infinite variety of postures and situations" (Hume [1739] 2000, 253). There is nothing unified, invariable and persistent behind all these perceptions that we can call "the self."

Hume's comment points out a paradoxical double role that the self plays in self-awareness: the self as the *subject* and the self as the *object*. According to Ludwig Wittgenstein, there are two different uses of the word 'I': "the use as object" and "the use as subject." When the word 'I' is used to pick out a particular person of which a description can be judged to be true or false, as in "I have a bump on my forehead," it is used as object; on the other hand, when 'I' is used to report a sense of agency, as in "I think it will rain," it is used as subject (Wittgenstein [1958] 1969, 66–67). In self-awareness or self-knowledge, both uses seem to be present. "*I* believe that *I* am the tallest person in the class"; "*I* know that *I* am not sad about her departure." How can there be two selves indicated in these self-reports, or is it just one self who knows, perceives, thinks about, or is aware of, *the same self*? How can the same self be both the knower and the known?

Hume's claim can be taken to be a rejection of the self as an object of knowledge, or a rejection of any such unified entity as *the self*. Both rejections have their defenders. In *Notebooks*, Wittgenstein exclaims: "The I is not an object. I objectively confront every object. But not the I" (Wittgenstein 1984, 80e). In *Beyond Good and Evil*, Nietzsche questions the Cartesian certainty in deducing the existence of an *I* from the act of thinking: "The philosopher must say to himself, 'When I dismantle the process which is expressed in the sentence "I think," I come upon a series of daring assertions whose grounding is difficult, perhaps impossible – for example, that *I* am the one who thinks, that there must be some general something that thinks, that thinking is an action and effect of a being which is to be thought of as a cause, that there is an "I."' ..." (Nietzsche [1886]

2009, Part 1, 16). Nietzsche also questions the unity of consciousness: "we always have only a semblance of unity" (Nietzsche [1901] 1968, 489). His hypothesis of the self is "the subject as multiplicity": the subject *I* is merely the sum of multiple perspectives, interpretations, and drives. Our customary use of the first-person word 'I' may have begun as a mere historical accident of grammatical habits of separating a subject and a predicate in our sentences, which later created an illusion that there really is a *self* to which we can refer.

In contemporary analytic philosophy, Daniel Dennett represents the skeptical, eliminativist view of a single self as the subject in consciousness. Based on current neuroscientific discoveries, Dennett argues against what he calls "the Cartesian Theater model." The Cartesian Theater model projects a single self as the observer of one's flow of consciousness, the *I* who is both the Cartesian thinker and the one who engages in self-inquiry. However, Dennett argues, neuroscience has discovered that "there is no single point in the brain where all information funnels in," and "there is no observer inside the brain" (Dennett 1992, 103). The correct picture of our consciousness is to think of parallel information processing tracks in the brain, producing constantly revised "drafts" that interpret and reinterpret what we are experiencing. Hence, we do not have a single narrative of our conscious life that belongs to a single agent; what we have instead are multiple drafts undergoing continuous "editorial revision."

While there are some contemporary analytic philosophers, like Dennett, who are skeptical of the self, there are far more who affirm its existence and seek to clarify its nature. Sydney Shoemaker (1986) agrees with Hume that there is no such thing as an introspective sense impression of the self. He argues that introspection involves relational knowledge that stands between an act and an object, but the self, being a mental *subject*, cannot itself be the object of introspective awareness. In other words, the self as the *I* cannot at the same time be the *me* of the same self. However, the word 'I' is more fundamentally used as subject than as object, according to Shoemaker. 'I' refers to the subject of statements and each person's system of reference has the person himself as an "anchoring point" (Shoemaker 1968, 567). Roderick Chisholm (1969) argues that Hume's mistake begins with his using "perception" as a mode of self-awareness, since the self is not supposed to be a perceivable object, but *that which* sees, hears, loves, or hates. He also points out that Hume's argument is self-defeating because in Hume's self-report, there was already an *I* who "stumble[s] on some particular perception or other, of heat or cold, light or shade, love or hatred, pain or pleasure" (Hume [1739] 2000, 252). This Hume-person who made the discovery is the subject *I* who apprehends all these perceptions in Hume's self-report. Therefore, that very Humean denial already proves an awareness of the self as subject. Even if the *I* cannot be an object of introspection, perception, or awareness, the *I as subject* seems indispensable.

Not only must there be an *I* who is the doer of deeds and the thinker of thoughts, but also there must be an unmistakable *I*, since an erroneous identification of the self is impossible. Wittgenstein argues that when 'I' is used as subject, there is no possibility of error in self-identification. If I say "I have a toothache," for example, it would be impossible that "I should have mistaken another person for myself" (Wittgenstein [1958] 1969, 67). Shoemaker (1968) also argues that when we use the word 'I' as the subject of our statements, we do not need to go through an identification process through which we identify ourselves as having the properties asserted in those statements. The reason is twofold: first, if we have to identify the self through some descriptive predicates, we must already possess a basic form of self-knowledge that we have these identifying features; second, identification goes with the possibility of misidentification, but in the case of the self, there is no possibility of misidentification. Therefore, basic self-knowledge is not based on identification of the self. For Shoemaker, self-knowledge or self-awareness comes in the form of self-predication: when one ascribes some particular predicates to oneself, such as "am hungry," "see a garden in front of me," "feel sad," "am in pain," one manifests self-knowledge or self-awareness. Shoemaker calls these special predicates *P**-predicates, "each of which can be known to be instantiated in such a way that knowing it to be instantiated in that way is equivalent to knowing it to be instantiated in oneself" (Shoemaker 1968, 565). Shoemaker argues that the self-ascription of these *P**-predicates is *immune to error through misidentification* – I cannot fail to identify *myself* when I use the word 'I' even though I could be mistaken about my beliefs about myself. If I ascribe to myself that I am in pain, for example, then I know that *I* am in pain. Self-knowledge is demonstrated in one's ability to use these *P**-predicates since using them presupposes having self-awareness. Our linguistic competence in self-ascribing *P**-predicates constitutes self-awareness.

In Shoemaker's analysis of self-knowledge, we see that self-reference is closely related to self-awareness. One could argue that our sense of the self is manifested in the linguistic usage of the first-person pronoun 'I,' which permeates our thinking and speaking. Even a person who suffers total amnesia is able to report: "*I* don't know who I am"; even a person with prosopagnosia would report, upon seeing her own image, "*I* don't recognize her." As long as a person can use the word 'I' in any statement, he or she has a sense of the self however meager the information is. As Gareth Evans claims: "the essence of self-consciousness is self-reference" (Evans 1982b, 191). Such a linguistic habit of using the first-person pronoun is not a mere "historical accident," as Nietzsche has assumed, but an inevitable development of our language because of the way we think about and talk about ourselves. Hector-Neri Castañeda argues for such inseparability between self-reference and the self: "[A] correct use of 'I' cannot fail to refer to the entity to which it purports to refer ... The first-person pronoun, without predicating a self-hood, purports to pick out a self *qua* self, and when it is correctly tendered it invariably succeeds" (Castañeda 1969, 161). Self-reference cannot fail to refer to the self, and this would then be the way to establish the self as subject. This is the classic Cartesian move, though not necessarily the Cartesian ego – an immaterial thinking substance. P. F. Strawson also claims that it seems to be "generally agreed" that an individual's use of 'I' is guaranteed against two kinds of failure: the failure of lack of reference and the failure of incorrect reference (Strawson 1994, 210).

G. E. M. Anscombe, however, disagrees. In "The first person," Anscombe argues that the word 'I' is not a referential term, and the use of 'I' does not guarantee that there is anything being referred to. She thinks that we derive a "grammatical illusion of a subject" from the seemingly self-referential nature of the first-person pronoun (Anscombe [1975] 1994, 159). Her argument can be defused by the view presented in John Perry's classic essay "The problem of the essential indexical." Perry analyzes 'I' as an essentially indexical term. An essential indexical depends on the context in which it is used to pick out the referent, and no other term could replace it without losing some of the explanatory force this term carries. The use of the first-person pronoun 'I' indicates a direct relationship between the speaker's conception and the speaker *herself*. His analysis of the referential nature of 'I' is externalistic and contextual: the usage of the 'I'-word itself, uttered by a particular speaker in a given context, secures the speaker as the referent. This view does not need to posit a Cartesian ego or any privately introspected self. Rather, it places the self in the midst of our language game and identifies the speaker as the subject. This is a self in the public sphere.

Galen Strawson (2009) points out a dual use of the word 'I' and its two associated conceptions of the self *as subject*: "when I think and talk about myself, my reference sometimes extends only to the self that I am, and sometimes it extends further out, to the human being that I am" (Strawson 2009, 31). The former use of 'I' refers to the subject of consciousness, as it is phenomenally presented to oneself, as how one conceives of oneself, how one is viewed or considered "from the inside"; the latter use of 'I' refers to the whole human being, spatially and temporally located in the world, as the subject of physical or mental attributes, the agent of actions, the owner of moral and legal responsibilities. We can call the former "the phenomenal I," and the latter "the public I." Or we can also say that the former is the *subjective self* while the latter is an important part of the *objective self.* Thomas Nagel (1983) proposes a conception of the objective self, according to which the self (TN) is projected into the *centerless* world, singled out by a complete set of publicly identifiable properties and viewed from an impersonal standpoint. Nagel argues that each one of us has, or should have, an objective self at our core. Owen Flanagan (this volume) depicts a conception of the person as he or she really is, *from God's point of view*, as the person's "actual full identity." The self one conceives from the first-person point of view in all likelihood does not reflect the whole person truthfully or completely, seen from the impersonal standpoint or from God's point of view. There are definitely gaps between what we represent ourselves to be and what we really are. The self viewed from the subjective standpoint and the person from an objective standpoint may not match up, and here we see that the notions of *self* and *person* diverge. This divergence also leads to possible problems in self-knowledge: what we think about ourselves, in terms of our mental states or psychological attributes, could have missed the mark of what kind of person we truly are and what kind of beliefs we truly have.

The reliability of self-knowledge can be subject to the same Humean skepticism: how do we *introspect* our own beliefs and desires? The question is again whether our own mental states could be the *object* of our knowledge. Gareth Evans (1982b) suggests that the way to gain self-knowledge is not "looking within," but to look at the outside world to form a judgment about the world. When the subject wishes to know whether he believes that *P*, he "does not in any sense gaze at, or concentrate on, his internal state. His internal state cannot in any sense become an *object* to him. (He is *in* it.)" (Evans 1982b, 204, original italics). Evans advocates an externalist view of self-knowledge: "In fact, we only have to be aware of some state of the world in order to be in a position to make an assertion about ourselves" (Evans 1982b, 207–08). Alex Byrne (2005) follows Evans and proposes an externalistic epistemic method of self-knowledge. He argues that reliable self-knowledge is easily obtainable if one simply follows a "self-verifying" epistemic rule, which he calls BEL: If *p*, believe that you believe that *p*. This rule is self-verifying because if one follows it, then one's second-order belief about one's own belief will be true. In other words, one gains reliable self-knowledge by following this epistemic rule. The advantage of Byrne's self-verifying principle is that it does not call for a special "internal mechanism" or an "inner sense" for our self-knowledge. As long as one perceives the conditions of the world and is rational enough to follow this epistemic rule, one *knows* what one believes.

Hume's concern about the introspectability of the self's presence and mental states can also lead to a question about the introspectability of the self's experiences, path of life, and *personhood* in general. Can we have a conception of the self that is not completely determined from the individual's point of view, the individual's self-ascription of beliefs, desires, and other psychological traits, and the individual's ownership of his or her deeds in memories? In other words, how do we establish an objective personhood that is not purely derived from the individual's phenomenal consciousness? The psychological account given by Locke seems insufficient as an account of personhood. Bernard Williams (1957) proposes that we use bodily continuity as a *necessary* condition of personal identity. He argues that the memory criterion cannot be divorced from the body criterion, since the only condition under which x has a veridical memory of y's doing A is that $x = y$, and for x and y to be the same person is to have the spatio-temporal continuity between their bodies. There may be imaginary cases of soul swapping or body switching, but if we go for a more realistic approach, according to Williams, "the facts of self-consciousness prove incapable of yielding the secret of personal identity, and we are forced back into the world of public criteria" (Williams [1957] 1999, 15). David Wiggins (1967) also uses spatio-temporal continuity as the criterion of personal identity. In recent literature, Eric Olson's (1999) account of personal identity appeals to the biological organism that human beings are, or biological continuity, as the criterion. He rejects the psychological criterion completely and suggests that a human person is just a living human animal. This view has been called "animalism." All these approaches can be seen as an attempt to establish personhood from an objective or at least *public* perspective, one that is not confined to the individual's consciousness.

The collected essays in this book continue these discussions in a new light. The first set of essays begins with the Humean denial. Some take up Humean skepticism about locating the self through our introspection while some aim to defeat it. The second set of essays deals with the issue of self-knowledge and the third set of essays explores the relation between personhood and one's consciousness.

David Rosenthal argues that Hume's denial of the self is based on an unfounded assumption that perception is the only means through which one could be aware of a self. Having an occurrent, assertoric thought about one's self as being present is another way for one to be aware of it. Rosenthal's HOT theory defines 'conscious mental state' as the mental state in which one has a suitable thought that one is, oneself, in that state. If one thinks that one is in a mental state, say, thinking about which movie to go see, then one not only is conscious of the thought but also is conscious of the thought as belonging to oneself. The sense of self emerges as the owner of these conscious mental states. Uriah Kriegel argues that self-awareness is always minimally in the "peripheral" of our conscious phenomenal experience. A phenomenal experience is how the experience is an experience *for me*, the subject of the experience. Without the subjective aspect, the experience itself would not even be an experience for anyone. We may not be able to find the subject in our phenomenal experience, but the subject is always there in our consciousness. Jesse Prinz, on the other hand, elaborates on Humean skepticism and argues against the possibility of finding, in our phenomenology, the self as the subject. Prinz rejects what he calls "the phenomenal I," not what he calls "the phenomenal me." According to Prinz, we never can have an experience of ourselves as the subject of our experiences; what we have are just our experiences, our mental states, our perceptions of the world. We do not experience ourselves as the "owner" of conscious mental states as Rosenthal claims; nor do we have any qualitative experiences associated with a subject *for whom* those qualitative experiences are experiences as Kriegel claims. All three views can be seen as examining the self as subject; in particular, the *subjective self*, or the self viewed "from the inside."

On the *public self*, we have essays by John Perry and Lucy O'Brien. John Perry examines the nature of "self-beliefs" or "I-thoughts," and places their origin in the world. One gathers "information" about oneself by multiple means, some of which are publicly assessable. The self does not have to be a private entity, knowable only to the subject. Lucy O'Brien focuses on the self-consciousness involved in one's awareness of others' gaze, which she calls "ordinary self-consciousness." On O'Brien's conception of the self, the *I* is both the object of others' scrutiny and the subject who experiences the variety of emotions associated with being thus self-aware. There seems to be a double role for the self here: the first self is the publicly observable person (the public *I*) while the second self is the subject *I* who is imagining how others examine the pubic self.

The gap between the subjective self and the objective self leads to the issue of authoritative self-knowledge. The issue of self-knowledge is another theme explored in this book. If there is a unified self within our consciousness, then to know what one thinks, what one believes, or what one desires should be the most reliable, immediate, and authoritative form of knowledge. The Cartesian claim of *infallible* self-knowledge has been taken to assume the subject's having a "privileged access" to the content of her own mind. However, even with the most honest intention, we do not have a complete grasp of ourselves. If personhood is construed purely subjectively, from the individual's self-conception, then it can deviate from the individual's real personality traits, moral character, true memories, and current intentions. Fred Dretske, Alex Byrne, and Eric Schwitzgebel examine different aspects of knowledge about one's self, including one's beliefs, desires, and moral attitudes. Dretske argues that "from the inside," the individual has no privileged evidence to the fact that she is thinking. Byrne suggests that we make judgments of *desirability* on the state of affairs in the world as a way to know our own desires. Schwitzgebel points out that our internal conception of ourselves frequently falls short of capturing our true selves. All three views can be seen as defending an externalist position on self-knowledge.

Finally, the last thread in this book is a reflection on the Lockean conception of personhood and persistence of the self in time on the basis of consciousness. Sydney Shoemaker defends a "neo-Lockean" theory of personal identity, using psychological continuity as the criterion for personal identity. Owen Flanagan appeals to William James' notion of *consciousness* and argues that personal identity should be based primarily on the Jamesian person. Even though the two views differ, they both appeal to the individual's consciousness to assign personal identity, and they both argue that the criterion cannot be determined purely "from the inside": for Shoemaker, it is the causal profiles of one's psychological properties; for Flanagan, it is the complete consciousness, the actual full identity not founded on the individual's autobiographical memories, that constitutes personhood.

SYNOPSIS OF CHAPTERS

In "Awareness and identification of self" David Rosenthal defends his higher-order thought (HOT) theory of self-awareness. Rosenthal addresses three concerns that the HOT theory may not be adequate as a theory of self-awareness. The first problem is that some of our thoughts about ourselves involve the so-called "essential indexical" – they are thoughts about one's referring to oneself with a first-person mode. These thoughts seem to be antecedent to one's having a higher-order thought about one's mental states; hence, some other account needs to be given to explain how we generate this form of self-awareness. The second problem derives from Sydney Shoemaker's well-known claim of "immunity to error through misidentification." According to Shoemaker, there is no possibility of misidentification of one's self as the subject of experience because *there was no identification of the self to begin with*. The HOT theory needs to provide a story about how this immunity is secured merely by higher-order thoughts. The third concern is that even if the HOT theory can explain our self-awareness of our *mental* states, it might not be able to explain our self-awareness as "physically functioning creatures"; namely, how we interact with other objects in the world, how we move, act, etc. There has to be unity between our awareness of our mental states and our awareness of ourselves as physical beings. It is unclear how the HOT theory can give us this unity.

Rosenthal's answer to all three objections is to separate a dispositional account of self-awareness from his actualist HOT account of self-awareness. In the case of essential indexicals, he argues that essential indexicals only involve one's *disposition* to identify oneself as the person having a particular thought, and not necessarily an actual self-referring thought with a specific identifying content. Therefore, it is not the case that a unique unmediated self-referring thought precedes any higher-order thought that involves self-awareness. Rosenthal further argues that since one has a disposition to identify one's self as the same agent being aware and having the experience, there is a form of identification of the self, *albeit* a "thin" self-identification, as he calls it. It is a thin self-identification because it is a mere disposition, not necessarily explicit in occurrent thoughts. If there is identification, then there is a possibility of misidentification, and thus one is not completely immune to error through misidentification. Rosenthal lists one case in which such misidentification does take place: the case of dissociative identity disorder, or what is more commonly known as "multiple personality disorder." He thinks that this case shows that we do have a disposition to identify the self as the agent with conscious mental states. Finally, with the issue of unity of self-awareness in both mental and physical conditions, Rosenthal's answer is that we identify ourselves with various means and in various contexts, and together these self-identifications form a unified sense of the self. These heterogeneous self-identifying thoughts reflect one's beliefs about oneself. These self-beliefs are typically cast in first-person terms in the mental analogue of the first-person pronoun 'I.' Our linguistic practice and our commonsense assumption are such that we use 'I' in our first-person thoughts to refer to the same individual. Rosenthal argues that identifying the same single self underlying all our conscious states is a disposition of ours, even though such a disposition is not always manifested; in other words, we do not always have occurrent thoughts about the unity of the self. It may even be the case that there is after all nothing that is a unified self, which underlies all our experiences. Nonetheless, our *disposition* to identify a single self explains why HOTs, which are first-person thoughts, generate a compelling sense of the unity of the self. In Rosenthal's theory of self-awareness, our linguistic practices involving the first-person pronoun 'I' as self-reference and our higher-order first-person thoughts about our own mental states are closely connected.

In "Self-representationalism and the explanatory gap," Uriah Kriegel explains how his self-representational theory of consciousness can handle the explanatory gap problem. The idea of self-representationalism is basically that a mental state is phenomenally conscious if and only if it represents itself in the right way. Kriegel thinks that there is a strong connection between phenomenal consciousness and self-consciousness: phenomenal consciousness involves essentially "a subtle, primordial kind of self-consciousness" (51). Self-representationalism takes phenomenally conscious states to contain two components: the *qualitative* character of the experience, which is how the perceived quality appears to be, and the *subjective* character of the experience, which is how the perceived quality appears to *me*, the subject of the experience. For an experience to be an experience, there has to be a self at the receiving end, processing the information. The experience is an experience "for me"; as Kriegel puts it, "its for-me-ness is what makes it an experience at all" (52).

Under self-representationalism, the subjective character of phenomenal consciousness presupposes a self at the center of the experience, since it is the self's awareness of the experience ("in the right way") that makes it a phenomenal experience. The agent's awareness of a mental state M is simply the agent's being in a mental state M* that represents M in the right way. The way self-representationalism differs from Rosenthal's HOT theory of consciousness is that M* is not a separate, higher-order state of M; rather, M* = M. Kriegel presents a *master argument for self-representationalism* in section 1 of his chapter. His basic idea is that M*, the mental state that represents an experience as an experience *for me*, is itself a conscious mental state. If M* is a separate state, however, then it requires a further mental state, call it M**, to represent it and to render it conscious. This further requirement would in the end bring us to an infinite regress of postulating higher-order mental states to make the lower-order states conscious. Since that is not an acceptable option, M* must not be a separate state from M. Therefore, M* = M. However, M is not a simple state, according to Kriegel, but rather a complex state that has two proper parts: M1 (the qualitative character) and M2 (the subjective character). M is *self-representing* iff M2 represents M1 directly, and thereby representing M (the complete phenomenally conscious state) indirectly. This complex structure gives Kriegel a clue on how to locate the neural structure that implements phenomenal conscious states.

Kriegel distinguishes two phenomena of self-consciousness: *transitive self-consciousness* and *intransitive self-consciousness*. The former depicts a relation between the subject and the experience the subject is conscious of having, as in, for example, "I am self-conscious of perceiving the laptop." The latter depicts the mode in which the subject has that experience, as in "I am self-consciously perceiving the laptop." Kriegel argues that these two are distinct phenomena, and it is the *intransitive self-consciousness* that captures the subjective character of phenomenal consciousness. The explanatory gap problem between phenomenal consciousness and physical properties turns out to be the issue of how to reductively explain the subject's intransitive self-consciousness in terms of the neural activities in her brain. Kriegel's solution to the explanatory gap problem is, in a nutshell, to find the neural structure that implements the self-representing nature of phenomenally conscious mental states. He hypothesizes that, in the case of visual perception, neural activation in the right part of visual cortex (V4) realizes M1 (*qualitative character*), while neural activation in the dorsolateral prefrontal cortex (dlPFC) realizes M2 (*subjective character*), and there is neural synchronization between them that joins M1 and M2 into a unified single state, M. The *binding* among neural activation in different brain areas constitutes a unified conscious experience. With this hypothesis about the neural foundations for phenomenal consciousness, in particular, for intransitive self-consciousness (i.e. subjective character of phenomenal consciousness), Kriegel embarks on his solution to the explanatory gap problem. Using the sorites series as an analogy, Kriegel first argues that the explanation of intransitive self-consciousness (or even phenomenal consciousness) in terms of neural processes follows a logical sequence, with each step closely connected to the previous step, but resulting in a huge gap between the first and the final step. What generates the explanatory gap is simply when we try to comprehend the whole sequence "in a single intellectual act," we cannot see the explanatory derivation (62). We may be inclined to conclude that the apparent gap exists only in our understanding, not in the explanation itself, and thus there is no genuine explanatory gap. However, this is not the approach that Kriegel takes. He actually acknowledges the existence of an explanatory gap, and suggests that what the logical explanatory sequence renders is *epistemic transparency*, but not *epistemic reduction*. The sequence of explanation gives reductive explanation step by step, but as he argues, "the relation of reductive explainability is not transitive" (65); hence, the whole sequence itself does not produce reductive explanation of intransitive self-consciousness in terms of synchronization with dlPFC activity, even though the former *is* ontologically reducible to the latter.

In "Thinking about the self" John Perry further develops his theory of self-belief – the belief one has about oneself *from the perspective of the self*. Perry begins by explicating the connection between belief, language, and the world. He thinks that beliefs in general are not fully determined internally and individualistically, because contents of beliefs involve circumstances in which the person situates, along with her relations to the objects and her relations to other thinkers or speakers. Beliefs, as well as other forms of cognition such as perception, are embedded in a system of information. The system of beliefs may be interrelated internally, but ultimately the function of belief is played out in what Perry calls the "information game": an agent picks up information about the external world in a given context, stores the information in the system, and later uses the information on a pertinent occasion. Perry describes different sorts of information games: straight-through, tracking, detach and recognize, and finally, communication. To him, beliefs play a causal role in storing and acting on the information that the agent picks up about objects in the world. Perry further explains the structure of belief: belief involves *notions* or *ideas*; the former are ideas of things while the latter are ideas of properties or relations. When the agent perceives someone or something and establishes an epistemic or pragmatic relation with the perceived object, the agent forms a "buffer," which is simply a notion attached to the perception of the object. Once the perceived object is out of sight, the original buffer becomes a "detached notion," which is stored for later use. Our beliefs, along with other forms of cognition, provide us with databases of buffers or detached notions of objects we interact with in our navigation through the world.

A belief is a representational state, and the content of the representational state specifies the conditions for its truth. These will be, roughly, the conditions under which an action, motivated by the belief in concert with a desire, will result in satisfaction of the desire. If the representational state represents a particular object, then the object is an "articulated constituent" of the content. If, on the other hand, the representational state is not explicitly about any object, yet the whole representational system insures that a particular object belongs in the content, then that object is an "unarticulated constituent" of the content. Either way, the object stands in an appropriate epistemic and pragmatic relation to the agent through the agent's belief.

Given this externalistic and pragmatic picture of belief, Perry examines the nature of self-belief. Self-beliefs are *typically* expressed with first-person self-assertions, but the first-person pronoun 'I' is not essentially involved in self-belief. Perry argues that our self-belief involves our *notions* about ourselves – our "self-notions," and we are either an articulated or unarticulated constituent of the content of our self-belief. Our self-beliefs are like other beliefs in certain ways: they also connect us to an individual who plays some epistemic and pragmatic roles in our lives, except that the individual bears an "identity" relation to ourselves. Perry calls our self-notions "self-buffers," but unlike other buffers, self-buffers do not get detached from the perceived object – my self-buffer will always be attached to my *self*. As Perry puts it: "Once you have the connection right, it is good for life" (93).

The method with which one obtains information about one's self and thereby forms a self-belief makes self-belief stand out from other kinds of belief. One could obtain information about oneself the same way one obtains information about others: looking them up on Facebook, or in a phone book, or the like. Perry argues that among the different methods one could use to pick up information about oneself, some are *normally* self-informative while some are *necessarily* self-informative. For example, seeing myself in the mirror is normally self-informative, but there are conceivably scenarios in which what I see is actually someone else. Having a pain sensation or having a thought about something, on the other hand, necessarily gives information only about one's self and only accessible from the perspective of the self. These methods are self-informative because they render information of oneself that is typically not available to others. However, if my self-belief is formed in a normally self-informative way, then I may still need some method of identification to learn that what I believe is true of *me*. If my self-belief is formed in a necessarily self-informative way, on the other hand, then my belief has the feature of *immunity to error through misidentification* since it is not possible that anyone but *me* could obtain this belief in the way I do. If I am thinking that I think that Picasso was a great painter (a case of Rosenthal's HOT), then there can be no mistake that *I* am the one having this thought – there is no possibility of *misidentification*. Perry thus argues that Rosenthal (this volume) fails to provide strong reasons to abandon Shoemaker's *immunity to error through misidentification* claim.

In "Ordinary self-consciousness," Lucy O'Brien explores another way in which one is self-conscious: under others' gaze (literally and metaphorically).

It is a kind of self-consciousness that involves one's being "conscious of oneself as an object represented by others" (101), and is closely linked to other self-conscious emotions such as embarrassment, shame, guilt, and pride. O'Brien argues that this kind of self-consciousness is a pervasive phenomenon in our daily experience; hence, she calls it "ordinary self-consciousness." Her usage is probably more in agreement with ordinary language than with philosophical terminology of 'self-consciousness.' According to G. E. M. Anscombe, the term 'self-consciousness' by the nineteenth century acquired a sense in ordinary language to mean "awkwardness from being troubled by the feeling of being an object of observation by other people" (Anscombe [1975] 1994, 145). This chapter gives a structured analysis of this mental phenomenon.

According to O'Brien, ordinary self-consciousness (OSC) involves a duality of perspectives – the perspective of the subject and the perspective of the evaluator (as seen or imagined by the subject). The structure of OSC thus includes several dimensions, from the identity of the evaluator, the nature of the evaluative schema, to the degrees of weight given to the evaluator or the evaluative schema. O'Brien takes OSC to be an affective state, whose intensity depends on how one gives weight to the others who are presumably judging oneself with their own evaluative schema. What she depicts in this chapter is the phenomenology of OSC, and the awareness of the self is placed in the center of one's evaluation of oneself through the eyes of the *projected* others.

In "Waiting for the self," Jesse Prinz brings up a position that could challenge all the above views about one's self-awareness. He argues against any separate phenomenal qualities associated with the subject of the self in addition to perceived qualities of things in the world, or sensations, and emotions. Prinz takes an eliminativist's stance on *I-qualia* – on his view, there is simply no qualitative experience of the self as *subject*, though he does not deny that one could experience the self as an *object*.

In this chapter, Prinz examines several recent studies in contemporary neuroscience that aim to locate the neural correlate of self-awareness. His targets include studies done by Goldberg *et al.* (2006) to find the difference in brain activities while the subject is engaged in self-related tasks and while the subject "lost herself" in rapid processing tasks, Damasio's (1999) hypothesis of a "core-self" as the background feelings of our various bodily states, attempts made by Blanke and Metzinger (2009) and Tsakiris *et al.* (2007), among others, to identify brain structures associated with the sense of body ownership, and the theory of authorship or agency (Wolpert *et al.* 1995; Frith *et al.* 2000; Hohwy 2007) of our own physical and mental acts.

In all these cases, Prinz argues, the authors fail to provide necessary and sufficient conditions for the experience of a self as *subject*. The brain areas identified as the neural correlate of self-awareness, the superior frontal gyrus (SFG), the right temporoparietal junction, the right posterior insula, or the posterior parietal cortex, all seem to be involved in other activities as well and thus the empirically established correlations do not substantiate the claim for self-awareness. The lack of corresponding phenomenal experiences, such as the background feelings of our bodily states or the integrated bodily representations, also does not prevent the agent from having a sense of the self. Furthermore, with the *ownership* theory in particular, Prinz argues that ownership is a two-place relation and we will be either going into infinite regress to find the thing that unifies the relata, or to acknowledge that we only have a bound whole, with no single part of the brain being responsible for self-awareness. Prinz acknowledges that the *authorship* theory seems to offer the best model for self-awareness, since agency and subjectivity are interconnected. However, he argues, even if the subject experiences a sense of control in comparing the anticipated act and the performed act, this experience generates merely a sense of self as *object*, not a self as *subject*, because what the subject perceives is the act, not the actor. There is no phenomenology of the *I* after all.

While Prinz questions the reliability of introspection in finding a subject *I* in one's thought, Fred Dretske continues to question the reliability of introspection in finding the act of thinking itself. In "I think I think, therefore I am – I think," Dretske goes back to Descartes' classic *Cogito* argument and challenges the very first premise: I am thinking. How do we *know*, he asks, that we are thinking? What evidence do we have for proving that we do think? Dretske argues that once we are pressed to supply a proof, we will come up empty-handed. The question is not about *what* we think, to which we do have a privileged access and on which we do have a unique authority; the question is about the fact *that* we think, and with this we cannot find proof. The former question is about the content of our thought; the latter is about the act of thinking itself. From the external point of view, other observers can point to evidence that we are thinking: our rational behavior, for example. We can appeal to the same set of evidence too. What Dretske argues is not skepticism about us as thinking beings, but skepticism about our having any *privileged* and *direct* access to the act of thinking. We do not have any internal sense with which to be aware of our own thinking. We do not feel anything special when we think, and there is nothing in particular that we are aware of. The act of thinking can be publicly observable, and there can be publicly identified evidence, but there is nothing *from the subject's point of view*, from the inside, that proves to the subject that she is thinking. There is simply no "phenomenology of thought."

Dretske's chapter leads into the issue of self-knowledge. Even though Dretske is skeptical of our self-knowledge of the fact that we think, he does not dispute that we have authority, and even a kind of infallibility, in our knowledge of the content of our thought. In "Knowing what I want," Alex Byrne extends his externalistic epistemic principle of self-knowledge of one's belief to self-knowledge of one's intention and desire. Byrne argues that on the principles of *economy* and *unification*, we should assume that one's epistemic capacities to know one's own mind should be the same across different mental categories: belief, perception, sensation, and desire, unless evidence speaks to the contrary. We have seen that with the case of belief, the epistemic rule one should employ to gain self-knowledge is BEL: If *p*, believe that you believe that *p*. The comparable epistemic rule Byrne comes up with for desire is DES: If φing is a desirable option, believe that you want to φ. If one follows this rule, then one gains knowledge of what one desires to do. Byrne's self-verifying principle seems to be based on realism with regard to both *truth* and *desirability* of states of affairs. If these features are "out there in the world," then as long as one is rational enough to acknowledge *p is true*, or *φing is desirable*, then one *knows* what one believes and what one desires. The underlying requirement for successful self-knowledge is human rationality and cognitive acuity. But the question is: are we really so rational and so perceptive? Eric Schwitzgebel next points to evidence that we are not.

In "Self-ignorance," Eric Schwitzgebel defends skepticism about self-knowledge and argues that we do not know much about the content of our stream of consciousness. Schwitzgebel focuses on the phenomenology of experience, and presents difficulties for self-knowledge based on how our experience is presented to us. We do not, for example, have a clear visual imagery of the content of our perception, and we cannot quite capture our ongoing "emotional phenomenology." Schwitzgebel cites some empirical studies that demonstrate people's fallibility in their judgments on what they think, how they feel, and the content of their perceptual experience. He thinks the problem is even more pronounced when it comes to our self-knowledge of our attitudes that reflect our general values and our background assumptions about the world. Covert sexists or racists would be a case in point. It is not that these people know what they are like and are in self-denial; it is rather that they do not really know their true beliefs. The problem is massive, according to Schwitzgebel, since it pertains to our self-knowledge (or the lack thereof) about other general features of our mentality, such as our intelligence, our moral character, our personality traits. If we use Perry's notion of *file* for self-beliefs, then we can say that we store many false self-beliefs in our file of ourselves.

The final two chapters in this book deal with the issue of personal identity – the same self in time. In "Personhood and consciousness," Sydney Shoemaker defends a "neo-Lockean" theory of personal identity and analyzes *the same self* in terms of the causal profiles of psychological properties. The causal profiles of psychological properties determine both the synchronic unity (as in the case of perception or action production) and the diachronic unity (as in the case of memory) relations of their instantiation tokens. In his chapter, Shoemaker's focus is on the diachronic unity of instances of psychological properties. He argues that just as one does not *introspect* the self as an object, one does not have a "past self" or "me-ness" in the content of one's memory either. We all claim to remember things that we *ourselves* have done or gone through, but the first-personal claim is not substantiated by our memory itself. There is no phenomenological difference between one's *veridical* memory and one's *seeming* memory of someone else's past experience – what Shoemaker calls "*quasi*-memory." The 'I' referred to in a memory statement "I went to China last year" could turn out to be someone else that I took to be myself.

To demonstrate the plausibility of quasi-memory, Shoemaker gives the story of *Parfit people*, which is a "spin-off from Derek Parfit's example of persons who reproduce by fission" (Shoemaker 2009, 88). Parfit people originate as we do, but around the age twenty-one, each of the Parfit people goes through a natural fission process. "In the fission a person's body divides into two exactly similar bodies, and each of the bodies is the body of a person psychologically continuous with the original person" (Shoemaker 2009, 88). One special feature of Shoemaker's Parfit people is that only one of the two successors is allowed to live on, while the other (randomly chosen) would be put to death painlessly shortly after the fission takes place. Furthermore, the surviving person would be unaware of what had happened and would inherit the original person's beliefs, attitudes, projects, and all personality traits as if no fission had taken place. Tyler Burge calls the sequence of an individual's total mental states a "mental career" of the agent (Burge 2003, 324). Shoemaker calls the career of the Parfit people a "quareer" – quasi-career, in that it consists of both the personal career of the original person and the personal career of the surviving offshoot. The two personal careers are linked by the surviving offshoot's *quasi*-memory of the original person's life plan. In other words, quareers are sustained by *quasi*-memories. The survivor's quasi-memory of the past would be like genuine memory "from the inside" – except that he and the original person were not the same person. In this case their use of the word 'I' should be translated as "I*" since it is not the same as our first-person pronoun. Reference using the first-person pronoun 'I' in a memory claim does not guarantee veridical designation of the *I*, when a proper causal theory can be devised as in the case of the Parfit people. In such a case, the subject is not immune to error through misidentification in his or her memory statement. Nonetheless, Shoemaker claims that in creatures *like us*, our memory statement preserves the same immunity to error through misidentification as our present-tense psychological judgments have. The conditions under which a memory is genuine and self-reference is successful in memory statements are not determined from the inside, from within the subject's consciousness, but are determined by causal facts about the subject and the subject's history – for example, the fact that we are *not* Parfit people. From the first-person perspective, one does not have the means to separate quasi-memories from genuine memories; in other words, one cannot judge with infallibility whether the remembered self is the same self. This is an externalist theory of personal identity.

Finally, in "My non-narrative, non-forensic *dasein*: the first and second self," Owen Flanagan defends a view of personal identity which he derives from William James' conception of *person*. He argues that the Lockean conception of *person*, which Shoemaker adopts as the starting point of his theory of personal identity, is "woefully inadequate" because it relies too much on autobiographical memories to constitute sameness of self. The problem with this account is that it appeals to a purely subjective condition, one's consciousness, to try to establish an objective forensic standard for *personhood*, which cannot be matched up by the subjective condition. One's complete personhood cannot be fully captured by one's autobiographical memories alone, since there are many important things that one has forgotten, has denied to oneself, or has never registered. There are also many insignificant events in our life that could have a causal impact on us, or are causally connected to things that matter to us. When the person's identity is conceived first-personally, on the basis of one's consciousness, as Locke has it, it is called "self-experienced identity (SEI)" or "self-represented identity (SRI)." On the other hand, a person's full life's history, viewed from *God's point of view*, would include everything the person experiences, whether he owns it or not. Flanagan calls it the person's "actual full identity (AFI)." If by 'person' we mean moral and legal agency, we cannot confine personhood to the subject's self-representations alone. For the notion of *person* to be used as a forensic concept, it has to include AFI.

William James provides an alternative conception of personhood, according to Flanagan, which can supplement Locke's conception. James depicts one's consciousness as "the free water of consciousness," which flows through both "substantive" and "transitive" states of mind in our daily life, not missing any detail. Even though the substantive part of our consciousness may be more important and more interesting to us, there is no exact science that tells us that those transitive states of mind do not have any causal impact on what makes us who we are. What Flanagan proposes in this chapter is to combine both accounts, and to place the Jamesian notion of personhood as primary ("the first self") while the Lockean notion would be derivative from this primary notion ("the second self"). The Jamesian persons need not be linguistic, conceptual, or social creatures; they could very well be cavemen and hunter-gatherers, as Flanagan sees it. They are "persons" because they have experiences and memories, but they are not "forensic persons" because "[t]he relevant legal and moral practices that define forensic persons into existence did not yet exist" (234). The Lockean notion of *person* is a modern invention that reflects our sense of legal and moral responsibilities, but the Jamesian notion of *person* depicts a fuller sense of the self, not just "from the inside."

Current literature on consciousness seems to manifest a fascination with issues such as phenomenal consciousness, qualia, the explanatory gap, the knowledge argument, reductionism or non-reductionism. All of these issues are grounded on the subject of consciousness, the subject *for whom* the experiences are experiences. Physicalism aims to give a full picture of the world, including the nature of human consciousness. But such an objective depiction from the third-person point of view seems bound to leave out the subjective aspect of experience and the subject *I* who has those experiences. From the first-person standpoint, there is undeniably a self of which one is conscious and to which one refers. No matter how current neuroscience can prove the absence of processors for the self in our brain's areas, the self is deeply rooted in our consciousness. Tell any person on the street that there is no single subject of her experience or that the self is a mere illusion created by our linguistic habits, she will just reply, "*I* don't believe it." Her very statement demonstrates her sense of the self. We human beings, as linguistic, cultural, and reflective persons, have this indubitable sense of the self. "From the inside," we may not know what we truly believe or desire, we may not have an accurate self-assessment of our personality and moral character, and we may not be able to tell whether our memory captures our true identity. Nonetheless, we *know* there is an *I* in our consciousness.

CHAPTER I

Awareness and identification of self

David Rosenthal

I. SELF-AWARENESS AND THE SELF

It is a crucial aspect of everyday mental functioning that we are in some way aware of ourselves. But it is far from clear at first sight just what this self-awareness consists in, and indeed just what the self is that we are aware of.

It is possible to give an answer to the second question that is mundane and unproblematic. The self one is aware of in everyday life is simply the individual that walks, talks, sleeps, and eats; the self one is aware of is, to echo Aristotle's provisional definition of the soul,[1] the living, functioning creature.

I will argue in the end that something in that spirit is correct and defensible. But many have held that this bland account of what the self is fails to capture what is important about the self, at least insofar as we are aware of that self. Thus Descartes argued that the self is that thing the awareness of which makes its existence indubitable, even if we doubt everything about the functioning and existence of physical reality.[2] And the self we are aware of is also typically taken to provide a kind of mental unity that binds together all of one's contemporaneous mental states. As Kant put it, for mental representations to be mine at all, they must "all belong to one self-consciousness" (Kant [1787] 1998, B132; cf. Shoemaker 2003, 59–71). It is something like that idea of the self that presumably underlies Ned Block's observation that there is a kind of "me-ishness" about at least many of one's conscious mental states (1995, 235). And the self that binds one's mental functioning into a unity may even thereby underwrite personal identity through time.

I am grateful to Myrto Mylopoulos for helpful comments on an earlier version.
[1] As "the form of a natural body having in it the capacity of life" (Aristotle, 1907, 412a20, 49).
[2] And, indeed, everything about mathematics and logic. See Descartes (1984, 17).

Hume notoriously challenged this notion of a self. "When I turn my reflexion on *myself*," he wrote, "I never can perceive this *self* without some one or more perceptions; nor can I ever perceive any thing but the perceptions." It is, he concluded, solely "the composition of these" perceptions that "forms the self" ([1739] 2000, Appendix, 399; emphasis Hume's). What metaphysicians call the self is "nothing but a bundle or collection of different perceptions" ([1739] 2000, I, IV, vi, 165).

It is worth noting that Hume does not just contest the existence of a self that independently binds our mental states into a unity; in denying that he perceives anything that could count as such a self, he denies that we have any reason to think that there is any such self. We lack, Hume urges, any subjective appearance that we could properly regard as the appearance of a self, at least a self that is anything distinct from "a mere heap or collection of different perceptions" ([1739] 2000, I, IV, ii, 137–38).

One may be tempted to respond to Hume's concerns by appealing to Kant's "transcendental unity of self-consciousness" (B132). But it is not clear how that addresses the issue at hand. Kant was well aware that "the empirical consciousness that accompanies different representations is by itself dispersed and without relation to the identity [that is, the unity] of the subject" (B133). In effect, he thereby followed Hume in holding that the way we are aware of our conscious states cannot, by itself at least, yield a subjective sense of mental unity or of the self. Even if we must, as Kant argued, posit a transcendental self to be able to think coherently about mental functioning, perhaps Hume is nonetheless correct to hold that there is no subjective appearance of any such self.

But we can undercut Hume's concerns without invoking a transcendental self that lies beyond any possible experience. Hume's way of assessing whether we are aware of a self negatively stacked the deck in a way that is seldom noticed. He assumed that the only way one could be aware of a self would be to perceive that self. But that assumption is unfounded. Perceiving things does make one aware of them, but perceiving is not the only way we are aware of things. We are also aware of something when we have a thought about that thing as being present to us. I am aware of an object in front of me if I see it or hear it; but if my eyes are closed and the object makes no sound, I can also be aware of it simply by having a thought that it is there in front of me.

Not all of our thoughts, of course, result in our being aware of the things those thoughts are about. Having thoughts about objects we take to be distant in place or time, such as Saturn or Caesar, does not intuitively make one aware of those objects. So the thought must be about the object as being present to one. And the thought must presumably have an assertoric mental attitude; having doubts or wondering about an object also does not make one aware of it. And the thought must be occurrent; simply being disposed to have a thought about something does not make one aware of it. But having an occurrent, assertoric thought about an object as being present does make one aware of that object.

Hume would have contested that the appeal to thoughts is a real alternative to perceptual awareness, since he maintained that thinking itself consists simply of pale versions of qualitative perceptual states. "All ideas," he insisted, "are borrow'd from preceding perceptions" (Appendix, 399). His problem about the self therefore rested on his view that all awareness is perceptual awareness.

But there is good reason to reject Hume's view about the perceptual nature of ideas and thoughts. For one thing, mental qualities cannot be combined to form thoughts with syntactic structure. In addition, intentional states have characteristic mental attitudes, such as mental assertion, doubt, wondering, and so forth, and there is nothing in perceiving that corresponds to mental attitude or even holds any hope for explaining it. And though mental qualities do arguably represent the perceptible properties that correspond to them (e.g. Berger manuscript; Lewis 1972, 257; Rosenthal 2005, chs. 5–7, 2011), the way they represent is unlike that of intentional states. Intentional states represent truth-evaluable units, such as states of affairs; by contrast, the impressions and ideas that Hume's view accommodates simply represent perceptible properties, which are not truth evaluable.[3]

Once we reject Hume's perceptual model of what thoughts consist in, a more promising way is available to understand just how we are aware of our mental selves. We are aware of ourselves by having suitable thoughts about ourselves, and aware of ourselves as mental beings by having thoughts that describe ourselves in mental terms. And because these thoughts are occurrent, empirical thoughts, we also avoid Kant's appeal to the transcendental.

The contrast between Hume's sensory approach and the alternative that relies on the thoughts we have about ourselves in mental terms reflects a crucial contrast between two views about what it is for a mental state to be conscious. The most widely held traditional view about the consciousness of

---

[3] Existence claims are truth evaluable. So perhaps impressions and ideas represent perceptible properties as existing, appealing to Hume's contention that the idea of existence "makes no addition" to "the idea of what we conceive to be existent" ([1739] 2000, I, ii, 6, 48). But representing something as existing requires being able to represent it as not existing, something that impressions and ideas cannot do.

mental states appeals to inner sense, and holds that a mental state is conscious if one senses or perceives that state.[4] The higher-order thought (HOT) theory, by contrast, holds that a state's being conscious consists in one's having a suitable thought that one is, oneself, in that state. On the version of the view that I have defended, the thought must be assertoric and non-dispositional. And because the thought has the content that one is, oneself, in that state, the thought automatically represents the target mental state as being present (Rosenthal 2002, 2005).

The difference between the inner-sense and HOT theories sheds light on the two models of self-awareness. If one's mental states were conscious in virtue of one's sensing those states, there would be for each conscious state a higher-order sensation that made one aware of that state. But sensations represent at best only corresponding perceptible properties; a sensation of red represents not the red physical object, but only its redness. So a higher-order sensation would represent only the target mental state, and not also a self to which that state belongs. So nothing in one's sensing a mental state could make one aware of such a self.[5]

Things are different if one is, instead, aware of one's conscious states by having thoughts about those states. One will then have a thought that one is in the state in question. And that HOT will thereby make one aware not only of that state, but also of a self that the HOT represents the state as belonging to. The HOT theory explains not only how we are aware of our conscious mental states, but also how it is that we are thereby aware of ourselves.

A sensation of a mental state would make one aware just of the state by itself, and not of the state as belonging to a self. That is what gives rise to Hume's professed inability to find a self "[w]hen," as he put it, "I turn my reflexion on *myself*." One might wonder whether a thought about a mental state could also make one aware of that state, as a sensation would, without making one aware of it as belonging to a self. But a mental state is in its very nature the sort of item that is a state of something. A perception or feeling or

---

[4] Kant ([1787] 1998) first used the term we translate as 'inner sense' (A22/B37), similar to Locke's "internal Sense" ([1700] 1975, II, i, 4, 105). Versions of the view are currently championed by Armstrong (1980) and by Lycan (1996, ch. 2, 13–43 and 2004).

[5] Sensing involves only mental qualities, and no intentional content, whereas perceiving involves both. So a higher-order perception of a mental state could make one aware of a self that a higher-order perception took the relevant states to belong to. But higher-order perceptions, like higher-order sensations, would have to exhibit higher-order mental qualities, and there is reason to believe that there are no higher-order mental qualities. Nor, *pace* Lycan (2004), is our higher-order awareness of conscious states in other ways more like perceiving than like the having of thoughts. See Rosenthal (2004b, §§2–3).

thought is always somebody's perception, feeling, or thought. So having a thought about a mental state is always to have a thought about that state as belonging to some individual. One might have a thought about a type of mental state, for example, a thought that you have the same feeling as I do; but a thought about a token mental state always ascribes that state to somebody.

Being aware of our mental states by having HOTs about those states results in our being aware of ourselves in mental terms. And being thus aware of ourselves explains why it appears to us that there is a self that is the subject of each of our mental states. The mental appearance of a self that eluded Hume is due to the HOTs we have about our various mental states.

There is, however, a stronger appearance of self than simply the subjective impression that each conscious state belongs to some self or other. In addition, it seems subjectively to us that each of our conscious states belongs to the same self as every other. This stronger idea of a unity of consciousness does not follow simply from the weaker appearance of a self for each conscious state. Nonetheless, it is tempting to hold that all one's conscious states do belong to a single unified consciousness. And we need to explain that appearance, which goes beyond the sense that each conscious state belongs to some self or other. Once again, Kant's transcendental unity of consciousness cannot help here, since that is only a unity we must posit, which cannot explain the robust subjective impression we have of a unity of consciousness.

Still, one might also have doubts about whether a HOT theory of how mental states are conscious can do justice to the particular way we are aware of ourselves. There are two main concerns, both reflecting the inviting idea that the way we are aware of ourselves is special in a way that simply having a thought about something cannot capture.

One worry stems from the well-known difference between a thought about somebody that happens to be oneself and a thought that is about oneself, as such, a thought that involves the so-called essential indexical.[6] If I have a thought that DR is in pain but do not know that I am DR, that thought would not result in my being aware of myself, as such. And that thought would not result in my pain's being conscious; HOTs must ascribe their target mental states to oneself, as such. But it may not seem obvious how to capture this essentially indexical aspect of HOTs. And that may lead one to suspect that having a thought about oneself, as such, requires some special awareness of the self that is antecedent to and independent of the thought.

[6] In John Perry's (1979) useful term.

In addition to that worry, many have followed Sydney Shoemaker[7] in holding that we are aware of ourselves in a way that precludes any error through misidentification of the self. And even if we can explain how HOTs can be about oneself in an essentially indexical way, it is unclear why having a thought that one is, oneself, in a particular mental state could be immune to error through misidentification of oneself. There would have to be something that goes beyond mere HOTs, it seems, to explain such immunity.

There is a third source of doubt about whether a view of self-awareness that relies on HOTs could be satisfactory. The way we are aware of ourselves as being in various conscious states may well be special in the respects just sketched. But our awareness of ourselves as being in conscious states must also somehow fit with our awareness of ourselves in ordinary, non-mental respects. Each of us is an individual that is in many conscious states. But each of us is also a creature that interacts with other objects in the world; we walk, talk, eat, and do many other non-mental things as well. And we are aware of ourselves not only as being in various conscious states, but also as engaging in these various physical activities. And it is unclear how the awareness of self that HOTs confer fits with awareness of ourselves as physical creatures.

It is not obvious, moreover, how to address this last concern about a HOT view of self-awareness without making things worse for the challenges that stem from the essential indexical and immunity to error through misidentification. Some special self-awareness seems immune to error through misidentification. But it may seem difficult to square any such special awareness with the way we are aware of ourselves as physically functioning creatures.

The sense of lack of fit between two types of self-awareness is especially vivid in connection with issues about unity. The unity that is relevant to our awareness of ourselves as bodily creatures is along the lines of the unity of enduring physical objects generally. There must be coherence of bodily properties and composition, and spatio-temporal continuity; the subjective unity that figures in connection with one's conscious states, by contrast, seems to rely on altogether different considerations.

In what follows, I argue that a model of self-awareness based on HOTs can meet all three of these challenges. In §II I show how HOTs can accommodate essentially indexical awareness of oneself without invoking any special,

---

[7] Shoemaker (1968). Page references below are to the reprinted version.

antecedent self-awareness. In §III, then, I argue that a crucial assumption
that underlies the claim of immunity to error through misidentification is
unfounded, namely, the assumption that no self-identification figures in our
awareness of our own conscious states. And in §IV I discuss the particular
kind of identification of self that figures in our higher-order awareness of our
conscious states and how that relates to the self-identification that underlies
our first-person thoughts generally.

II. ESSENTIALLY INDEXICAL SELF-AWARENESS

The way we are aware of our own conscious states requires essentially
indexical self-reference. So if we are aware of those states by having
HOTs about them, HOTs themselves must somehow incorporate the
essential indexical. Is such self-reference, in thought and speech, basic and
unanalyzable? Or can it be discharged by appeal to more ordinary kinds of
reference?

Consider John Perry's well-known example, in which I see a trail of sugar
apparently spilling from somebody's grocery cart and, not realizing that it is
spilling from my cart, think that the person spilling sugar, whoever it is,
is making a mess. Though I am that person, having that thought does
not imply that I think that I myself am making a mess.[8] Reference to
oneself, as such, uses what Perry dubs the essential indexical, called by
traditional grammarians the indirect reflexive because it plays a role in
indirect discourse played in direct quotation by the first-person pronoun.[9]

For a mental state to be conscious, it will not do simply for one to be
aware that somebody that happens to be oneself is in that state; one must be
aware of oneself, as such, as being in that state. As noted earlier, if I am in
pain but aware just that DR is in pain, that would result in my pain's being
conscious only if I were also aware that I am DR. If I thought instead that
you were DR, my awareness that DR is in pain would not result in any
pain's being conscious; it would not make me aware in any relevant way of
myself as being in pain.

Essentially indexical self-reference is one way in which our awareness of
ourselves and our conscious states is special. So if we are aware of ourselves

---

[8] Perry (2000). There is an extensive literature on this phenomenon; see, e.g., Geach (1957); Prior
(1967); Castañeda (1968); Anscombe (1975); Lewis (1979); Boër and Lycan (1980); and Chisholm (1981,
chs. 3–4).
[9] And it is indirect discourse that matters in specifying the intentional content of HOTs.

as being in particular mental states by having HOTs that we are, those HOTs must refer to oneself in this essentially indexical way. HOTs cannot represent the states they are about as belonging to oneself described in some inessential way; they must represent those states as belonging to oneself, as such.

It is sometimes argued that this requirement undermines any HOT account of what it is for a mental state to be conscious (e.g. Zahavi and Parnas 1998, §III). So it is crucial to see just what such essentially indexical self-reference consists in, and whether HOTs can refer to oneself in that special way. An essentially indexical thought or speech act about myself has the content that I myself am *F*. But what is it that results in its referring to oneself in an essentially indexical way?

Essentially indexical self-reference occurs not just with HOTs, but also with all our first-person thoughts. It does not matter whether the property the first-person thought ascribes to oneself is that of being in a mental state or something else. So let us consider the general case. Suppose I think that I, myself, have the property of being *F*. My thought that I, myself, am *F* in effect represents as being *F* the very individual who thinks that thought.

It is this tacit identification of oneself as the thinker of the first-person thought that underlies one's reference to oneself, as such. I refer to myself, as such, when I in effect refer to something as the individual that does the referring. That is why essentially indexical self-reference and self-awareness forge a referential connection that seems intuitively to be independent of any intentional content.

In Perry's case, I begin by thinking that somebody is spilling sugar and I come to realize that I, myself, am that very person. What I discover, in effect, is that the individual who is spilling sugar is the very same as the individual who thinks that somebody is spilling sugar; the person that is being said or thought to spill is the very person who says or thinks that somebody is spilling. By tacitly identifying the individual that a thought purports to be about with the individual who thinks that thought, the essential indexical links what the thought purports to be about to that very act of thinking.

HOTs make essentially indexical self-reference in just this way. Suppose I have a pain, and that the pain is conscious; I am aware of myself as having that pain. On the HOT theory, I have a HOT to the effect that I have that pain. My HOT succeeds in referring to me in an essentially indexical way by in effect ascribing the pain to the very individual who has that HOT.

HOTs are just a special case of first-person thoughts. But there is a complication that affects HOTs alone. We are seldom aware of our HOTs;

HOTs typically are not conscious thoughts.[10] Indeed, that is just what the HOT theory predicts; a HOT would be conscious only if one were aware of having that HOT, and that would happen only when one has a third-order thought about it. And we evidently seldom have such third-order thoughts.

This is where the complication with HOTs comes in. Consider the case of conscious pain. If a HOT had the explicit content that the individual who thinks this thought is in pain, that would make one aware not just of the pain, but of the HOT itself. And since HOTs are seldom conscious, they cannot have explicit content of that sort. So it cannot be that the HOT explicitly identifies the individual that is in pain as the thinker of that HOT; rather the HOT identifies the individual in that way tacitly, only in effect. But what exactly does that amount to?

A HOT must represent tacitly that a pain belongs to the individual who has that HOT, but the HOT cannot have the explicit content that the pain belongs to the individual that has that HOT. Instead, the HOT's content describes the pain as belonging to some particular individual, and the individual that has that HOT is, in addition, disposed to identify the individual the HOT refers to as the individual that has that HOT. The content of each HOT refers to the individual it asserts to be in pain by the mental analogue of 'I.' Though the HOT does not describe that individual as the thinker of the HOT, the individual is disposed to do so should the question ever arise. Needless to say, the question seldom if ever does arise; so the individual that has the HOT may never actually perform that identification. But the disposition to do so constitutes a tacit identification of the self that the HOT ascribes pain to. And that constitutes the essentially indexical self-reference.[11]

---

[10] HOTs need not be conscious thoughts to make one aware of the mental states they are about. For one thing, the target states do not inherit the property of being conscious from the HOTs that are about them; rather, HOTs make one aware of being in the target states, and that is what it is for a state to be conscious. A state is conscious if one is aware of being in that state in a suitably unmediated way. There is, moreover, no difficulty in a non-conscious state's making one aware of something; indeed, this is just what happens in subliminal perception. Subliminal perception has distinctive psychological effects, e.g., in one's subsequent expectations, decisions, and psychological processing. These effects would not be possible unless the subliminal perceiving made one aware of the thing perceived, though not of course consciously aware of it. On subliminal perception, see, e.g., Marcel (1983a, 1983b) and Breitmeyer and Öğmen (2006).

[11] This disposition to identify the individual that each HOT refers to explains how HOTs can refer to oneself in an essentially indexical way and yet seldom be conscious. But why think that we have any such disposition? The question about who it is that has a HOT is a question as to which individual is aware of being in a particular mental state. And it will not address the force of that question to specify the individual by way of such individuating properties as the having of a particular name or location. If this question does arise for an individual that has a HOT, the initial response will doubtless be simply that it is I that has the HOT. But if pressed by oneself or another for more, it will then be natural to reply that the HOT refers to the individual that has that HOT.

Indeed, that is exactly how things work in Perry's sugar case. When I discover that I am the one who is spilling sugar, the thought that embodies that discovery refers to myself in thought in an essentially indexical way. But I do not on that account have a thought with the explicit content that the person spilling sugar is the person that has this very thought. Rather, I come to be disposed to identify the individual that is spilling sugar in that way, that is, as the individual who has the thought I can express by saying that I am spilling sugar. In ordinary circumstances, I would never have a thought that explicitly identifies the individual who is spilling sugar as the individual who has that thought; but my disposition to perform that identification suffices for my essentially indexical self-reference. So it is with the essentially indexical reference that occurs in HOTs.

This disposition to identify an individual as the thinker of a thought explains why essentially indexical reference seems to operate independently of any particular way of describing or characterizing oneself. It is not that no description of oneself is relevant to secure such reference; the relevant description is oneself as the thinker of a particular thought. But because essentially indexical self-reference relies on a disposition to identify the relevant individual in that way, and not on any explicit identifying content, such self-reference seems to be independent of self-description altogether. And this helps explain the intuitive elusiveness both of essentially indexical reference and what such reference picks out.

A thought about oneself as such refers, by way of a disposition to identify oneself, to the individual that thinks that thought, though the content of such a thought does not explicitly describe one in that way. Since essentially indexical thoughts refer independently of any particular description that occurs in their content, it is tempting to see them as referring in an unmediated way, a way that might thereby provide the foundation for all other referring.[12] If so, perhaps we need some special awareness of the self, antecedent to any thoughts we might have about it, to underlie any essentially indexical self-reference.

But such reference is mediated by a disposition to identify oneself as the thinker of a particular thought; it does not rest on or constitute some independent access to the self, but simply on a disposition to have another thought. So essentially indexical self-reference cannot provide any foundation for the identifying of anything else.

---

[12] For such a claim, see, e.g., Shoemaker (1968); Chisholm (1976, ch. 1, §5 and 1981, ch. 3, esp. 29–32); and Lewis (1979).

And it is independently implausible that essentially indexical self-reference is required for identifying anything other than oneself. We rarely identify other objects by reference to ourselves; we almost always identify other things by some local frame of reference that we fix in turn by appeal to various objects we perceive and know about, independently of ourselves. Such local frames of reference occasionally fail, but when they do the solution is seldom to refer back to ourselves. Essentially indexical self-reference cannot underwrite foundationalist epistemological leanings.

There is a sense we sometimes have of ourselves that can make it seem difficult to see ourselves, insofar as we are conscious selves, as located among the physical furniture of the universe. And it might be thought that essentially indexical self-reference is responsible for this appearance of mystery about the subjects of conscious experience, since the essential indexical occurs ineliminably only in describing such subjects. (See, e.g., Anscombe 1975 and Nagel 1965, §v.) The present account suggests an explanation. It may be that the self seems to elude our objective framework because essentially indexical self-reference is secured not by explicit descriptive content, but only by a disposition to identify the individual a thought is about with the thinker of that thought.

Reference to an individual, as such, occurs in cases other than the first person. I can describe others as having thoughts about themselves, as such, and the same account applies. I can describe you as thinking that you, yourself, are F, and your thought is about you, as such, just in case your thought, cast in the first-person, refers to an individual that you are disposed to identify as the thinker of that thought.

Thoughts need not be conscious, and essentially indexical reference to oneself can occur even when they are not. I realize that I, myself, am the one spilling sugar if I would identify the person I think is spilling sugar with the person who thinks that thought; in that case, my thought makes essentially indexical reference to myself. If the thought fails to be conscious, my realization will fail to be as well.

Does essentially indexical self-reference make a difference to the way beliefs and desires issue in action? David Kaplan's catchy example of my essentially indexical thought that my pants are on fire[13] may make it seem so, since I might behave differently if I thought only that some person's pants are on fire without also thinking that I am that person. Similarly, my

---

[13] "If I see, reflected in a window, the image of a man whose pants appear to be on fire, my behavior is sensitive to whether I think, 'His pants are on fire' or 'My pants are on fire', though the object of thought may be the same" (Kaplan 1989, 533). See also Lewis (1979, 543).

thinking that I, myself, should do a certain thing might result in my doing it, whereas my merely thinking that DR should do it might not result in my doing it if I did not also think that I was DR.

Such cases require care. My doing something when I think I should arguably results from that belief's interacting with a relevant occurrent desire I have to do what I should. Since I likely would not desire to do what DR should do if I did not think I was DR, I would in that case have no desire that would suitably interact with my belief that DR should do that thing. And if, still not recognizing that I am DR, I nonetheless had for some reason a desire to do what DR should do, my belief that DR should do something would then very likely result in my doing it, all without any essentially indexical self-reference. The belief must refer to oneself in an essentially indexical way only if the relevant desire does as well.

The situation is the same with thinking that one's pants are on fire. Even disregarding perceptual asymmetries, the desires that would pertain to my belief that my pants are on fire will doubtless differ in relevant ways from desires that would pertain to my belief that your pants are on fire. Similarly with my belief that DR's pants are on fire if I do not know that I am DR.

Many of our beliefs and desires, however, do not refer to oneself at all, as such or in any other way. I might want a beer and think that there is beer in the refrigerator. And the content of my desire might refer to me; it could be a desire that I have a beer. Things might then be different if instead I simply had a desire just that DR have a beer.

But the relevant desire need not refer to me at all; its content could be simply that having a beer would be nice. And that desire would likely lead to my going to get a beer not because the content of the desire refers to me, but because I am the individual that holds the desiderative attitude toward that content. Essentially indexical self-reference is not needed for beliefs and desires to issue in action.

It is sometimes objected to the HOT theory that non-linguistic beings, including human infants, could not have HOTs. But this is far from obvious. Many non-linguistic beings likely do have some thoughts, and the conceptual resources that HOTs use to describe their mental states could well, in the case of infants and non-human animals, be fairly minimal. Such beings would not, for example, have to conceptualize their mental states as being mental to be aware of those states in a way that results in their being conscious states. Perhaps language is required for HOTs about purely intentional states, such as thoughts. (See Rosenthal 2005, ch. 10, §v.)

But it is also far from obvious that our pretheoretic view about non-linguistic creatures requires ascribing to them conscious intentional states. Non-linguistic creatures and human infants might well be in intentional states, but it may also be that only their qualitative mental states are conscious.[14]

Essentially indexical self-reference involves a disposition to identify oneself as the individual that thinks a particular thought. So if one cannot be aware of oneself as being in intentional states unless one has language, essentially indexical self-reference will be available only for individuals that have language. And if HOTs require the essential indexical, creatures without language would not, on the HOT theory, be able to be in mental states that are conscious.

But weaker requirements arguably figure for the HOTs of non-linguistic creatures. The requirement that HOTs must refer to oneself in an essentially indexical way is to exclude irrelevant, inessential ways of referring to oneself. If I have a thought that DR is in pain without also thinking that I am DR, that will not result in my pain's being conscious. I will not in that case be aware of myself, as such, as being in pain.

But human infants and non-linguistic animals have no irrelevant, inessential ways of referring to themselves in thought. They do distinguish themselves from everything else, and can thereby refer to themselves in thought. But their HOTs do not require the essential indexical, since distinguishing themselves from everything else provides the only way they have to refer to themselves.

HOTs must make essentially indexical reference to the self to which they ascribe mental states. So if essentially indexical self-reference required special access to the self, a form of self-awareness would be needed that is more immediate and direct than the awareness of self that HOTs can deliver. But since we can explain essentially indexical self-reference by appeal to a disposition to identify the self that each first-person thought refers to with the individual that thinks that thought, we need not appeal to any such special, unmediated self-awareness. The reference to a self that occurs in each HOT, together with a disposition to identify that self with the thinker of that HOT, will suffice.

---

[14] More precisely, perhaps the mental states of non-linguistic creatures and human infants are conscious only in respect of their qualitative character and not, in addition, in respect of their intentional properties.

III. SELF-AWARENESS AND IMMUNITY TO ERROR

It has often been held that our awareness of our conscious states is both infallible and exhaustive, that no conscious state fails to have any feature that we are aware of it as having, and it has no mental feature of which we are unaware.[15]

Few today explicitly assert that our access to our own mental states is privileged in such a strong way. Still, there is a tension that affects some thinking about this issue. Some authors are tempted to hold that the reality of conscious mental states automatically coincides with the way they appear to us in consciousness, and even that it is groundless to distinguish appearance from reality in the case of conscious states.[16]

But the appearance of conscious states simply is the way they are from a first-person point of view, what it is like for one to be in those states. So it is not clear how the appearance of conscious states could coincide with their reality unless our access to our conscious states is, after all, exhaustive and infallible. And if the way conscious states are from a first-person point of view invariably coincides with the reality of those states, the way they appear to us will be both accurate and exhaustive.

But it is plain that it is not. There is doubtless much about the mental natures of our conscious states that we are unaware of, and much that we are, occasionally at least, wrong about. Often, for example, we are aware of a color experience in a relatively generic way, perhaps just as a perception of some red or other, though we have good reason to think that our visual sensations register exact shades.

Nor is our access to our conscious states infallible. There is robust experimental evidence that we are sometimes wrong about what thoughts and desires have led to our choices and actions. People often confabulate having thoughts or desires that explain their choices in situations in which we have independent evidence that the reported states could not have been operative.[17] And expectations can affect subjective qualitative experience, even as regards qualitative experiences such as pain (e.g. Koyama *et al.* 2005). In this kind of case, we become aware of ourselves as being in states that differ in their mental properties from the states we actually are in.

---

[15] The qualification about features that are mental is to allow the possibility that mental states are each identical with some physical state, in which case each mental state would have, in addition to its mental properties, some physical properties that are not mental.

[16] E.g., Nagel (1979, 174). I discuss difficulties with this view in Rosenthal (2011).

[17] The classic study is Nisbett and Wilson (1977). See also Johansson *et al.* (2005); Hall *et al.* (2010); Frith (2007); and Schnider (2008).

If awareness of our conscious states were infallible or exhaustive, that would be surprising and would call for some special explanation. And it is unclear what explanation would be credible. If a mental state's being conscious is due to a distinct higher-order awareness of that state, whether a HOT or any other kind of awareness, perhaps that higher-order awareness is typically accurate. But there is no guarantee that it will invariably be so.

Some theorists have urged that this higher-order awareness is intrinsic to the states it represents one as being in.[18] And it might seem tempting to hold that a higher-order awareness of a state that is intrinsic to that state would have to represent it correctly.[19] If a higher-order awareness were intrinsic to the state, perhaps nothing could mediate between the state and awareness of it, and perhaps nothing could then interfere with the accuracy of the awareness.

But misrepresentation remains an open possibility whether the awareness is intrinsic to or distinct from the state it is about. If they are distinct, it is clear that the awareness can misrepresent, since extraneous factors could interfere with the awareness. But even if it is intrinsic, the awareness would be only one of the state's mental properties, and the awareness might still misrepresent the state's other mental properties. Since the awareness, even if intrinsic to the state, is distinct from the mental properties it represents the state as having, there can still be no guarantee that the awareness represents those other properties accurately or fully. Whatever our account of consciousness, awareness of one's own mental states is neither infallible nor exhaustive.

But accurately and fully representing a state's mental properties is not the only type of privilege that is been proposed. Even if I may be wrong about the intentional content and qualitative character of my mental states, there is something else, Shoemaker has argued, that I cannot be in error about in connection with my mental states. "[I]t cannot happen," he urges, "that I am mistaken in saying 'I feel pain' because, although I do know of someone that feels pain, I am mistaken in thinking that person to be myself."[20]

---

[18] E.g., Kriegel (2009) and Gennaro (2006). It is unlikely that any higher-order awareness can be intrinsic to the state it is about. For one thing, that awareness typically occurs slightly after the state itself; see, e.g., Libet (2004, ch. 2) and Libet et al. (1979). Timing to one side, the higher-order state must be assertoric to result in one's being aware of the first-order state, and the first-order state will often have a non-assertoric mental attitude or, in the case of sensations, none at all. And a difference in mental attitude points to distinct states.

[19] As Kriegel (2009, ch. 4, §II) and Gennaro (2004, §2) urge. For convincing counter-arguments see Weisberg (2008).

[20] Shoemaker (1968, 8). Shoemaker urges that such immunity applies even when I take myself to be performing some action. See also Evans (1982a) and Bermúdez (1998).

Perhaps I can be wrong in such a case about whether it is pain that I feel. But I cannot be wrong in thinking that I consciously feel pain because, and only because, though I am right that somebody consciously does feel pain, I misidentify that person as being me. Such first-person thoughts would, in Shoemaker's classic phrase, be "immune to error through misidentification," specifically with respect to reference to oneself.

Shoemaker appeals to a well-known passage in *The Blue Book* in which Wittgenstein distinguishes two ways we use the first-person pronoun. On one use, which Wittgenstein labels "the use as object" ([1958] 1969, 66), I might believe that my arm is broken, and I could in that case be mistaken about whether the arm that is broken is actually mine; it might be the arm of another person. But Wittgenstein maintains when I say that I have a pain, this is a distinct use, on which "there is no question of recognizing [which] person" it is that is in pain. "To ask 'are you sure it is *you* who have pains?' would be nonsensical" ([1958] 1969, 67; emphasis Wittgenstein's).

Since no recognition figures in using 'I' in the second way according to Wittgenstein, he evidently holds also that when 'I' is used in that way, its use does not involve one's identifying oneself, as such or in any other way. And since no identification of oneself occurs in connection with one's using 'I' in that way, misidentification is not a possibility. There can be no failure of identification if there is no identification to begin with.

Shoemaker evidently sees things this way as well. Sometimes we refer to ourselves in a first-person way that does require identification of oneself. I may see somebody reflected in a mirror and identify the person thus reflected as myself. But sometimes the first-person reference one makes to oneself is, Shoemaker insists, "reference without identification." In such cases, he writes, "[m]y use of the word 'I' as the subject of my statement is not due to my having identified as myself something of which I know, or believe, or wish to say, that the predicate of my statement applies to it" (Shoemaker 1968, 9). And since "identification necessarily goes together with the possibility of misidentification" (13), when no identifying figures in first-person reference to oneself, no misidentification is possible either.

One might suppose that introspection enables us to identify ourselves in a way that precludes possible misidentification. It seems difficult to see how one could misidentify oneself in introspection. But Shoemaker argues that no identification occurs even in connection with introspective self-awareness. Suppose I am aware of a pain I have. For self-identification to figure in introspective awareness, Shoemaker urges, such awareness would have to be parallel to perception. And "[a]n essential part of the explanation of my perceptual awareness that John has a beard is the fact that the observed properties of the man I perceive, together with other things I know, are sufficient to identify him for me as John" (13).

But that model cannot, Shoemaker maintains, apply to my awareness of my pain. If there were a property that served to identify myself as myself, I would have not only to be aware of it, but also to be aware that it is I who is aware of it. "[I]n order to identify a self as myself by its possession of *this* property, I would have to know that *I* observe it by inner sense, and *this* self-knowledge, being the ground of my identification of the self as myself, could not itself be grounded on that identification" (14). No properties that one is aware of could, Shoemaker concludes, identify the possessor of those properties with the self that is aware of them.

I urged earlier that Hume's denial of awareness of a self resulted from his adoption of an exclusively perceptual model of awareness. Shoemaker construes Hume as rather having had in mind this concern about identi-fication. He sees Hume's insistence that we are never aware of a self[21] as amounting only to a denial that when one is aware of one's mental states, the resulting awareness of oneself rests in any way on some identification of oneself. It is unlikely that Hume meant no more than that, given his repeated explicit denial of awareness of self, though that denial does carry with it a denial that our awareness of our conscious states involves any identifying of a self.

Apart from how we understand Hume, the issue about identification is independent of whether our higher-order awareness of our conscious states is perceptual or due to HOTs. On a HOT theory, one is aware of each conscious state by having a HOT with the content that one is in that state. So Shoemaker's insistence that no identification underlies our awareness of ourselves raises a challenge that a HOT theory must address. The theory must explain what ensures that each HOT refers to the right self, that is, to the same self as the self that has that HOT. And it may seem that any such explanation would have to appeal to some prior awareness of self that does not itself rest on any kind of identification of the self. If so, HOTs cannot explain consciousness without appealing to the very awareness without identification that Shoemaker and Wittgenstein describe.

Our awareness of ourselves seems to differ in important ways from our awareness of everything other than ourselves. And it may be tempting to explain that intuitive difference by appeal to the idea that self-awareness and self-reference depend on no identification of self. But explaining the

---

[21] Shoemaker appeals to Hume's statement that "I never catch *myself* at any time without a perception, and never can observe anything but the perception" ([1739] 2000, 1, iv, 6, 165; emphasis Hume's).

difference in that way does not square with the way we actually operate when we assert that we are in some mental state or we are aware of ourselves as being in that state.

When I assert that you are in pain, I must identify the self I ascribe pain to in some way independent of your simply being in pain. But there is no similar need, according to Shoemaker, to identify the individual I take to be in pain when I assert that I am in pain or am aware of myself as being in pain. But it is far from clear that this is so. For one thing, when I am aware of myself as being in pain, I identify the individual I take to be in pain as the individual that is aware, in a distinctively first-person way, of being in pain. Such identification is very thin, and does not take one far. But if I am aware of myself as being in pain, it does distinguish the individual I take to be in pain from you, as well as any other person.

Such thin identification is seldom explicit. As noted in §11, if my higher-order awareness of a pain had the explicit content that the individual I am aware of as being in pain is identical with the individual that is thus aware, that higher-order awareness would itself be conscious. Since such higher-order awareness is seldom itself conscious, it cannot have that content. So the tie between the self one is aware of being in pain and the self that is thus aware must be due to a disposition to identify them, a disposition that is sometimes exhibited in an occurrent thought, though not all that often.

But this disposition is nonetheless sufficient to provide a way of identifying the individual that one is aware of as being in pain. When I am aware of being in pain or assert that I am in pain, I am disposed, if the question arises, to identify the individual I say is in pain as the individual that asserts or is thus aware. Needless to say, the question hardly ever arises, perhaps occurring only in theoretical discussions about self-identity and the like. But that hardly shows that awareness of oneself as being in a conscious state is not accompanied by a disposition to reply in that thin way, and perhaps with some impatience, to a question about who it is one is aware of as being in pain.

This thin self-identification operates along the same lines as essentially indexical self-reference. When I realize in an essentially indexical way that I, myself, am the one who is spilling sugar, I am disposed to identify the person that I think is spilling sugar with the person that thinks that thought. Similarly, when I am aware of myself as being in pain, I am disposed to identify the individual I am aware of as the very individual that is doing the identifying. That disposition to identify, thin as it is, distinguishes that individual I am aware of as being in pain from other candidates.

Because such identifying is so thin and because it is almost always a mere disposition to identify, it is natural to overlook it altogether and assume that no identification underlies one's awareness of oneself as being in a conscious state. But a total lack of any underlying identifying runs the risk of reducing the self in question to nothing. That indeed is the picture of self that figures in Wittgenstein's *Tractatus Logico-Philosophicus*: "The self does not belong to the world: rather, it is a limit of the world" (Wittgenstein 1974, 5.632: 69). And it is natural to assume that this picture remains operative in *The Blue Book* in connection with Wittgenstein's insistence that when I say that I have a pain, "there is no question of recognizing [which] person" it is that is in pain.[22]

Is a mere disposition to identify enough to undermine Shoemaker's claim that there is no need to identify, and Wittgenstein's that there is no question of recognition? Compare again Perry's sugar case. When I realize that I am the person spilling sugar, I have no thought to the effect that the person spilling is the person who thought somebody was spilling; it is just that I am now disposed to have that thought.

And compare a case of my identifying you as the person who is in pain; perhaps somebody cried out in pain and after looking around I see that it was you. I might have a thought with the explicit content that you, grasping your foot, are the person who cried out, but more likely I just have a thought that you are in pain, with an underlying disposition explicitly to identify you with the person that cried out. Most identifying, whether first or third person, takes place by way of dispositions to think identifying thoughts.

There is another reason to hold that awareness of oneself as being in a conscious state is sustained by a disposition to identify in some way the individual one is aware of as being in that state. When I am aware of, or refer to, myself as being in pain, I am aware of or refer to something that you can be aware of and refer to as well. The self I am aware of as being in pain is a self that you too can be aware of as being in pain. When you are aware of me as being in pain, it will not be the seemingly unmediated awareness characteristic of one's awareness of one's own pain, but we are nonetheless aware of the very same thing as being in pain. And when I say of myself that I am in pain, I refer to the very same self that you speak of when you say of me that I am in pain. Otherwise my statement that I am in pain would not say the same thing as your statement, 'You're in pain,' addressed to me, nor would that statement of yours contradict my statement that I am not in pain.

Immunity to error through misidentification occurs if I cannot be wrong in thinking that I consciously feel pain because, and only because, though

---

[22] Cf. what P. F. Strawson labels the no-ownership view of the self (1959, 95–98), and Strawson's reasons for seeing Wittgenstein as having held that view (1959, fn. on p. 95).

I am right that somebody does consciously feel pain, I misidentify that person as being me. And Shoemaker argues no such misidentification can occur in such a case because no identification figures in the first place.

But a disposition to identify oneself does underlie one's awareness as being in pain or some other conscious state. One is disposed in any such case to identify the self that one is aware of as being in the relevant conscious state as the self that is thus aware. Since that disposition to identify does underlie one's awareness of being in conscious states, we would need some other reason if we are to rule out misidentification.

One reason might be that it is conspicuously difficult to come up with a case in which misidentification seems to occur. It is not easy to describe a credible case in which, though I am right that somebody consciously feels pain, my sense that I am the one that is in pain is based solely on my having misidentified that person as being me. Assume that when I have a conscious pain, I identify the individual I am aware of as being in pain with the individual that is thus aware. But when it is somebody else that actually has a pain, what would lead me to misidentify that individual as myself? What circumstances can we describe in which such misidentification might occur?[23] One way to explain why it seems hard to specify such circumstances is to hold that misidentification in that kind of case simply is not possible.

But there is another explanation for why such cases are hard to come by, which rests on the compelling subjective sense we have that when we are in a conscious state, nothing mediates between the state one is aware of and one's awareness of that state.

Consider a conscious pain. There is a compelling subjective sense when a pain is conscious that nothing mediates between that pain and one's awareness of it; they seem subjectively to be of a piece. And since one is disposed to identify the individual that is in pain with the individual that is aware of pain, that awareness is tied to oneself. So it seems subjectively as though nothing comes between the self that is aware of the pain and the pain itself; the subjective sense of immediacy appears to forge an unbreakable tie between self and conscious state.

It is this appearance of an unbreakable tie between pain and oneself that makes it inviting to hold that misidentification of that self cannot occur.

[23] In (2005, ch. 13, §6) and (2004a, §4) I argued against immunity to error through misidentification based in part on an alleged counter-example. I am grateful to Myrto Mylopoulos for noting that the case I described in those places is not a counter-example and for pressing other points, which together led to my developing the present treatment. What I say here is similar in spirit to my earlier discussions, though with substantial differences in the argument.

If one ascribes a pain to oneself, it cannot be because one is right to ascribe pain to somebody, but mistaken about whether it is oneself.

But we have no reason to think that the lack of mediation in question is more than subjective appearance. For one thing, actual immediacy is not needed to explain our subjective sense of immediacy. When we are aware of being in a conscious state, we are unaware of any mediation; we are unaware of any observation that led to our being aware of the states, and unaware of any inference that led to that awareness. And that yields our subjective sense of immediacy; since we are not aware of any mediation, it is tempting to conclude that none occurs.

But there is much in our mental functioning that we are unaware of. That is especially so for mental processes, which lead from one mental state to another; we are seldom if ever aware of such intervening processes. So our not being aware of mediation is little reason to suppose that there isn't any. Only if we assumed that the mind is transparent to itself in respect of such mental processes could we explain apparent immediacy by appeal to actual immediacy.

It is tempting to hold that our awareness of our conscious states is always accurate about those states. And perhaps that would provide some reason to conclude that nothing mediates between those states and our awareness of them.[24] But the subjective sense that our awareness of our conscious states is always accurate is not reliable. We know that our awareness of what mental states we are in is sometimes mistaken. The appearance that we are never mistaken stems from our never having any first-person resources by means of which we might check and correct our first-person access to our mental states. The subjective sense that consciousness is the last word on our mental life does not support the view that nothing mediates between our conscious states and our awareness of them.

Nonetheless, the subjective appearance that no mediation occurs does make it difficult to construct a credible case in which one would ascribe a conscious state to oneself solely because one misidentified somebody else as oneself. Any case we describe as involving such misidentification is hard to see as also involving a subjective appearance that nothing mediates between the conscious state and oneself.

But since the subjective appearance that nothing mediates is unfounded, we should be wary of trusting the conclusion that no such misidentification can occur. Still, if such misidentification is possible, we should be able to describe a situation in which it is credible that it does occur. And it turns out

---

[24] Though even immediacy cannot guarantee reliability without other substantive assumptions.

that there is such a case. In multiple personality disorder, now better known as dissociative identity disorder (DID),[25] there are several apparent personalities, so-called alters, that inhabit a single body, or host. Each alter is dominant at different times from the others. These alters have different memories and different conscious access to mental states, though these states typically overlap somewhat and one alter often has access to the mental functioning of others, but not conversely.

These alters function in various ways as distinct selves. As with ordinary selves, the experiences, memories, thoughts, and desires of each alter are well integrated and connect in characteristic ways with the social ties and behavior patterns distinctive of that alter. And the awareness each alter has of those states will also be well integrated into its own mental life and behavior. But one alter will sometimes have subjectively unmediated awareness of the mental states of another; one alter will disavow being in particular mental states, ascribing them instead to another alter. In such cases, one alter has HOTs, reasonably well integrated into its own mental life, that describe the other alter as being in various mental states. (For more, see Ross 1997 and McAllister 2000.)

Because some alters have access not only to their own memories and experiences, but to those of other alters as well, there is room for confusion about which state belongs to which alter. So when one alter but not another actually has a pain,[26] it may happen that the other alter is sometimes wrong in being aware of itself as being in pain because, and only because, the alter that is aware of itself as being in pain misidentifies the other alter as itself.

What is it for conscious states that occur in a host body to belong to one alter rather than another? In ordinary cases, we rely on identifying the organism in question, but that is not available here. Nonetheless, we do have a robust commonsense test. A state belongs to one alter rather than another if it is suitably integrated with a range of other states characteristic of a particular alter, and not other alters. The range of mental states that anchor an alter's identity would include awareness of various mental states, where both the states and the awareness of them fit together in the way characteristic of a self. So for an alter to be aware of some particular state as belonging to itself, and not another alter, would require awareness of the state as belonging to an individual identified by appeal to the relevant range

---

[25] The newer designation supplanted the older one in DSM-IV (1994).

[26] If a pain or other mental state is integrated into the mental life and behavior of one alter but not another, it counts as belonging to the first and not the second.

of mental states. Some means of identification must underlie each alter's awareness of a mental state as belonging to itself.

Despite the strangeness of DID, we have no reason to doubt that the awareness of their own conscious states that alters enjoy is psychologically on a par with the awareness that occurs in ourselves. Whatever explanation we adopt for ourselves will have, with suitable adjustment, to work for them as well. And because their first-person awareness of conscious states sometimes requires identification of a relevant self, it is open that this holds also for normal cases.[27] And where identification can occur, there is a possibility of misidentification.

DID is a controversial subject, on which theorists and clinicians do not agree. But it is natural to see the phenomenon clinicians describe as involving multiple functioning selves. And that, together with the theoretical considerations that support the occurrence of self-identification in connection with our awareness of our conscious states, gives ample reason to doubt that we are immune to error through misidentification.

IV. SELF-IDENTIFICATION AND SELF-AWARENESS

If no disposition to identify oneself occurred in connection with our awareness of ourselves as being in conscious states, such self-ascription would be immune to error through misidentification. But a disposition to identify does arguably underlie one's awareness of one's own conscious states and reference to oneself as being in those states. One's awareness of one's conscious states consists in having a HOT that one is in that state, and the reference to oneself that such HOTs make is secured by a disposition to identify the relevant self as the individual that is thinking that very HOT.

Actual identifying is not required to undermine immunity to error through misidentification. Substantive misidentification does not require an actual identification; a disposition to identify is sufficient for misidentification to be possible. However one is disposed to identify the self that one is aware of as being in the conscious state, one could instead be disposed to identify that self in some other way instead.

But even though reliance on a disposition to identify does not raise a difficulty, perhaps the particular disposition appealed to in the foregoing

[27] Some theorists have speculated that even in normal cases there is something like multiple selves that must be suitably integrated within the overall psychological functioning relevant to a single individual person. On the possibility of something like multiple selves, see, e.g., Gazzaniga (1985) and Ornstein (1986).

proposal does. For the relevant misidentification to be possible, a disposition is needed to identify the self one is aware of as being in a particular conscious state. But is a disposition to identify that self merely as the self that is thus aware sufficient? A champion of immunity might well argue that such a thin type of identification cannot sustain the possibility of substantive error through misidentification. If the disposition to identify amounts to nothing more than that, perhaps substantive immunity is sustained after all.

One reason to doubt that such thin identification can undermine immunity is that it seems by itself not to anchor the self in any satisfactory way. When one is in a conscious pain, one is disposed to identify the individual that one is aware of as being in pain with the individual that is aware of the pain. But who is that individual? Such thin identification does not by itself seem to go beyond the uninformative Tractarian picture of the self as merely "a limit of the world."

Such thin identification faces another difficulty as well. There is a compelling subjective sense that all our conscious states belong to a single unified self, rather than there merely being one self for each conscious state. This is reflected in Hume's bundle metaphor itself, on which the self is "nothing but a bundle or collection of different perceptions"; Hume casts his very denial of awareness of a self in terms of a metaphor of unity. And it is what Kant insisted on in positing a "transcendental unity of self-consciousness" (B132). But the thin identifying of the self each conscious state belongs to with the self that is aware of that particular state cannot account for such unity and such bundling.

But that thin identification is not all we have to go on. We identify ourselves in ways that rely on a large and heterogeneous collection of factors, ranging from highly individual considerations to others that are fleeting and mundane. We appeal to location in time and place, current situation, bodily features, the current and past contents of our conscious mental lives, and various psychological characteristics and propensities, indeed, to all the properties we take ourselves to have. The factors that figure in our identifying ourselves are mostly theoretically uninteresting and have little systematic connection. There is no magic bullet by which we identify ourselves, whether in connection with conscious states or in any other respect. There is only a vast and heterogeneous collection of considerations, each of which is by itself relatively unimpressive, but whose combination is enough for us to identify ourselves whenever the question arises.

Each of these factors reflects some belief one has about oneself, ranging from what one's name is, where one lives, and what one's physical dimensions and location are to what the current contents are of one's consciousness. We can be in error about any of these beliefs about ourselves; indeed, we could be in error about most of them. One could be wrong about all one's personal history, background, and current circumstances. One might even be mistaken about one's location relative to other objects if, for example, one lacked relevant sensory input[28] or the input one had was suitably distorted.

One can be wrong even about what conscious states one is currently in. One may take oneself, in a distinctively first-person way, to have beliefs and preferences that one does not actually have and to lack those one does. And one may be wrong about the sensations or emotions one is aware of oneself as having.

But how does this multitude of ways in which we identify ourselves help? How do these many ways of identifying oneself give substance to the disposition to thinly identify the self one is aware of as being in conscious states with the self that is thus aware?

Identifying oneself always consists of saying who it is that one is talking or thinking about when one talks or thinks about oneself, that is, when one has first-person thoughts or makes first-person remarks that express those thoughts. One picks out the individual those first-person thoughts are about by reference to a diverse collection of contingent properties, such as those mentioned above. The reference any new first-person thought makes to oneself is secured by appeal to the descriptive content of other, prior first-person thoughts, which gradually enlarges the stock of self-identifying thoughts available to secure such reference.

This applies to HOTs, which are themselves cast in the first person, no less than to other, more mundane first-person thoughts. Each HOT refers to a self as being in a particular mental state, and we are in every case disposed to identify that self with the individual that thinks the HOT. But we are also disposed to identify that self with the individual that all our other first-person thoughts refer to. So the disposition to thinly identify the self one is aware of as being in a particular state with the individual that is thus aware is supplemented by the disposition to identify that individual with the referent of a multitude of other first-person thoughts.

First-person thoughts are cast in terms of the mental analogue of the first-person pronoun, 'I.' That includes HOTs, whose content is that I am in a particular state. And 'I' and its mental analogue function somewhat as do proper names. We routinely take distinct tokens of a proper name all to

---

[28] As Anscombe imagines (Anscombe 1975, 58).

refer to the same individual unless something overrides that default assumption. Similarly, we take all tokens of the mental analogue of 'I' in our first-person thoughts also to refer to the same individual. It is by no means easy, moreover, to override this default assumption for the mental analogue of 'I,' though as suggested in §III, this seems to happen in cases of DID. 'I' and its mental analogue refer to whatever individual says or thinks something in first-person terms, and we also take them to refer to one and the same individual across various first-person thoughts or speech acts.

G. E. M. Anscombe (1975) has urged that 'I' does not function as proper names do, maintaining that the first-person thought that I am standing, does not predicate the concept *standing* of a subject, but instead simply exhibits a wholly unmediated conception of standing. But if that were so, we would be unable to explain the incompatibility of my thought that I am standing with your thought that I am not. Similarly for awareness of one's conscious states; my HOT that I am in pain is incompatible with your thought that I am not.

The reference HOTs make to a self rests on a disposition to identify the self each HOT refers to as being in a particular mental state as being the self that thinks that HOT. But your thought that I am not in pain presumably makes no appeal, nor are you in any way disposed to appeal to the self that is aware of being in pain. So if my disposition to identify the self my HOT refers to as being in pain did not connect with more substantive ways of identifying myself, there would be nothing that could ground the incompatibility of my HOT that I am in pain with your third-person thought that I am not.

But because HOTs are first-person thoughts, my disposition to identify the self that is in pain as the thinker of a HOT relies for additional identifying characteristics on the battery of other first-person thoughts I have. We are disposed to take our first-person thoughts and speech acts as referring to the same individual from one first-person thought to another. Since my HOTs are cast in the first person, my disposition to take the mental analogue of 'I' to refer to a single individual provides a basis for the default assumption that my conscious states all belong to a single self.

Although the disposition to identify the self that each HOT refers to cannot sustain our subjective sense of a single unified self, the pervasive practice of taking first-person thoughts to refer to a single self does. Each awareness of a mental state as belonging to a self that is referred to in the first person is tied to every other such awareness. And each such awareness is backed by a disposition to identify the self one is aware of as being in the state in question as the self that is thus aware. Our default practice with

first-person thoughts explains the compelling subjective sense we have of
the unity of consciousness.

This conscious sense of unity does not require having an explicit, conscious thought that all occurrences of the mental analogue of 'I' refer to a
single thing. We typically have a sense that we are talking about one and the
same individual when we use different tokens of a proper name and their
mental analogues, but we seldom have any actual thought to the effect that
such co-reference obtains. Such a thought would arise only if something
seemed to challenge or override the default of taking tokens of the same type
to refer to the same thing. The same holds for talking or thinking about
oneself using different tokens of 'I' or its mental analogue. We are disposed
to take all our first-person thoughts to refer to a single individual, though it
is rare that one has a thought that has that explicit content.

Explaining our conscious sense of unity in dispositional terms fits with
our subjective experience. We seldom have any occurrent awareness of
ourselves as unified, though we are disposed to regard our conscious states
as belonging to a single unified self. That our subjective sense of unity is
dispositional fits also with Kant's having described the unity of self-
consciousness as transcendental;[29] it is something we must assume for our
actual mental lives even to be possible. And he maintains only that the
representation 'I think' must be able to accompany all other representations,
not that it actually does (B131–2; cf. B406).

We are disposed to take our first-person thoughts to be about the same
individual from one thought to another, and the HOTs in virtue of which
we are aware of our conscious states are first-person thoughts. This enables
identifying of the self one is aware of as being in various conscious states
in ways that go well beyond the thin identification as the self that is aware
of those conscious states. We are disposed to identify the self our HOTs
refer to as the self that figures in a multitude of heterogeneous, contingent
first-person thoughts that have nothing to do with what conscious states
we are in.

Indeed, it is hard to imagine a case in which somebody is aware of being
in pain but is wholly unable to identify in any other way the individual that
person is aware of as being in pain. What sort of awareness could it be that is
not sustained by some independent way of identifying the individual one is
aware of as being in pain?

These informative ways of self-identification, which go beyond what
conscious states one is aware of, underwrite the conceptual ties that hold

---

[29] The representation 'I think' is a non-empirical (B132) or transcendental (B401, A343) representation.

between my HOTs about my own conscious states and your thoughts about what mental states I am in. My HOT that I am in pain contradicts yours that I am not in pain because we are both disposed to identify the self in question by suitably overlapping batteries of heterogeneous, contingent thoughts about myself. My disposition to identify the self I am aware of as being in various conscious states with the self that is thus aware is buttressed by a multitude of other, more mundane first-person thoughts. The result is a substantive identification of the self that one is in each case aware of as being in a conscious state. And that substantive identification undermines immunity to error through misidentification.

There is nothing special or mysterious about the way we are aware of our mental states or the individual they belong to that issues in our subjective sense that our conscious states all belong to a single self. That subjective sense results simply from our commonsense assumption that the heterogeneous collection of ways in which we identify ourselves combine to pick out one individual, that the mental analogue of 'I' in all our first-person thoughts refers to a single self.

Nonetheless, some theorists have urged that since the identification of everything apart from ourselves is ultimately relative to our awareness of ourselves, that awareness must be unique and special (e.g. Shoemaker 1968; Lewis 1979; and Chisholm 1981, ch. 3, esp. 29–32). And if that is so, we would be unable to identify ourselves by appeal to a heterogeneous battery of properties relying on the multitude of first-person thoughts we have about ourselves. Self-awareness would then provide a fixed point, independent of any need to identify and by appeal to which we identify all other things.

But we seldom do appeal to ourselves when we identify other things. Identifying objects perceptually does depend on the perceptual relationship one has to the objects we perceive, but no self-awareness underlies such perceptual identifying. Indeed, one can identify perceived objects even when the perceiving is not at all conscious. One's bodily location does provide the origin for the coordinate system within which one locates and identifies other objects. But that coordinate system reflects the sensory field of the relevant perceptual modality, and does not derive from some awareness of oneself. We may occasionally identify things perceptually relative to ourselves, but that is rather unusual; we typically identify the things we perceive relative to a larger scheme of things that contains the target object. And when appeal to that larger framework fails to identify for whatever reason, nothing about the way we are aware of ourselves independently of that larger framework will come to our rescue.

Each HOT represents the mental state it is about as belonging to some individual. One secures informative reference to that individual by way of a large collection of other, heterogeneous first-person thoughts. And we identify in that way the self to which each HOT ascribes its target as being the same from one of an individual's HOTs to another. Indeed, this provides an answer, which Hume despaired of giving, to his challenge "to explain the principles, that unite our successive perceptions in our thought or consciousness" (Appendix, 400).

Each of us is aware of our conscious states as all belonging to a single self. But by itself that does not show that the self that we are aware of our conscious states as belonging to actually exists. Perhaps one's HOTs do not, after all, refer to the same self for all of an individual's HOTs.[30] The mental analogue of 'I' in each HOT refers to whatever individual thinks that thought. But perhaps that individual is different for a particular person's HOTs from one HOT to another or between groups of HOTs; perhaps there is nothing underlying whatever functional integration obtains that we can reasonably call a self. But whatever the case about those questions, the natural practice of identifying a self by appeal to the referent of an individual's first-person thoughts is sufficient to explain the compelling sense each of us has of a unified center of consciousness.

---

[30] It is convenient to posit a single self when an individual's mental life and behavior is suitably well integrated. Similarly, we countenance multiple alters in DID when such integration breaks down and there are instead several independent streams of mental states in a single individual, each of which is relatively self-contained and well integrated.

For challenging doubts and useful references about whether there is normally a single, unified self for each individual, see Klein (2010).

CHAPTER 2

Self-representationalism and the explanatory gap

Uriah Kriegel

INTRODUCTION

According to the self-representational theory of consciousness – *self-representationalism* for short – a mental state is phenomenally conscious when, and only when, it represents itself in the right way. Part of the motivation for this view is a conception of phenomenal consciousness as involving essentially a subtle, primordial kind of self-consciousness. A consequence of this conception is that the alleged explanatory gap between phenomenal consciousness and physical properties is *eo ipso* an explanatory gap between (the relevant kind of) self-consciousness and physical properties. In this chapter, I consider how self-representationalism might address this explanatory gap. I open with a presentation of self-representationalism and the motivation for it (§1). After introducing the explanatory gap, and suggesting that on self-representationalism it would apply to self-consciousness (§2), I present what I take to be the most promising self-representational approach to the explanatory gap (§3). That approach is threatened, however, by an objection to self-representationalism, due to Levine, which I call the *just more representation* objection (§4). I close with a discussion of how the self-representationalist might approach the objection (§5).

I. SELF-REPRESENTATIONALISM

In *Subjective Consciousness: A Self-Representational Theory* (henceforth, SC), I develop and defend a specific version of self-representationalism. Self-representationalism can be formulated as follows:

(SR) Necessarily, for any mental state M, M is phenomenally conscious iff M represents itself in the right way.

Different versions of SR can be obtained by unpacking "in the right way" in different ways. My own version construes "the right way" as "non-derivatively, specifically, and essentially."[1]

What motivates SR, at least to me, is a certain conception of the structure of phenomenal character. As I look at the blue sky, I undergo a conscious experience, and there is a bluish way it is like for me to undergo that experience. This "bluish way it is like for me" is the experience's phenomenal character. As Levine (2001) notes, there is a conceptual distinction to be drawn between two components of this "bluish way it is like for me": (i) the bluish component, and (ii) the for-me component. I call the former *qualitative character* and the latter *subjective character* (Kriegel 2005, 2009). To a first approximation, the experience's bluish qualitative character is what makes it the experience it is, but its for-me-ness is what makes it an experience at all. A better, if initially less clear, approximation is this: my experience is the experience it is because it is bluish-for-me, and is an experience at all because it is somehow-for-me (or qualitatively-for-me).[2] Thus qualitative character is what varies among conscious experiences, while subjective character is what is common to them.

Many philosophers have assumed that the core of the problem of consciousness is qualitative character, but an interesting result of the above conception of the structure of phenomenal character is that it is actually subjective character that is more central (Levine 2001; Kriegel 2009). Although it is important to understand what accounts for the differences among conscious experiences, it is more central to the problem of consciousness to understand what distinguishes conscious experiences from non-conscious mental states. According to Levine and me, the deeply mystifying feature of phenomenal consciousness is that when I have a conscious experience, the experience does not occur only *in me*, but also *for me*. There is some sort of direct presence, a subjective significance, of the

---

[1] I explain what these qualifications mean toward the end of chapter 4 of the book. Their exact nature will not matter here, so I will not go into it here. It does matter, however, that there *exist* such qualifications, meaning that not any old self-representation is supposed to be sufficient for phenomenal consciousness, only a specific variety. Prinz (this volume) objects to self-representationalism that self-representation cannot suffice for phenomenality, since the word 'word' represents itself but is not phenomenal. This specific example is actually discussed in SC chapter 4 by way of motivating one of the three qualifiers. For Prinz's objection to work, it would have to cite not just any old instance of non-phenomenal self-representation, but an instance of non-phenomenal self-representation that is non-derivative, specific, and essential.

[2] The latter is a determinable of which the former is a determinate. As is common, what makes X the X it is, is a determinate of what makes it an X at all.

experience to the subject. This is of course not uncontroversial, but I will not argue for it here. What I want to focus on is the inference *from* this conception of the structure of phenomenal character *to* self-representationalism.

Self-representationalism is essentially an account of subjective character: it claims that a mental state has subjective character just in case, and because, it represents itself in the right way.[3] The argument for this can be thought of as proceeding in three stages. Here I will only sketch the argument.[4]

First, for a conscious experience to be not only *in* me, but also *for* me, I would have to be *aware* of it. The awareness in question need not be particularly focused or attentive. But there must be some minimal awareness of a mental state if the state is to be described as exhibiting "for-me-ness." So we can reason as follows:

(1) Necessarily, for any mental state M and subject S, such that S is in M, M is phenomenally conscious iff M has subjective character (is *for* S).

(2) Necessarily, for any mental state M and subject S, such that S is in M, M has subjective character (is *for* S) iff S is aware of M in the right way. Therefore,

(3) Necessarily, for any mental state M and subject S, such that S is in M, M is phenomenally conscious iff S is aware of M in the right way. (1,2)

This is the first stage of the argument. It takes us from phenomenal character to awareness.

The second stage employs crucially a pair of relatively uncontroversial lemmas, to the effects that (a) being aware of something is a matter of representing it and (b) representing something is a matter of being in a mental state that represents it:

(4) Necessarily, for any entity X and subject S, S is aware of X in the right way iff S has a representation of X of the right kind. (Lemma)

(5) Necessarily, for any entity X and subject S, S has a representation of X of the right kind iff there is a mental state M*, such that (i) S is in M* and (ii) M* represents X in the right way. (Lemma) Therefore,

(6) Necessarily, for any mental state M and subject S, such that S is in M, M is phenomenally conscious iff there is a mental state M*,

---

[3] Here the 'because' must be understood as denoting a constitutive rather than causal explanation. That is, it is not the 'because' of "I am a bachelor because I never met the right woman," but the 'because' of "I am a bachelor because I am an unmarried man."

[4] For details, see ch. 4 of SC.

such that (i) S is in M* and (ii) M* represents M in the right way.
(3,4,5)

This is the second stage, which takes us from awareness to representation.

The third stage takes us from representation to self-representation. It does so by first setting up a dilemma – are the conscious state and its representation numerically distinct or numerically identical? – and then offering considerations in favor of the latter horn. Thus:

(7) For any mental states M and M*, either M = M* or M ≠ M*. (Excluded middle)

(8) Necessarily, for no mental state M and subject S, such that S is in M, M is phenomenally conscious iff there is a mental state M*, such that (i) S is in M*, (ii) M* represents M in the right way, and (iii) M ≠ M*. Therefore,

(9) Necessarily, for any mental state M and subject S, such that S is in M, M is phenomenally conscious iff there is a mental state M*, such that (i) S is in M*, (ii) M* represents M in the right way, and (iii) M = M*. (6,7,8)

The conclusion, Proposition 9, is equivalent to SR. The negation of Premise 8, while not equivalent to the so-called higher-order theory of consciousness, is a commitment of that theory.[5] What is needed to complete the argument are considerations that support Premise 8.[6]

In chapter 4 of SC I offer a battery of considerations against higher-order theory, hence in favor of Premise 8. I cannot go through all of them, and anyway many are familiar from the literature. But the consideration which is least familiar, yet which personally has been most persuasive to me, can be put thus: for-me-ness is internal to the phenomenology of conscious experience – it is a component of phenomenal character, after all – and this cannot be accommodated by higher-order theory, only by self-representationalism. There are two parts to this.

The first part is the claim that for-me-ness is internal to the phenomenology – that it is itself a conscious phenomenon. This seems to me self-evident. The very reason to believe in the for-me-ness of experience is fundamentally phenomenological: it is derived not from experimental research, nor from conceptual analysis, nor from any other sources, but

---

[5] For higher-order theory, see (most notably) Rosenthal (1990, 2005).

[6] The argument is in actuality a little more complicated than this, because there are in fact three possible views here of what makes mental states phenomenally conscious: (a) that each is represented by itself; (b) that each is represented by a numerically distinct state; (c) that some are represented by themselves and some by numerically distinct states. Ruling out (b) is thus insufficient. Ruling out (c) is part of the argument for (a). For details, see SC ch. 4.

rather from a certain first-person impression. This suggests that for-me-ness is phenomenologically manifest.[7]

The second part is the claim that only SR can accommodate the phenomenological manifest-ness of for-me-ness. The reasoning here is this. If the for-me-ness of a conscious mental state M is itself conscious, then the mental state that represents M, i.e. M*, must be a conscious mental state. If M* is numerically identical to M, as per SR, it is predictable that M* be conscious, since M is conscious and M* = M. But if M and M* are numerically distinct, as per higher-order theory, M*'s being conscious is not only inexplicable, but in fact leads straightforwardly to an infinite regress: M*'s being conscious requires the postulation of a third-order M**, and so on.

This argument is developed in much greater detail in SC, chapter 4. It amounts to splitting Premise 8 in the above argument into two parts:

(8a) Necessarily, for any mental state M and subject S, such that S is in M, M is phenomenally conscious iff there is a mental state M*, such that (i) S is in M*, (ii) M* represents M in the right way, and (iii) M* is conscious. (Phenomenological observation)

(8b) Necessarily, for no mental state M and subject S, such that S is in M, M is phenomenally conscious iff there is a mental state M*, such that (i) S is in M*, (ii) M* represents M in the right way, (iii) M* is conscious, and (iv) M ≠ M*. (On pain of infinite regress)

Together, 8a and 8b entail 8. With 8 in place, and given our starting point in 1 and 2 and the relatively uncontroversial lemmas in 4 and 5, we obtain 9. Call this the *master argument for self-representationalism*.

2. SELF-CONSCIOUSNESS AND THE EXPLANATORY GAP

I mentioned that, according to the conception of phenomenal character that motivates self-representationalism, the core of the problem of consciousness pertains to subjective character. This can be put in terms of the so-called explanatory gap (Levine 1983): while there may be some perplexity as to how we might reductively explain differences in phenomenal character in terms of neural activity, surely the heart of the philosophical anxiety

---

[7] Note that claiming that for-me-ness is phenomenologically manifest need not be the same as claiming that for-me-ness is *introspectively* manifest. In SC ch. 5, I argue that for-me-ness is actually not introspectible, even though it is phenomenologically manifest in a non-introspective manner. How exactly this could be is something I cannot go into here, but observe that it will address Prinz's (this volume) objection that he does not find any for-me-ness when he introspects his own phenomenal experience.

surrounding consciousness concerns how we might reductively explain the very existence of phenomenal character. It is the existence conditions of phenomenality, not its identity conditions, which present the deep mystery.

If this is right, then the core of the philosophical problem of consciousness is the explanatory gap between subjective character – the for-me-ness of conscious states – and physical properties. This is a surprising result, insofar as there is clearly a close connection between subjective character and self-consciousness, and yet it is a staple of recent discussions of consciousness that the explanatory gap is properly applied to phenomenal consciousness but *not* self-consciousness. In this section, I want to explore the connection between subjective character and self-consciousness, and its implications for the explanatory gap. More specifically, I want to argue that there are two different phenomena of self-consciousness, and while one of them is at most *contingently* connected to subjective character, the other is *essentially* connected.

The distinction between two phenomena of self-consciousness that I have in mind can be brought out by contrasting two types of *report* of self-consciousness:

(R1) I am self-conscious of perceiving the laptop.
(R2) I am self-consciously perceiving the laptop.

In R1, the self-consciousness term (if you please) is a transitive verb. If we take the surface grammar at face value, this suggests a *relation* between me and my perceiving. In R2, however, the self-consciousness term is an adverb, which suggests an *intrinsic modification* of my perceiving. That is, in R2 the self-consciousness term does not denote a state of standing in a relation to my perception (or my perceiving), but rather designates the *way* I am having (or doing) my perceiving. We may call the self-consciousness reported in R1 *transitive self-consciousness* and that in R2 *intransitive self-consciousness* (Kriegel 2003, 2004).

To draw a terminological, or even conceptual, distinction between transitive and intransitive self-consciousness is not to beg the question of whether they are two distinct and irreducible properties. Indeed, a natural thought is that intransitive self-consciousness is analyzable in terms of transitive self-consciousness. For example, one might hold that I am self-consciously perceiving x iff I (i) am perceiving x and (ii) am self-conscious *of* perceiving x. On this suggestion, to perceive self-consciously is simply to perceive *and* be self-conscious of doing so.[8]

---

[8] A variation on this view would have it that I am self-consciously perceiving x iff (i) I am perceiving x and (ii) I am *disposed* to become self-conscious of doing so.

However, this particular analysis is belied by an important feature of the surface grammar of R1 and R2. In R1, the state of self-consciousness takes one's perception as an object. So the perception of which I am self-conscious and the state of self-consciousness itself are treated as two *numerically distinct* mental states. By contrast, in R2 there is no numerical distinction between the perception and the state of self-consciousness: the perception *is* the state of self-consciousness. Since the adverb 'self-consciously' denotes a *way* I am having my perception, no *extra* act of self-consciousness need take place *after* the perception occurs. Rather, self-consciously is *how* the perception occurs.

The conceptual distinction between transitive and intransitive self-consciousness does not *entail* a corresponding metaphysical distinction, but it does create a *prima facie* case, or presumption, in favor of one. We may think of it as producing defeasible evidence for the metaphysical distinction. Until the evidence is actually defeated, by the presentation of a viable analysis of intransitive in terms of transitive self-consciousness, we ought to proceed on the assumption that these are two different properties. Elsewhere, I develop a more sustained argument to the effect that they are indeed two different properties (Kriegel 2004).

It is interesting to note a certain parallelism between the kind of phenomenon intransitive self-consciousness is and the nature of subjective character according to self-representationalism. In the former, there turns out to be numerical identity between the conscious state and the state of self-consciousness; in the latter, between the conscious state and the subject's awareness of it. This may suggest that there is an intimate connection between intransitive self-consciousness and subjective character. The *simplest* account of this connection would be a certain *identity thesis*: subjective character *just is* intransitive self-consciousness. On this view, the fact that a conscious experience is *for the subject* and the fact that the subject self-consciously undergoes the experience is one and the same fact: to say that there is a way it is like for me to perceive the sky is to say that I self-consciously perceive the sky.

The reasoning we have pursued leads to an interesting conclusion: the core of the problem of consciousness is the explanatory gap between a certain kind of self-consciousness – namely, intransitive self-consciousness – and physical properties. It is the fact that we cannot reductively explain in terms of neural activity that makes it the case that a subject not only perceives *x*, but does so *self-consciously*, without quite being self-conscious *of* doing so, that is at the source of the philosophical anxiety surrounding consciousness.

In SC chs. 6–8, I suggest a potential neural reducer of subjective character. My strategy is to first specify the abstract structure involved in a mental
state's self-representing, and then identify a neural structure that realizes
this abstract specification. This means, in the first instance, getting clear on
what is involved in self-representation, preferably in naturalistic terms. The
natural approach to this challenge is to consult naturalistic theories of
mental representation, and suggest that whatever natural relation they
identify as underlying mental representation – informational, teleological,
or what have you – is the kind of relation that mental states can sometimes
bear to themselves. Call the kind of self-representation this would be *crude
self-representation*. The problem with crude self-representation is that when
we actually consult such theories as Dretske's (1981, 1988), Millikan's (1984),
and Fodor's (1990), we find that they identify natural relations that are anti-
reflexive: nothing can bear them to itself. At its heart, the problem is that
these relations typically involve causal relations, and those are often anti-
reflexive.[9]

In chapter 6 of SC, I offer an account of self-representation intended
to make it consistent with naturalistic accounts of mental representation.
To a first (and rough) approximation, the story is this. First, there is a
distinction to be drawn between direct and indirect representation. For
example, I might represent a house by representing its façade. In this case,
I represent the façade directly and the house indirectly. Secondly, for M to
self-represent is for M to have two parts, M_1 and M_2, such that M_2
represents both (i) M_1 *directly* and (ii) M *indirectly*. (M_2 represents M *by*
representing M_1, just as a picture represents the house by representing its
façade.) Thirdly, a naturalistic theory of mental representation can have two
components: one accounting for *direct* representation in terms of the
natural relation identified by the best naturalistic theory, and one accounting for *indirect* representation in terms of the combination of the relevant
natural relation and some story about what makes it the case that a direct
representation of x is also an indirect representation of y. Presumably, some
relation must hold between x and y when and only when any direct
representation of x also serves as an indirect representation of y; we may
call the relation R that x bears to y just when this is so the *representation-
transmission* relation.[10] For example, a picture might represent a façade in

---

[9] Certainly the causal relation of "x causes y" is anti-reflexive, since nothing can cause its own
   occurrence, but other, subtler causal relations are often anti-reflexive as well, and as I argue in SC
   chapter 6, those adverted to by Dretske, Millikan, and Fodor in fact are.
[10] What the representation-transmission relation actually is needs to be addressed by a full account;
   I discuss this matter, somewhat preliminarily, in SC chapter 6.

virtue of bearing the right teleo-informational relation to it, and represent the house of which it is a façade in virtue of (i) bearing that relation to the façade and (ii) the façade bearing the representation-transmission relation to the house. When we put together all three elements into an overall account of self-representation, we obtain the following: a self-representing mental state is a mental state with two parts, such that one part bears the right natural (e.g. teleo-informational) relation to the other part and this second part bears the representation-transmission relation to the whole of which they are both parts. More precisely: M represents itself iff there are states M_1 and M_2, such that (i) M_1 is a proper part of M, (ii) M_2 is a proper part of M, (iii) M_1 bears the right natural relation to M_2, and (iv) M_2 bears the representation-transmission relation R to M. To distinguish it from crude self-representation, call this *subtle self-representation*.[11]

Once this relatively specific structure has been identified, we can seek brain structures and processes that implement it: neural structures we have good reasons to describe as involving two parts one of which bears the right natural relation to the other while the other bears the right representation-transmission relation to the whole of which they are both parts. Although an endeavor of this sort is extremely speculative at present, I indulge in it in ch. 7 of SC. With the aid of several empirical claims, the speculative hypothesis I arrive at is this: a conscious experience of blue, say, is realized by neural synchronization of activation in the right part of the visual cortex – V_4, as it happens – and the dorsolateral prefrontal cortex (dlPFC). The V_4 activation realizes M_1, the dlPFC activation realizes M_2, and the neural synchronization between them realizes the cognitive-unity relation between M_1 and M_2 in virtue of which they are parts of a single state rather than two separate states. Thus a brain state such as this realizes the perceptual experience's qualitative character through the specific activation in sensory cortex (in this case, the right subpopulation of neurons in V_4) and its subjective character, or intransitive self-consciousness, through the neural synchronization with dlPFC activation.

Observe that this account of the neural implementation of self-representation, founded as it is on a distinction between crude and subtle self-representation, casts self-representation as neurobiologically perfectly plausible. Prinz (this volume) complains of neurobiological implausibility

---

[11] One worry that arises immediately here is in what substantive way this subtle self-representation is different from standard higher-order representation: what exactly makes (non-conventionally) M_1 and M_2 two parts of a single mental state rather than two distinct mental states. I address this too in SC chapter 6, requiring a robust and psychologically real relation of cognitive unity between M_1 and M_2. (For more detail, see SC chapter 6.)

in self-representationalism, on the grounds that neurons do not appear to represent themselves. This objection misfires, however, as subtle self-representation does not require, and in fact shuns, the notion that some neurons represent themselves. What self-represents is not this or that neuron, but a structured neural state, which moreover self-represents only insofar as some part of it represents the whole of it.

In any case, given the argument of this section, the above account of neural implementation suggests that the alleged explanatory gap between consciousness and matter comes down to a much more specific explanatory gap between intransitive self-consciousness and synchronization with dlPFC activation. The problem of consciousness can thus be distilled into the problem of bridging the explanatory gap between intransitive self-consciousness and synchronization with dlPFC activation.

3. EXPLANATORY GAPS AND EXPLANATORY SEQUENCES

How *could* those brute and blind processes unfolding in the dark corners of the dorsolateral prefrontal cortex constitute a subject's not only perceiving something, but perceiving it self-consciously, in a way the blindsight patient who perceives the same thing does not?

Consider a sorites series that takes you from a yellow circle to a red circle. As you are force-marched through the series, any pair of adjacent circles are visually indistinguishable to you, yet the first and last circles are very much distinguishable. In other words, when the steps in a sequence of this sort are small enough, the relation of visual indiscriminability will hold between the two sides of each step but not between the start and end points of the sequence. The relation of explainability – or perhaps just reductive explainability (as distinguished, say, from causal explainability) – might exhibit similar behavior, though perhaps for different reasons (not because it is vague). A series of claims can be envisaged, such that every claim $n+1$ is a reductive explanation of claim n, but there is no reductive-explanatory relation between the first and last claims.

In light of the previous sections, we might wish to consider the following sequence of proposed explanatory steps:

Step 1:   explain subjective character/intransitive self-consciousness in terms of a certain type of awareness

Step 2:   explain this type of awareness in terms of representation

Step 3:   explain the relevant kind of representation in terms of self-representation

Step 4: explain the naturalistic possibility of self-representation in terms of subtle self-representation

Step 5: explain subtle self-representation in terms of synchronization with dlPFC activation

Each step seems to involve an explanatory move that does not strike us immediately as outlandish: the gap between explanandum and explanans does not seem obviously unbridgeable. So the relevant explanation relation *does* hold within each step.[12] Yet the explanatory gap looms ominously when we consider, in one intellectual act as it were, intransitive self-consciousness and synchronization with dlPFC activity. The same sense of mystery obtains if we add:

Step 0: explain phenomenal consciousness in terms of subjective character/intransitive self-consciousness

This is the more familiar explanatory gap, between phenomenal consciousness and neural activation, which I claim is due to the more specific gap concerning subjective character or intransitive self-consciousness.

In any case, on this line of thought the explanatory gap arises because of an unwarranted expectation that a complex sequence of explanations could be appreciated in one intellectual act. When we look at water and H_2O, a single intellectual act would leave us equally puzzled about how it is that the right interlocking of an oxygen atom and two hydrogen atoms could make something *wet*. It is a general feature of the relationship between the manifest image and the scientific image that structures and processes from the latter do not illuminate ones from the former in such a direct way. The illumination is not provided in a single encompassing act of apprehension. Rather, it is appreciated indirectly through patient consideration of a sequence of local explanations too long or complex to grasp at once (see Pollock and Cruz 1999).[13]

---

[12] In the first step, it is based on the first-person impression that motivates the conception of the structure of phenomenal character presented above; in the second and third steps, it is based on some kind of *a priori* reasoning; in the fourth step, on various forms of philosophical argumentation (namely, those that undermine higher-order theory); in the fifth step, on another kind of philosophical argumentation (from the prior commitment to naturalization); and in the sixth, by a combination of empirical and speculative considerations. Note that with the exception of the very last step, all steps in this reasoning can be understood as broadly *a priori*.

[13] Again, compare the proof of Fermat's Last Theorem. Having read through the 100-page proof, one does not find oneself in a position to enjoy the experience of direct grasp of *why it should be* that $x^n + y^n \neq z^n$ whenever x, y, and z are non-zero integers and $n > 2$. But with sufficient acumen in Number Theory, one might just find oneself in a position to trust that the theorem does in fact hold.

Note as well that we are familiar, in everyday life, with two kinds of understanding. Sometimes we understand something in a purely intellectual, somewhat cold-blooded manner. On other, relatively rarer occasions, we understand something in a more visceral way, where we feel like we can *see* the truth (or plausibility) of some notion. Indeed, it sometimes happens that we understand something first in the cold-blooded manner and suddenly in the more visceral way. The latter experience of understanding is much more phenomenologically impressive, and is also more *satisfying* and more confidence-imbuing. But it is also rarer, and there is no reason to suppose that it is always available: there may be areas where the human cognitive system does not have the resources that would allow us to undergo the experience of this more visceral variety of understanding. We must there rest content with the phenomenologically lamer variety of understanding – and remember that it is still a variety of *understanding*.[14]

Taking these considerations into account, one may suggest that the explanatory gap is an illusion grounded in the attempt to take in a complex sequence of explanations in a single intellectual act.[15] The sequence may simply be too complex for us to do so successfully, in a way that summons the visceral phenomenology of understanding. But the other variety of understanding, the more "cold-blooded" variety, can still be enjoyed when we consider patiently the sequence of explanatory steps presented above, perhaps precisely because we do experience the visceral variety whenever we consider any single step in the sequence.

On this interpretation of the line of thought under consideration, there is no genuine explanatory gap between intransitive self-consciousness and synchronization with dlPFC activity. There *is* in fact a reductive explanation of the former in terms of the latter. It is just that this reductive explanation is not such as to elicit in us a visceral phenomenology of understanding.

The analogy with the sorites series points to a different interpretation, however. In that series, the red circle *really is* dissimilar to the yellow. The two are *not* visually indistinguishable. It is just that the continuity between them, which would otherwise be surprising, can be appreciated through the series. If we take the analogy at face value, intransitive self-consciousness

---

[14] I should state that almost everything I know about the connection between the explanatory gap, on the one hand, and the nature of understanding and its phenomenology, on the other, I learned from my friend and student Brian Fiala (see Fiala, forthcoming).

[15] I am assuming here a tight connection between explanation and understanding. One possibility is that explanation be construed as that which produces an appropriate state of understanding. Another is to reverse the order of explication here and construe understanding as the state which an appropriate explanation is supposed to elicit. Either way, we can treat explanation and understanding as correlatives.

really is unexplainable in terms of synchronization with dlPFC activity. There is no reductive explanation to be had of the former in terms of the latter. What there is, however, is a sort of intellectual domestication of consciousness without reductive explanation of it. This admittedly elusive intellectual domestication may allow us to accept that intransitive self-consciousness reduces to neural processes even though it is not reductively explainable in terms of them.

To clarify this approach, let me position it within the familiar dialectic around explanatory gap arguments. Start with the distinction between *ontological* and *epistemic* reduction. Let us say that F is *epistemically reducible* to G iff there is no explanatory gap between F and G; and that if there is an explanatory gap between F and every other property, such that F is not epistemically reducible to anything, then F is *epistemically primitive*. Correspondingly, let us say that F is *ontologically reducible* to G iff there is no ontological gap between F and G; and that if there is an ontological gap between F and every other property, such that F is not ontologically reducible to anything, then F is *ontologically primitive*. In these terms, the explanatory gap argument for dualism may be formulated as follows:

(1) Intransitive self-consciousness is epistemically irreducible to physical properties;

(2) If intransitive self-consciousness is epistemically irreducible to physical properties, then it is ontologically irreducible to them as well;

(3) If intransitive self-consciousness is ontologically irreducible to physical properties, then intransitive self-consciousness is ontologically primitive; therefore,

(4) Intransitive self-consciousness is ontologically primitive.

Since the argument is valid, there are only three ways to deny it. Some materialists would deny Premise 1, rejecting any explanatory gap for intransitive self-consciousness. Other materialists would deny Premise 2, conceding an explanatory gap but rejecting the inference to ontological irreducibility. Finally, certain neutral monists would deny Premise 4, namely, those who posit a third type of property, neither physical nor conscious, and attempt to reduce both to it. Accepting all three premises, by contrast, leads one to dualism about intransitive self-consciousness.[16]

---

[16] In terms of Chalmers' (2002) scheme for classifying positions on the metaphysics of consciousness (or rather in terms of a parallel scheme for positions on intransitive self-consciousness), denying Premise 1 is a form of type-A materialism, denying Premise 2 a form of type-B materialism, and denying Premise 4 a form of type-F monism.

Sociologically speaking, most materialists would deny Premise 2: they would concede an explanatory gap but insist on ontological reducibility.[17] What dualists find objectionable about such denial is that it allows for reduction that is not *epistemically transparent* (see Chalmers and Jackson 2001). The connection between two facts, p and q, is epistemically transparent to subject S just in case S can see why p should be the case given that q is the case.[18] According to Chalmers and Jackson, ontological reduction requires epistemically transparent connections between reduced and reducer. Even in the case of water and H_2O, although their identity is *a posteriori*, it is nonetheless epistemically transparent, in that a subject who knew all the non-identity truths about water and all the non-identity truths about H_2O would be in a position to establish the identity of water and H_2O. However, Chalmers and Jackson argue, once the connection between reduced and reducer is epistemically transparent, the reduction is not only ontological but also epistemic: one is in a position to *explain* the facts about the reduced in terms of the facts about the reducer.[19]

Applying Chalmers and Jackson's reasoning to the above argument for dualism about intransitive self-consciousness, we obtain the following defense of Premise 2 in the argument: (2.1) We are justified in holding that one property ontologically reduces to another only if the connection between them is epistemically transparent; but (2.2) When the connection between two properties is epistemically transparent, we are also justified in holding that one *epistemically* reduces to the other; therefore, (2.3) We are justified in holding that one property ontologically reduces to another only if we are also justified in holding that one *epistemically* reduces to the other; so, (2) If intransitive self-consciousness is epistemically irreducible to physical properties, then it is ontologically irreducible to them as well. What materialists typically reject in Chalmers and Jackson's reasoning is Premise 2.1: they insist that the paradigmatic ontological reductions (e.g. of water to H_2O) are epistemically opaque (see Block and Stalnaker 1999). The debate then centers on the proper treatment of paradigmatic instances of ontological reduction.

The approach suggested above to the explanatory gap avoids such debates. For instead of denying Premise 2.1, it denies Premise 2.2, allowing

---

[17] This seems like a generally safe strategy, founded as it is on the widely recognized heuristic that we should avoid deriving ontological conclusions from exclusively epistemological premises.

[18] For Chalmers and Jackson, epistemic transparency is achieved through *a priori* entailment: if p entails q, then the connection between them is epistemically transparent. Thus *a priori* entailment is sufficient for epistemic transparency. It is less clear whether it should be taken as necessary for it as well. In any case, *a priori* entailment does not seem to be *definitional* of epistemic transparency.

[19] Thus, a subject who is in a position to establish the identity of water and H_2O is also in a position to explain the water facts in terms of the H_2O facts.

that epistemic transparency can arise even in the absence of epistemic reduction. On the emerging view, a sequence of explanatory steps may be such that there is a genuine explanatory gap between the first and last items in the sequence, but the continuity that can be traced between them through consideration of the intermediary steps generates epistemic transparency in the entire sequence: the connection between the first and last items in the series is epistemically transparent to any subject who can follow each explanatory step in the series. Thus because every step in the series with which I opened this section is an instance of reductive explanation, and we can follow the sequence, the identification (or ontological reduction) of intransitive self-consciousness to synchronization with dlPFC activity is epistemically transparent; but because the relation of reductive explainability is not transitive – whether for reasons of vagueness or some other reasons – intransitive self-consciousness is not reductively explainable in terms of synchronization with dlPFC activity. This seems to be the correct analogy with the sorites series of circles.

On this interpretation, the explanatory gap between intransitive self-consciousness (or subjective character) and synchronization with dlPFC activity is real, in that we cannot explain why the "subjective facts" (the facts of intransitive self-consciousness) are what they are in terms of the neural facts being what they are. Intransitive self-consciousness is genuinely epistemically irreducible to synchronization with dlPFC activity. Nonetheless, it does not follow that an ontological reduction of intransitive self-consciousness to synchronization with dlPFC activity must be epistemically opaque, leaving us with no insight into why it should be that intransitive self-consciousness is nothing but synchronization with dlPFC activity. On the contrary, by tracing a sequence of reductive explanations step by step, we can come to appreciate why it should be that intransitive self-consciousness is nothing but synchronization with dlPFC activity, say – even though contemplating the notion that it is in a single intellectual act produces in us only the phenomenology of incredulity.[20]

---

[20] We have here the reduction without reductive explanation – reduction in the face of persistent explanatory gap – that is the hallmark of type-B materialism. But unlike typical type-B materialism, which embraces ontological reduction as brute and epistemically opaque, and is to that extent widely acknowledged to leave something to be desired, the present variety of type-B materialism offers epistemically transparent ontological reduction, and merely denies that epistemic transparency brings in its train epistemic reduction. We may distinguish between type-B1 and type-B2 materialism. The former is the more common variety, embracing epistemically opaque ontological reduction. The latter is the variety suggested by the present interpretation of the line of thought explored in this section, the variety that exploits the sorites-like behavior of reductive explanation. What I am proposing here is in effect a self-representational variety of type-B2 materialism.

To conclude. I started this section with an analogy between a sequence of (reductive) explanations leading from intransitive self-consciousness to the neural process of synchronization with dlPFC activity, on the one hand, and a sequence of visually indistinguishable pairs of circles leading from a yellow circle to a red one, on the other. I then offered two interpretations of the analogy. On the first interpretation, the explanatory gap between intransitive self-consciousness and synchronization with dlPFC activity is illusory: there is no explanatory gap between the two, but the appearance of such a gap arises from the unwarranted expectation that we undergo a visceral phenomenology of understanding upon contemplating the start and end points of the explanatory sequence.[21] A tighter analogy is offered by the second interpretation: the explanatory gap is genuine, in that we really do not understand how intransitive self-consciousness could be nothing but synchronization with dlPFC activity, but nonetheless it is so reducible, and moreover in an epistemically transparent manner (thanks to the sequence of reductive explanations connecting the two). I am happy with either interpretation, but find the second vastly more satisfactory, insofar as it manages to respect rather than dismiss the force of the explanatory gap intuition.

4. LEVINE'S "JUST MORE REPRESENTATION" OBJECTION

This self-representational approach to the explanatory gap can be resisted in two main ways. One is to deny the general claim that a series of reductive explanations can underlie an epistemically transparent physicalistic reduction of intransitive self-consciousness even in the absence of reductive explanation of it in physical terms. The other is to claim that, however the general issue turns out, one of the five individual steps of reductive explanation I described in the previous section fails. The most acute criticism of self-representationalism that takes this second form is developed by Levine (2006), who argues that the for-me-ness of experience cannot be recovered by self-representation, because the kind of awareness involved in it cannot be accounted for in terms of the notion of representation at play in the relevant type of self-representation. This is to reject Step 2 in the explanatory sequence (explaining awareness in terms of representation).

---

[21] This is, in effect, a form of type-A materialism about intransitive self-consciousness.

For Levine, self-representation cannot account for for-me-ness, because just as something needs to bestow for-me-ness – a "subjective significance" – on any old representation, so something needs to bestow that subjective significance on *self*-representations. As long as self-representing representations represent themselves in the same sense in which other-representing representations represent things other than themselves, it is not clear what would make the former "for the subject" even though the latter are not. Levine writes (2006, 194):

Subjectivity, as I described it earlier, is that feature of a mental state by virtue of which it is of significance for the subject; not merely something happening within her, but "for her." The self-representation thesis aims to explicate that sense of significance for the subject through the fact that the state is being represented. But now, what makes that representation itself of significance for the subject, and thus conscious?

The answer to this question cannot be, of course, that a self-representing representation is of significance to the subject because it represents itself to be self-representing. That would quickly lead to an infinite regress. The suspicion Levine raises is that there may not be a way to answer his question without invoking phenomenality.

Certainly what makes a representation "for the subject" cannot be what it represents. It cannot be that when a representation represents *x*, it is not for the subject, so that the subject does not self-consciously represent *x*, but when it represents *y*, it is. And at a first pass, it might seem that this is precisely what self-representationalism claims. It claims that what makes some representations "for the subject" is that what they represent is themselves. Yet the fact that a state represents itself rather than something other than itself does not dissolve the mystery involved in it representing whatever it does *to oneself*, i.e. in a self-conscious sort of way. Much more plausible is that representations endowed with subjective character, in virtue of which the subject represents self-consciously, are of a categorically different kind from other representations. If this is right, then what gives such representations their subjective character, or intransitive self-consciousness, is an aspect not of *what* they represent, but of *how* they represent – not their *object* of representation, but their *manner* of representation.

However, the heart of Levine's objection cannot be that representations have subjective character in virtue of how they represent and not what they represent. For this is something that standard versions of self-representationalism can accommodate. Compare "I am happy" and "my mother's nieceless brother's only nephew is happy." Both statements represent me as happy, but there is a sense (perhaps elusive, perhaps not) that the former does so *essentially* whereas the latter *accidentally*. In specifying what makes a "suitable" self-representation – the kind of self-representation that bestows subjective character or intransitive self-consciousness – it is natural for the self-representationalist to insist that only the essential variety is relevant. Only essentially self-representing states are "for the subject" and hence intransitively self-conscious. Merely accidentally self-representing states are not. The point is that *what* is represented in both essential and accidental self-representation is the same, so what accounts for the fact that only the former involves subjective character must be the *manner* of representation (*how* what is represented is represented).

The heart of the objection is therefore not the what/how (object/manner) distinction. Rather, it must be the thought that there is no way to account for the right *manner* of representation in non-subjective terms, as would be required for any ontological reduction of subjective character. Even if a certain non-subjective, non-phenomenal specification of the right manner were extensionally adequate, such that no counter-example could be found to the thesis that necessarily, a mental state has subjective character/intransitive self-consciousness iff it self-represents in that manner, we would still have on our hands an explanatory gap between subjective character/intransitive self-consciousness and this non-phenomenal specification of the relevant manner. It would still be unclear how this specific kind of self-representation, understood in non-phenomenal terms, could give rise to the distinctive kind of awareness of one's conscious experiences that is imbued with subjective significance and constitutes intransitive self-consciousness. Thus as long as representation is understood in non-phenomenal terms – certainly as long as it is understood in purely physical terms – it does not help to appeal specifically to *self*-representation.

The problem with self-representation, then, is that it is *just more representation*. As Levine (2006, 195) puts it,

Somehow, what we have in conscious states are representations that are intrinsically of subjective significance, "animated" as it were, and I maintain that we really don't understand how that is possible. It doesn't seem to be a matter of more of the same – more representation of the same kind – but rather representation of a different kind altogether.

The awareness we have of our conscious experiences, in virtue of which they are "for us," involves a kind of direct acquaintance with those states that brute representations simply do not seem to replicate, not even when they are representations of themselves. For a self-representation as for an other-representation, we can always ask: why is there something it is like *for me* to have this representation? Call this the *just more representation objection*.[22]

This objection undermines the self-representational approach to the explanatory gap presented in the previous section. For suppose it is true that epistemically transparent ontological reduction of intransitive self-consciousness can proceed without closing the explanatory gap, that is, without epistemic reduction. Suppose it is true that through a sequence of more local reductive explanations, we can obtain an epistemically transparent ontological reduction that does not quite amount to epistemic reduction. Still, this kind of epistemically transparent ontological reduction, although possibly available in the case of water and H_2O, is not available for intransitive self-consciousness and physical phenomena, because the reductive explanation of awareness in terms of representation (in Step 2 of the above explanatory sequence) fails.[23] What Levine's line of objection seems to press is the need for a *sui generis* notion of *representation-for-me*, a kind of primitive intentional relation borne by subjects, rather than by subjects' internal states. The problem with positing such a relation is that it seems to resist physicalist reduction.

---

[22] We can, of course, countenance a phenomenal notion of representation that casts some representations as inherently subjective (see Loar 1987, 2003; Horgan and Tienson 2002). With this phenomenal notion of representation, one could certainly account for our awareness of our conscious experiences in terms of their manner of representing themselves: they represent themselves *phenomenally*. But the result would be a kind of non-reductive self-representationalism. Conversely, there may be *a* notion of awareness that can be accounted for in ordinary representational terms – essentially, a *non-phenomenal* notion of awareness. However, the kind of awareness we have of our conscious experiences, in virtue of which they are "for us" in the relevant sense, is inherently phenomenal, being as it is a component of phenomenal character. So even if we account in self-representational terms for a *non-phenomenal* awareness, that would not help us account for the for-me-ness of conscious experience, since the latter is constituted by a *phenomenal* awareness. The upshot seems to be that while we can reductively explain the phenomenal kind of awareness in terms of a phenomenal kind of (self-)representation, and can reductively explain non-phenomenal awareness in terms of a non-phenomenal kind of (self-)representation, there appears to be no way to reductively explain phenomenal awareness in terms of a non-phenomenal notion of representation. For appealing to a non-phenomenal notion of (self-)representation in the context of explaining the phenomenal notion of awareness falls prey to the just more representation objection.

[23] This is where the explanatory sequence is derailed, it is natural to suppose, because this is the step that happens to involve the attempt to transition from the phenomenal sphere to the non-phenomenal sphere. But the more general point is that *some* step in the explanatory sequence that leads from phenomenal consciousness to physical phenomena (such as synchronization with dlPFC activity) has to involve such a transition, and therefore *some* step in the explanatory sequence is bound to fail.

The upshot, in any case, is that the self-representational approach to the explanatory gap developed in §3 fails.[24]

5. SELF-REPRESENTATIONALISM AND EPISTEMIC OPACITY

I think this is the deepest objection to self-representationalism. In fact, I am persuaded by Levine that there is something fundamentally mysterious about for-me-ness, hence intransitive self-consciousness, which is not removed simply by citing self-representation. Levine is right that the question of subjective significance applies with equal force to self-representation as to other-representation. For a self-representing state too, we can ask what it is about the state that makes it represent itself *to me*, rather than merely represent itself *in me*. In this section, I present the reaction I think a self-representationalist ought to have to Levine's objection; the reaction is more concessive than confrontational.

The first thing to point out is that although I would be keen to defend a version of self-representationalism that embraces epistemically transparent ontological reduction, self-representationalism as such admits of many varieties: a dualist variety, a materialist variety with epistemically opaque ontological reduction, a materialist variety with epistemic reduction, and even a neutral-monist variety.[25]

Recall that according to dualism about intransitive self-consciousness, intransitive self-consciousness is ontologically irreducible to any other properties, and is therefore ontologically primitive. An irresponsible kind of dualism would maintain that intransitive self-consciousness is completely dissociated and insulated from the physical realm. A responsible dualism would connect intransitive self-consciousness to the physical realm via laws of nature – probably causal laws – that dictate what instantiations of intransitive self-consciousness are caused (under what conditions) by what

---

[24] The deep reason for this failure seems to be that while reductive explanation may exhibit sorites-like behavior, phenomenality does not: there is no way to get from the non-phenomenal to the phenomenal in a series of sorites-like steps. Because of this, some step in any relevant explanatory sequence must involve a discrete leap from the non-phenomenal to the phenomenal. Whatever step that is, we can expect reductive explanation to fail there, due to the explanatory gap, thus vitiating the sequence of reductive explanations that enables an epistemically transparent reduction. Of course, if phenomenality *could* be shown to exhibit sorites-like behavior, then the worry would dissipate and the self-representational approach to the explanatory gap might be viable after all. It is just that the possibility of going from something non-phenomenal to something phenomenal in a sorites-like series of steps seems on its face rather implausible.

[25] In terms of Chalmers' framework and the additions made to it in notes to §3, the kind of type-B2 self-representationalism I would like to have is only one variety, others being type-B1, type-A, type-F, and dualist self-representationalism.

physical property instantiations. Because intransitive self-consciousness is ontologically primitive, on this view, these laws of nature would be themselves primitive. As a result, intransitive self-consciousness would supervene upon physical properties with *nomological* necessity, but not with *metaphysical* necessity. This is a sort of responsible dualist self-representationalism.[26] This dualist self-representationalism is not threatened by Levine's just more representation objection.

This is not surprising, since the objection is not *meant* to threaten them. But it does bring out the difference between self-representationalism as such and self-representationalism as an attempt to address the explanatory gap. The following two theses are obviously different:

(T1) Self-representationalism neutralizes the explanatory gap.[27]
(T2) Self-representationalism is true.

Levine's objection threatens T1, but not T2. It is thus not an objection to self-representationalism as such, strictly speaking. It is an objection to something else.

This is important, because the master argument for self-representationalism (from §1) can be readily reframed in such a way that it does not *require* that the relevant kind of inner awareness be recovered by self-representation. The premises of the argument involve a modal operator, but while it is natural to interpret the modal force in those premises as *metaphysical*, the argument can be reframed as involving rather *nomological* necessity – without commenting

---

[26] Given the distinction between phenomenal and non-phenomenal notions of (self-)representation, dualist self-representationalism can come in two varieties. The first combines metaphysical supervenience of intransitive self-consciousness upon self-representation, construed phenomenally, with nomological supervenience of self-representation, so construed, upon microphysical properties. The second, more interesting variety combines nomological supervenience of phenomenal consciousness upon self-representation, construed *non*-phenomenally, with metaphysical supervenience of self-representation, so construed, upon microphysical properties. In the former, the primitive laws of nature connect microphysical properties with a phenomenal self-representation, which is seen to be part of the phenomenal structure of consciousness. In the latter, there is a kind of self-representation that is fully reducible to the microphysical, and it is only this kind of self-representation that *causally* brings about phenomenal consciousness, in accordance with some primitive laws of nature. Thus, a type-E (say) dualist, who holds that phenomenal properties are causally inert, could be a self-representationalist, and in two kinds of ways. Type-E1 self-representationalism is the view that self-representation is part of the phenomenal structure of consciousness, which nomologically supervenes on the microphysical. Type-E2 self-representationalism is the view that a microphysically reducible self-representation is the causal basis (hence nomological supervenience base) of phenomenal consciousness.

[27] I use the term 'neutralizes' to cover two possibilities: that the explanatory gap is bridged, and that the explanatory gap becomes something we can live with, say because we have an epistemically transparent reduction that illuminates why there is an explanatory gap, as in the approach to the explanatory gap sketched in §2. Thus both type-A and type-B2 materialism "neutralize" the explanatory gap, even though only the former *bridges* it (or "closes" it).

on whether it is *merely* nomological necessity. Thus Premise 4 in the master argument could be reconstrued as follows:

(4*) Nomologically-necessarily, for any entity X and subject S, S is aware of X in the right way iff S represents X in the right way.

With this weakened premise in place, and leaving all other premises untouched, we can obtain the following weakened conclusion:

(9*) Nomologically-necessarily, for any mental state M and subject S, such that S is in M, M is phenomenally conscious iff there is a mental state M*, such that (i) S is in M*, (ii) M* represents M in the right way, and (iii) M = M*.

This guarantees that *at least* a dualist variety of self-representationalism is right. The weakened master argument thus concedes that self-representationalism may not recover for-me-ness, or subjective character, but insists on the following two points: (a) self-representationalism can at least *accommodate* this for-me-ness; (b) no other theory of phenomenal consciousness can accommodate it. This is not everything a self-representationalist might want, but it is not all that weak a conclusion either.

Of course, not only dualist versions of self-representationalism fail to neutralize the explanatory gap; materialist versions that embrace epistemically opaque reduction do as well.[28] And so a self-representationalist might consider reverting to this sort of materialist self-representationalism in light of the just more representation objection, conceding that the reduction of subjective character, or intransitive self-consciousness, to self-representation is epistemically opaque – due to the epistemic opacity of explaining awareness in terms of representation. Thus someone who is impressed with both the weakened master argument for self-representationalism and the just more representation objection could still embrace the disjunction of this hard-nosed materialist self-representationalism and dualist self-representationalism. Both are forms of self-representationalism that cohabits with a persisting explanatory gap.

What would lead one to prefer such a materialist self-representationalism to dualist self-representationalism is, of course, an antecedent commitment to physicalism. Consider what Perry (2001a) calls "antecedent physicalism,"

---

[28] This is what I call above Type-B1 materialism, the view that insists on the ontological reducibility of consciousness to physics but accepts that the reduction is epistemically opaque and leaves the explanatory gap untouched. As Chalmers and Jackson (2001) note, the metaphysical supervenience it posits between consciousness and physics is as epistemically primitive as the nomological supervenience posited by dualism: there is no explanation of it, merely brute assertion.

the view that physicalism should be our default position – we should be physicalists pending reasons not to be (physicalism is innocent until proven guilty, if you will). Someone who is impressed with both the weakened master argument for self-representationalism and the just more representation objection, but also embraces antecedent physicalism, would be naturally led to what we may call "antecedent materialist self-representationalism."[29]

For my part, this is indeed where I find myself led. I have already indicated why I am impressed with the weakened master argument for self-representationalism and the just more representation objection. As for antecedent physicalism, it should not be confused with physicalism as an unargued-for article of faith, nor with physicalism as an attitude rather than a thesis (Ney 2008), both of which do not call for argumentation.[30] An argument for antecedent physicalism is needed, but the argument needed is not nearly as strong as the argument needed to establish all-things-considered physicalism. What it calls for is a *prima facie* rather than *ultima facie* case for physicalism. This is a burden we can certainly meet. Thus, citing Occam's razor as a reason to adopt a single type of properties over a duality thereof, while an underwhelming argument for all-things-considered (*ultima facie*) physicalism, is a perfectly cogent argument for antecedent (*prima facie*) physicalism. Likewise, the inductive argument that physicalism turned out to be true about many other initially recalcitrant phenomena (e.g. life) is underwhelming as an argument for *ultima facie* physicalism but an overwhelming one for *prima facie* physicalism.[31]

Of course, *antecedent* materialist self-representationalism does allow that, given appropriate reasons, one might have to relinquish materialist self-representationalism. So if one were inclined to reject epistemically opaque reduction as incoherent, or as otherwise necessarily false, say for Chalmers and Jackson's reasons, one would have to reject this version of materialist self-representationalism. Thus someone who is impressed with both the weakened master argument for self-representationalism and the just more

---

[29] More specifically, this would be antecedent type-B1 materialism.

[30] This is true of Ney's physicalism-as-an-attitude because the latter is not truth-apt, and argumentation – in the relevant sense, involving the notion of validity (where true premises would necessitate true conclusion) – is only called for where a truth-apt statement is at stake.

[31] This seems to be the view that Levine should adopt as well. Since he endorses the thought of embracing ontological reduction without epistemic reduction (Levine 1993), and at the same time seems to hold that self-representationalism comes closest to meeting the explanatory burden of physicalism and is the climax of physicalist attempts to address the explanatory gap (Levine 2001), he should certainly embrace something like antecedent type-B self-representationalism (of one of the two kinds).

representation objection, but also accepts Chalmers and Jackson's argumentation, would be naturally led to dualist self-representationalism.

The dialectical upshot seems to me to be this. The issue of whether there is a case for self-representationalism and the issue of whether there is a case for materialism are orthogonal, since one can be a self-representationalist without being a materialist or a materialist without being a self-representationalist. The problem of the explanatory gap is relevant to the issue of whether there is a case for materialism, not to the issue of whether there is a case for self-representationalism. Given the "just more representation" consideration, epistemically transparent reduction of intransitive self-consciousness, and therefore of phenomenal consciousness, seems elusive. Whether *some* reduction may nonetheless be achieved depends on whether there is another kind of reduction to be had. That is, it depends on the general viability of epistemically opaque reduction (or whether it may sometimes make sense for us to believe that feature F reduces to feature G even though we cannot quite see how it could). However this debate is resolved will determine whether a self-representationalist ought to be a materialist self-representationalist or a dualist self-representationalist.[32]

CONCLUSION

In this chapter, I have been concerned to establish two main claims. The first is that the explanatory gap between phenomenal consciousness and physical properties is at its core an explanatory gap between a certain mode of self-consciousness – intransitive self-consciousness – and neural activity (probably) in the dorsolateral prefrontal cortex. The second is that the problem of the explanatory gap is not directly relevant to the issue of whether there is a case for self-representationalism: in a weakened form, the master argument for self-representationalism (presented in §1) does not require that the subjective character of experience, its intransitive self-consciousness, be *recovered* by self-representation, but only that it be *accommodated*.

To be sure, one might have wished that self-representationalism would neutralize the explanatory gap (that would certainly constitute a major advantage for the view). But this turns out to be unlikely. Although consideration of the sorites-like behavior of explanatory sequences inspires

---

[32] It is worth keeping in mind that, given antecedent physicalism, in this debate the physicalist is playing defense and the dualist offense. Thus as long as the debate is unresolved we are free to adopt the physicalist position.

initial confidence, upon closer examination the prospects dim as the failure of reductive explanation of awareness in terms of representation comes to the fore.[33] My hesitant inclination, on the basis of the entire array of considerations examined here, is to adopt an antecedent materialist self-representationalism with epistemically opaque reduction.[34]

---

[33] Nonetheless, there may yet be hope for a materialist variety of self-representationalism, namely, if either epistemically opaque reduction turned out to be possible or phenomenal consciousness turned out to exhibit the sorites-like behavior that reductive explanation does. The former would prop up what I called type-B1 self-representationalism, the latter what I called type-B2 self-representationalism.

[34] For comments on a previous draft, I am greatly indebted to JeeLoo Liu and Brian Fiala, ongoing interaction with whom has influenced the chapter. I am also grateful to Shaun Nichols for another set of comments on an earlier draft and have benefited from interactions with Stephen Biggs, David Chalmers, Jennifer Corns, Angela Coventry, and Sebastian Watzl.

CHAPTER 3

Thinking about the self

John Perry

INTRODUCTION

Suppose that when Bill Clinton moved to the White House he was unaware that the Secret Service used the acronym "POTUS" to refer to the president. In his morning briefing summary he sees the sentence "POTUS meets with the Queen of England at noon." This upsets him. Who is POTUS? Why is this person meeting with the Queen, instead of Clinton? He says to Hillary, "POTUS is meeting with the Queen; who in the world is POTUS, and why is he meeting with the Queen instead of me?" It seems that the person Clinton is asking about is Clinton himself; the right answer for Hillary to give is, "You are POTUS." Clinton *said* something about himself, without realizing it. And, indeed, it seems that Clinton *believed* something about himself, without realizing it. I will say that Clinton had a belief that was *merely* about the person he happened to be. This is a self-belief, in that the truth-conditions of the belief impose conditions on the believer. But it is not what we would normally call having a belief about oneself.

It seems then, that we can make a distinction between saying something about yourself in the sense in which that merely said something about the person you happen to be, and saying something about yourself in the sense of making what we might call a "self-assertion," which implies not only that the person you referred to was you, but also that you knew this and intended to convey it. Use of the word 'I' indicates that one is self-asserting. And an analogous distinction may be made at the level of belief. We have the phrase "self-knowledge"; I will supplement it with the phrase "self-belief." Clinton had a belief about the person he happened to be, but it was not a self-belief.

Hector Neri-Castañeda (Castañeda 1966) noticed that reports like "Clinton believes he is meeting the Queen for lunch" and "Clinton said he was meeting the Queen for lunch," are in some way ambiguous. These reports could be construed so that they are true in our opening case, even before Clinton realized that he was POTUS. Usually, however, we would take such reports to imply more than this, that is, we would take them as reports of self-belief and self-assertion. Castañeda uses an asterisk to mark the difference, and so will I. Thus, "Clinton believes that he* is meeting the Queen for lunch" would not be true before he learned that he was indeed POTUS, but would be true after he learned this. And in the imagined situation, "Clinton said that he* was meeting the Queen for lunch" would not be true, but if he had said "I am meeting the Queen for lunch," it would have been true. Castañeda thought that 'he*' was a different word than 'he,' or at the very least marked an ambiguity. One might be skeptical about this, and suppose the added information is a matter of Gricean implicature. This issue will not matter in this essay.

Self-beliefs are typically expressed with self-assertions, and hence with the first person. Here is a simple account of how the first person works: an utterance of the word 'I' stands for the person who utters it. The word 'I' is thus one way that Bill Clinton has of referring to himself. He can also call himself 'Bill Clinton,' or even, in the appropriate circumstances, 'that man.' If he is expressing a self-belief, then using the word 'I' is the natural way for him to refer to himself. If, on the other hand, he is expressing a belief that happens to be about himself, but is not a self-belief, we would not expect him to use the first person.

But it does not seem very satisfactory to explain self-belief in terms of the first person. It seems like there is something about self-beliefs that makes them correctly and naturally and appropriately expressed with the first person; the difference between self-beliefs, and beliefs that are merely about the person one happens to be, as I shall put it, is somehow reflected in the difference between first- and third-person ways of referring to oneself, but not constituted by it.

My first goal in this chapter is to construct an account of self-beliefs that distinguishes them from beliefs that are merely about the person one happens to be. Such an account should explain the close connection between self-belief and the first person. My second goal is to consider issues raised by David Rosenthal in his chapter in this volume about what he calls the "essential indexicality" of HOTS. HOTS are Higher-Order Thoughts about our own mental states and activities. Rosenthal's account involves giving up Sydney Shoemaker's (Shoemaker 1968) principle that a person is immune to certain sorts of errors about her own mental states, namely, whether it is she* that is having them. I will argue that we should not give up Shoemaker's principle, and that we need not do so to account for the feature of HOTS that Rosenthal calls their "essential indexicality." These issues are crucial for those who are inclined to accept Rosenthal's account of consciousness, in which HOTS play a crucial role.

THE CAUSAL ROLE AND CONTENT OF BELIEFS

Before looking into what is special about self-beliefs, we need to fix some ideas about beliefs in general. I take it that beliefs are particular states of the brain; I assume that they are physical states, but a property dualist, who thinks that belief states are not physical in some important sense, could agree with everything I say here, so long as she is not an epiphenomenalist.

I use the word 'state' in two ways, for particular states in the mind of a particular person, and for types of such states, that get at their internal, non-circumstantial properties. In either sense, states can be total or partial.

I conceive of brain states, in the first sense, as non-basic particulars of a certain sort for which some philosophers in the seventeenth and eighteenth centuries used the flexible term *mode*.[1] In this use, a mode is not a basic particular, but one that involves a more basic particular (God, or Nature, perhaps), or more basic particulars (atoms, perhaps), or complexes of more basic particulars, or successions of complexes of more basic particulars. I will not assume that the more basic particulars have to be completely basic particulars, or even that there are any of those. Earlier stages of a mode of given kind will pass along traits and patterns of traits to later stages in more or less predictable and often quite useful ways.[2] The ripple that flows across the lake is a mode, involving successive complexes of water molecules, rising and falling in predictable ways. A dent in a fender is a mode; left alone, it will not change much with time. Ripples and dents are not universals but particulars. They begin to exist at a certain time, say when someone tosses a rock into a lake, or backs into another car in a parking lot. They last for a while, and then may cease to exist, say when the ripple reaches shore, or the fender is repaired, or the car goes to the junkyard and is crushed.

Another example of a mode is a bump in a carpet, of the sort that inevitably occurs when an amateur tries to lay a large carpet, and gets a pocket of air trapped under it. You can push the bump all around the carpet. But it is the same bump. You can refer to it: "I have been trying to get rid of that bump for an hour." You are not likely to think of it as a metaphysically basic object; you could get by without referring to it, and just talking about

---

[1] See Locke (1689), Book II, Chapter XII, section 4; Spinoza (1677), Part I, Definition V.
[2] Everything I say is consistent with Dan Giberman's "Glop Theory," for example (Giberman 2010).

the carpet, and how various parts of it rise and fall over time, as the trapped air is pushed about. But it is natural to talk about it and refer to it.

Modes that preserve waveforms – sound waves, radio waves, and the like – can preserve information about their sources. The movement and preservation of the waveforms, and thus information, occurs naturally. The technology of preserving computer-generated files to disks uses preservation of structure, at some appropriate level, to preserve information, even as the file is moved about the disk by the operating system, in ways that lose other kinds of structure – a single file may end up being stored in various discontinuous regions, for example. So such files are modes.

Computer files change over time. When things go right this is due to additional input by those who use them; when things go wrong it is due to malfunctions of various sorts, and the files are corrupted. Although the files are designed and created to preserve information, the information they carry is not an essential property of them; it may be changed or lost, while the file continues to exist. I think beliefs and other cognitions, and the ideas that comprise them, are modes in this sense.

In this sense, modes are not universals. They instantiate universals, that is, modes have properties and stand in relations of various sorts. The dent may be oval; the ripple may diminish in size as time passes; the file may be small when it begins to exist, and then grows large. Here the second use of 'state' is useful. In engineering and science, the state of a system is constituted by its local properties, those that it has in virtue of the intrinsic properties of its parts, and the ways they are related. A state can be total or partial. And we can speak in either sense of states of the whole system in which we are interested, or states of its subsystems, or parts of the system. The state of an engine is constituted in part by the states of its crankshaft and camshaft, for example. The state of the solar system, at a certain time, is constituted by the way the planets are oriented to the Sun and to each other, where they are in their rotations and their orbits, and things like that. The solar system may have other important properties at a given time; perhaps it is now coming closer to a black hole that will eventually suck it up and destroy it. That is an interesting fact about the solar system, but not a part of the state of the solar system.

The states of a system, in this sense, do not exhaust its properties, for a system will have many properties in virtue of relations of things inside the system to things outside the system. The lake is in the state of having a ripple, but it came to be in that state because a boy threw a rock into it; that is a property of the lake, a fact about the lake, but not a state it is in. The car has lost value, not simply in virtue of the dent, but because people prefer cars without dents. The solar system will soon be annihilated, not because of the state it is in, but of a property it has to things outside of itself, namely because of its proximity to a black hole. An idea may be of a certain property, or thing, because of the circumstances in which it was formed, its association with certain words, and the way it influences action. A belief may be true or false because of the way the external object its ideas are of are related to one another.

Individual beliefs are parts of a system of beliefs and other cognitions and the properties of the cognitions and their relations constitute a person's *cognitive state* at a given time. The states of individual beliefs and other cognitions make *incremental* contributions to the state of the whole cognitive system. We are quite adept at characterizing these contributions, and predicting what sort of difference they will make to the whole system, and the activities of the person to which it belongs, in spite of our relative ignorance of their intrinsic nature. For example, a normal human being comes into a bookstore, and the clerk asks what she is looking for. If she says "Mysteries," he will lead her to one part of the store; if she says "Philosophy," he will lead her to another part of the store. The choice of one word rather than another indicates the presence of one desire rather than another, and this difference, which one supposes must be a very tiny physical difference in the whole system, gives the clerk good evidence about where he is likely to make a sale.

When we make such inferences, from bits of language or other small behaviors, we manage to do so in spite of our ignorance of the intrinsic nature of cognitive states. We deal with such states indirectly, in terms of a rather remarkable conceptual apparatus, our system of *contents*.

Contents are a system of abstract objects, usually propositions, that philosophers and others have developed to model and systematize our practice of describing cognitive states by the conditions in which they are true, in the case of beliefs and other doxastic attitudes, or satisfied, in the case of desires and other pro-attitudes. A system of propositions will encode such conditions, given a scheme of interpretation. For example, the ordered pair of the property of being an orator and Cicero might constitute the proposition that Cicero is an orator, where the scheme of interpretation is that the proposition is true if the second object instantiates the first. Propositions encode the truth- and satisfaction-conditions of attitudes that are reported with utterances like "She believes that Cicero was a Roman Orator," or "He hopes that Cicero was a Roman orator (because that's what he said on his exam)" and the like.

I say that this is how we describe and classify belief states, but these little perturbations of the brain clearly do not have their contents intrinsically.

Their contents depend on their relation to other perturbations, the way the whole system functions, and its historical and practical connection to the external world. Properties like *believing that Santa Cruz is east of Berkeley*, or *wanting to help relieve one's arthritis*, are not fully determined by the cognitive states of the person of whom they are properties, but also involve circumstances that the person is in, that relate him to the things his thoughts are about, and to other thinkers and language users.

Returning to Clinton, imagine him to be at a barbecue. He sees a man at a grill in the distance flipping burgers. His brain changes in a certain way. He acquires a belief, which he might express with "That man is making hamburgers." What he believes, the content of his belief, is that a certain man, the one he sees, is making hamburgers. The intrinsic nature of his cognitive system does not determine which man the belief is about and which proposition serves as its content. That depends on who it is Clinton sees. The little change in his brain makes an incremental contribution to the state of Clinton's cognitive system, which itself occurs in a certain brain, of a certain person, on a certain patio, with eyes pointed in a certain direction, and a certain man flipping hamburgers in the distance. When we use a singular proposition to classify Clinton's cognitive properties, we are not directly describing his cognitive states, but describing them given external factors, such as whom he is looking at.

Thus the little change that Clinton's new cognition makes combines with all sorts of other facts, to make it the case that Clinton believes what he does, namely, that a certain man, the one he in fact sees, is making hamburgers. So we have here a state of Clinton's brain, caused by perception, and causing various things, perhaps a smile at the anticipation of eating a hamburger.[3] The content of the belief depends on the relations of this state to other things inside of his brain and a lot outside of his brain. It is a belief about hamburgers because it involves Clinton's idea of a hamburger; it is about a certain chef because he is the person Clinton perceived, and so on. The content of Clinton's belief is not in his head, although it is the content of something that is in his head. This I take it is the lesson we should learn from "externalism."[4]

To emphasize a possibly counterintuitive aspect of the view I advocate, the contents of ideas and beliefs are *not* intrinsic to them. Cognitions, such as beliefs and desires, have the contents they do in virtue of the causal roles

---

[3] This example is apparently out of date, since, according the *The National Enquirer*, Clinton has become a vegan.
[4] See Kripke (1980); Putnam (1975); Burge 1979.

that belong to states in virtue of their types, and in virtue of particular connections they have to objects outside of the system of which they are a part. My belief that water is a liquid is true because H_2O is a liquid; it has the content that H_2O is a liquid. If things were as Hilary Putnam imagined, and I was on twin earth, I could be in the same state, but its content would be that XYZ is a liquid (setting aside problems that result from Putnam's choosing water, one of the main things of which I am composed, as an example). If my basic "operating system" were different, then the same state might have different causes and effects in my brain, and have a different content.

So, I take it that beliefs and other cognitions are modes, particular states of brains, parts of a system of cognitions, each with intrinsic properties and systematic connections to other cognitions. The system as a whole and its parts have extrinsic properties, most importantly those which derive from the particular chain of events that causes them, the particular chains of effects that they cause, and the effects they would have in various counterfactual situations. Content properties give us a powerful, if indirect, way of describing beliefs and other cognitions largely based on their extrinsic properties.

INFORMATION GAMES

I seek an account that tells us three things about self-beliefs: their causal role, their content, and the connection between the two. That is, I want an account that relates a self-belief's incremental contribution to causal properties of the cognitive system of which it is a part, and its incremental contribution to the contents of that cognitive system of which it is a part, and explains how and why these fit together.

Let us start by thinking about the function of beliefs and cognitions in general. It seems pretty clear that an important function of perception and belief formation is to help guide action. That is, if things go right, we pick up information in perception that tells us what we have to do, to act successfully. What counts as success depends on our beliefs, desires, and needs.

So, for example, a chicken needs to eat seeds and bugs and similar things to survive, and if it has not had any food for a while, it will be hungry and desire to get some. It has eyes that are very good at spotting seeds, and the ability to peck at the spot where it sees a seed. When it sees a seed its cognitive system, such as it is, changes, and as a result of this change, it pecks at that spot, and gets nutrition.

This is an example of what I call an *information game*. In an information game, a system gets information, typically about the world around it, and then uses that information, in the sense that it acts in ways that will be successful, given the information. What characterize different information games are the relations between the agent, time, and place where the information is picked up, and the agent, time, and place where it is used. The chicken's game I call the "straight-through" information game; the agent, time, and place are pretty much the same for the pick-up and the use. The chicken learned *that there was a seed in front of it*, and it engaged in an action that was successful, for the purpose of getting nutrition, in virtue of the fact *that there was a seed in front of it*. I think the concept of an information game helps us see how different sorts of doxastic states fit into human activities, in a way that illuminates the structure they have, and our rather amazing ability to indirectly characterize them, with our system of contents, in useful ways. The system depends on attributing a certain local rationality, even to chickens. We think that the contents of their inner states will mesh with their causal roles. Basically, we attribute pro-attitudes and doxastic states in a way that makes sense. We see the chicken as motivated by pro-attitudes and doxastic attitudes of a primitive sort. The effect of a pro-attitude and a doxastic attitude – the actions the chicken performs – will promote the satisfaction of the pro-attitude, if the doxastic attitude is true. The chicken will get something to eat, if there is a kernel of corn or a grain of millet at the spot where it perceives one to be.

People engage in far more complex information games than this one. Like many animals, including chickens I suppose, we track objects, and accumulate information about them. A thief watches me take money from the ATM; he picks up the information that I have cash on me. Then he tracks me, looking for an opportune moment to mug me and take the money. As he tracks me, he may accumulate more useful information: where I put the money; how fast and strong I am (or am not); whether I am carrying any weapons. He accumulates information about the object he is tracking, and when he strikes all of this information, obtained at different times, may be brought to bear on how he acts.

A third kind of information game I call "detach and recognize." It is of great importance in human life, although probably not uniquely human. Perhaps rather than tracking me, the thief merely notes some identifying characteristics about me: what I look like and what I am wearing. Later in the day, in a dark and secluded spot, he recognizes me as the person who took cash from the ATM; he infers that since I had a lot of money, I likely still have some, and this information motivates his attack. He picks up information about me at one time; he breaks off his perception of me – that is what 'detach' means – then later he uses some of the information he picked up about me to recognize me, and other bits of information to guide his action; because I had cash, I probably still have cash, and am worth mugging.

Finally, there is an even more characteristically human information game that depends on the detach and recognize game: communication. The thief sees me walking from the bank down Hamilton Avenue toward my home; he phones a confederate lurking at the corner of Hamilton and Guinda, and tells him what I look like and that I am loaded with cash; the confederate waits until he sees a shabby, gray-haired, tweed-jacketed pedagogue, and then mugs me. Information picked up at one time, by one person, is *applied* – that is, guides the action of – another person at another time.

In all of these information games we can distinguish between what I call the *source* and the *applicandum* of a game. The source is the object the information is picked up about. The applicandum is the object the action guided by the information is directed at. In these stories, I was both the source and applicandum; I was the object the original thief picked up information about, and the object that was eventually mugged by one thief or the other.

But clearly, things do not always go as they are supposed to; the source is not always the applicandum. Some other gray-haired, tweed-coated shabby pedagogue who has not been to an ATM and is in fact quite penniless may make it to the corner of Guinda and Hamilton before I do; the second thief may mug this fellow and come up penniless. In this case, I was the source; the other poor fellow was the applicandum. In the detach and recognize information game, our detached beliefs – the ones not tied to any perception – have two duties. First they should help us to recognize the source – ideally insuring that the source is the applicandum. This went wrong in the present example; the second thief's identifying information the first thief had wasn't detailed enough. The second duty is to provide information that helps the agent choose among various actions. The original thug sees what I look like, which will aid in recognition; he sees that I have cash, which provides a motive for mugging me.

Desires are a species of a wider class of "pro-attitudes," including wants, hopes, sudden urges, yens, and the like. Beliefs are also a species of a wider class of doxastic (pro-) attitudes, including perceptions, memories, conjectures, knowings-how, and the like. The word "belief" is sometimes used as a portmanteau phrase for all of these, but I will not use it that way. I will use belief for the sorts of states humans get themselves in: beliefs have truth-conditions that depend on what the world is like, but are *not* tied tightly to our position in the world at a given time; they may be caused by perceptions, but are typically retained for later use. Beliefs are connected to our detach and recognize information game, and especially to communication. So chickens have doxastic attitudes but not beliefs in this narrow sense; they see that a seed is in a certain relative position; but (as far as I know) they do not store this information for later use; they act on it or not, and then it is gone. On the other hand, suppose I give my dog a bone and she buries it. She will return to the same spot days later, when the bone is properly aged and cured through the effects of bacteria in the dirt, dig it up and enjoy it. It seems that she has a sort of a belief about where she buried the bone, that remains after the perceptions of the buried bone and the tree it is under are gone.

NOTIONS AND IDEAS

All of our information games are based on what I call *epistemic roles* and *pragmatic roles*. An object plays an epistemic role in our life, when it stands in a relation to us that affords picking up information about it; most obviously, when we can see it, hear it, touch it, or in other ways perceive it. An object plays a pragmatic role in our lives, when it stands in a relation to us that affords acting upon it, that is, acting in ways that affect it, or at least in ways whose success depends on facts about it. Basic epistemic roles and basic pragmatic roles are typically linked by natural facts; the things I can see and touch are likely to be things I can have some effect on, or things whose properties may affect my actions. If a chicken sees a grain of millet it can peck it; if it sees a fox, it can try to avoid it.

Nature provides us with basic epistemic and pragmatic relations; technology, in the broad sense, provides us with many more, and in these cases the epistemic and pragmatic are not always closely linked. By knowing a name, we often have access to pools of information[5] about a person or thing, stored in books, other people's minds, and now files around the world accessible through the internet. For example, if I look up your name in "Who's Who" I can find out things about you, due to a complex relation I have with you, involving the mediation of language, books, libraries, publishing companies, and the like. This relation will enable me to think about you and say things about you, but it may not put me in a position to

[5] In this essay I use 'information' loosely, so some misinformation counts as information. I am using 'information' the way David Israel and I use 'informational content' in Israel and Perry (1990).

affect you in any more significant way. I can find out a lot about Aristotle, for example, by consulting various works, but there is not much I can do to him. Modern weaponry is a depressing example of how we can be in pragmatic relations to objects without being able to learn much about them. A sniper that has me in his sights has the ability to end my life, although his knowledge is limited to what he gets from a fleeting glance. Modern world leaders can unleash weapons that will destroy thousands of lives, in spite of abject ignorance about the people who live them.

Embedded deeply in folk psychology and cognitive science is the concept that our beliefs, desires, and other cognitions have structure; that we have ideas, that are involved in a variety of combinations, in many different cognitions. I have beliefs about Stanford, desires involving Stanford, I make conjectures about Stanford, and experience emotions that concern Stanford. My idea of Stanford is a common element of all of these cognitions. Similarly I believe that Harvard is a university, Princeton is a university, MIT is a university, the University of California at Riverside is a university, and so on. My idea of the property of being a university is a common element of all of these. My belief that Stanford is a university has a structure; it involves these two ideas.

For my purposes in this essay a rather crude taxonomy of ideas will suffice. I distinguish between *notions*, ideas of things, and ideas of properties and relations, which I will just call "ideas." Among notions, I will distinguish between *buffers* and *detached notions*. Being a buffer is a status a notion has, when it is being affected by perception, and shaping volition, in virtue of being associated with epistemic or pragmatic relations. I notice a familiar looking person at a party, and form a buffer of him. I notice more things about him, and eventually recognize that it is, say, David Rosenthal, looking a bit older, grayer, and wiser than last time I saw him. My notion of David Rosenthal, until then a detached notion, becomes attached to the perceptions I am having; it ceases to be detached and becomes a buffer. If I am certain of my identification, the original buffer ceases to have a separate existence. To ask whether it is merged with my old Rosenthal notion, or uploads its information and disappears, or uploads and remains for reassignment, is to press my theory (or model, or metaphor, or fantasy) for more details than are provided by the mixture of folk psychology, reflective common sense, and phenomenology that motivates it. (I realized this when François Recanati noted inconsistencies in different presentations of the theory, and pressed the questions.) There is a pretty clear difference, however, between cases where the recognition is tentative and reversible, and the buffer and detached notion coexist for a while, and cases where it is quite definite (although perhaps, nevertheless, incorrect) and only one notion survives.

Cognitions like beliefs involve notions being associated with various ideas and other notions. The cognitions are about the objects the notions are of. It is possible that a single notion, perhaps developed through a series of misidentifications (imagine Rosenthal has a twin), is of two objects, or, to put it more carefully, is related to two objects in ways that would suffice to be of either of them, in the absence of the other. Then we have what I call a "mess," a technical concept that is developed further in Perry (2001b).

The basic picture is this. Our beliefs, and other cognitions, provide us with two connected databases, which correspond to the attached and detached distinction alluded to in the phrase "detach and recognize." Buffers are perceptual; they are attached; they are of objects that we perceive, or are at least actively keeping track of, so we know where they just were and have expectations about where they will be found again.[6] As we navigate around the world, we are constantly filling up buffers with information about objects we perceive; objects we see and hear, things we pick up and handle, and so forth. A second database involves detached notions, those we have of objects that we do not perceive at a given time, notions that are typically the results of previous encounters. Links are made between the databases, as we recognize the objects of which we have formed buffers, as the very objects of which we already have detached notions – or mistakenly think we do. Here is a striking individual at my office door; an intelligent face; a kind demeanor; a strong athletic build; a well-clipped moustache; who could it be? Maybe Omar Sharif? Or John Fischer? What would Omar Sharif be doing at my office? And wouldn't he look older by now? It must be John Fischer. Information flows from my detached file to my buffer; this fellow I see is the one I know from the past, the one named "John Fischer"; the one who is chair of the department, the one who seems

---

[6] As Recanati has pointed out, I actually employ (at least) two pictures, or metaphors, or models, which aren't entirely consistent. Sometimes I think of detached notions as *file-folders*. Here it is natural to think of the file-folders as having two different uses, as buffers and as detached files. When the student is in your office and the folder is in your hand and you are making notes, or giving advice, it is functioning as a buffer. When it is put away in the file cabinet it is functioning as a detached notion. The second is of a three-story house, with file folders on the third floor, and in-boxes and out-boxes on the first, and the second full of wiring to connect and disconnect the first-floor boxes and the third-floor file-folders, when detachment, recognition, or misrecognition occur. On the second metaphor, buffers are not phases of notions but separate entities connected or unconnected to them. Both metaphors emphasize the key distinction, between notions (or phases of notions) that are tied to various epistemic and pragmatic roles (introduced below) and those that are not. For full generality, the file-folder limps badly when we get to relations. The second metaphor is more at home with the idea of linked databases.

obsessed with moral responsibility and Stanford football. And information is piped up from buffer to notion: this fellow looks young and energetic. The combined information leads to inferences: being chair, being devoted to Stanford football, and obsessing about moral responsibility, is not aging as much as one might have expected.

An important part of the picture, or pictures, is the concept of *know-how*. We know how to do things involving objects, to achieve effects, conditional on what the objects are like. I know how to shake hands, or startle, or irritate, or find out more about, the object in front of me, or to my right, or in the next room. The chicken has know-how; it knows how to peck the grain of millet in front of it, or flee the fox it sees. We have a more complex repertoire of doxastic states, in virtue of the ability to detach notions and store information, which enables us to play more complicated information games.

SELF-BELIEF

I distinguish three levels of self-knowledge; one can have knowledge of the same fact in all three ways. I have mentioned two of them. Knowledge about the person one happens to be is the sort that Clinton had in the POTUS example, when he knew that POTUS was going to have lunch with the Queen, but before Hillary explained how the term 'POTUS' was used. When he realized that he* was POTUS, he had self-knowledge of the second kind of the same fact. The third kind of self-knowledge is really the most basic sort. I call it knowledge from the perspective of a self.[7] This is the sort of self-knowledge that a chicken has about itself.[7] Each time the chicken learns through perception that there is a kernel of corn in front of it, it is learning something about itself, for the chicken is the "it" that the kernel is in front of. But the chicken does not need a representation, file, or notion of itself, because it does not need to keep track of which chicken the information it picks up is about. All of the information it picks up is about itself and how things are related to it. I say that the chicken is an "unarticulated constituent" of the things it knows about itself.

The chicken might have notions of all sorts of things without needing a notion of itself. It might recognize the barn, the farmer, and even a rooster

---

[7] Since I said that selves are persons, and that humans are paradigmatic persons, and I do not believe that chickens are persons, talking of the self-knowledge of chickens is mildly inconsistent, but, I think, not irreparably so.

or two. But it does not need to think "the farmer's coming toward me with an ax"; it just needs to think "the farmer's coming toward with an ax."

In thinking about this most basic level of self-representation, it is important to keep the distinction between a representational state, and the content of a representational state, clearly in mind. I am not sure how sophisticated chickens are, but let us suppose that they can distinguish between corn and millet, and prefer corn. Our imaginary chicken goes into state M when it perceives a kernel of millet, and into state C when it perceives a kernel of corn. In state M, it will peck at the millet, unless it is also in state C. In state C, it will peck at the corn whether or not it is also in state M.

Given these causal roles for states M and C, what account of content would mesh? We might plausibly suppose that each chicken has a fixed desire to eat when it is not sleeping, and would prefer corn to millet. Given that, can't we simply say that M represents millet and C represents corn? Or better, M represents millet-in-front, and C represents corn-in-front? But this will not quite do. We want the content of each state to capture the conditions under which the act caused will succeed in satisfying the motivating desire. For the pecking to succeed, it is not enough that there is a kernel of millet in front of some chicken or other; there has to be a kernel of millet in front of the very chicken that is doing the pecking, the very chicken that is in state M. If we are talking about Bertha the Leghorn doing the pecking, then the condition under which that pecking will succeed is that there is a grain of millet in front of Bertha the Leghorn.

Here is how I think of it. The content is an abstract object that *encodes* truth-conditions or success-conditions. An object can be a constituent of the content of a state or event for two different reasons. There may be a part of the representation that has the job of representing that *that* object, rather than some other, is the one that has to meet certain conditions for the representation to be true, or to be successful. Or it may be that architecture of the representational system insures that this object belongs in the content, without an explicit part of the representation having that job. In the former case, I say the representation is *about* the object, and it is an *articulated constituent* of its content. In the latter case, I say that the representation *concerns* the object, which is an *unarticulated constituent* of the content.[8]

A simple example of what I am getting at is the needle on a speedometer on the dashboard of a car. It has the job of indicating the miles per hour that

[8] See Perry (1986).

the very car in whose dashboard it sits is traveling. The speedometer is set up to discriminate among different speeds, but not among different cars that are going that speed. But if the needle points to '60,' for the speedometer to be correct the very car in which it sits must be going 60 mph. Its content, its truth or veridicality conditions, are not simply that *some* car is going that fast. So the car is an unarticulated constituent of the content of the speedometer; the speedometer provides us with representations that *concern* the car.

What makes it the case that a particular car is the one the speedometer concerns, and tells us about, is a relational fact, that the speedometer is mounted in the car, and connected in the usual way to the car's drivetrain. That does not mean that the speedometer somehow contains a representation of the car in question as the car that meets that condition.

But we of course do have a concept of ourselves as ourselves, the same being at different times and in different places. We have an idea, or notion of ourselves. Our thoughts do not merely *concern* ourselves, but are often fully *about* ourselves; we are articulated constituents of our thoughts – at least some of the time. We have a notion of ourselves, which I call "the self-notion." We have thoughts in which we are explicitly represented, by our self-notions, and not just thoughts that concern ourselves like chickens and many other animals and I suppose children up to a certain age. This is the second kind of self-knowledge.

Let us return to Clinton. The first thing to observe is that Clinton does play a very important role in his own life, the role we call "self." One's neighbor is the person who stands in the relation *living next door* to one. One's mother is the person who stands in the relation *female parent of* to one. These are important roles. One's self is the person who stands in the relation *being identical with* to one. This is an even more important role.

Identity is an epistemic and a pragmatic relation, and self an epistemic and a pragmatic role. There are certain ways of knowing about the person who is one's self, that do not normally work for anyone else; I call them *normally self-informative*. And there are certain ways of doing things to and with one's self, that do not work for anyone else; I call these *normally self-effecting*.[9] The chicken's method of finding out about kernels of corn is normally self-informative. What makes the chicken's perception veridical is that there is a kernel of corn in front of a certain chicken, and whenever it has such a veridical perception, the chicken the kernel is in front of is the chicken doing the perceiving.

---

[9] 'Normally self-effecting' is shorthand for something like "normally self-effecting, or at any rate productive of effects whose nature depends on one's own properties and relations."

I call these methods "*normally* self-informative" because in abnormal circumstances, particularly of the sort philosophers like to imagine, one may pick up information about someone else in spite of using them. Imagine Clinton looking to see if he has spilled ketchup on his shirt. Compare this with the method Hillary might use to see if Bill has spilled ketchup on his shirt. Clinton lowers his head, the way one examines one's own shirt, the normally self-informative procedure for seeing whether there is a ketchup stain there. Hillary looks at Bill's shirt, more or less at her eye-level, which is normally a way of finding out if the person in front of you has spilled ketchup on his shirt.

But philosophers can invent examples where methods of knowing that are normally self-informative actually provide information about someone else. Perhaps a trick mirror is set up, so that when a person looks into it he do not see himself, but the person standing to his right. If that person was chosen to resemble the person doing the looking, he might be fooled. Clinton might think he has seen ketchup on his own shirt, when he has really seen it on the shirt of his double. Arguably, some methods are not just normally but necessarily self-informative, such as one's methods for finding out whether one is in pain, or whether one likes hamburgers better than salmon burgers, or, at least, whether one thinks one likes hamburgers better than salmon burgers. When I say a method is normally self-informative (or self-effecting) I do not mean to rule out its being necessarily so.

Now my suggestion about self-belief is this. We each have what I call a *self-buffer*, that is the repository of information picked up in normally self-informative ways, and that is also the motivator of actions done in normally self-effecting or self-involving ways. Self-belief is belief involving these buffers, which we can call "self-notions." A self-notion will always be associated with normally self-informative methods of knowing and normally self-effecting ways of acting, and so it will always be a buffer.[10]

One of the reasons we need a self-buffer is that in addition to normally self-informative ways of getting information about ourselves, we have other methods. Basically these were involved in what I earlier called "knowledge about the person one happens to be," like Clinton had before he knew what 'POTUS' meant. If we pick up knowledge about the person we happen to be, and recognize that we are that person, such knowledge will be integrated

---

[10] The self-buffer will not always be associated with the same methods of knowing and acting. Injuries or philosophical imaginations may deprive a real or imagined agent of many of the normal methods, but not, as far as I have been able to imagine, all of them at once, without simply putting the agent in a state where obtaining knowledge or acting in any way is impossible.

into our self-notion, and be an instance of the second kind of self-knowledge. (In such a case I say that the person still has knowledge of the person he happens to be, but no longer *mere* knowledge of that sort.)

Perhaps Clinton ran his office like this. Each morning a schedule was printed out for Clinton and his senior staff, a grid with the names on the left and the hours of the day across the top. At about 4 p.m. Clinton would glance at his copy to see where he was supposed to eat dinner. He looked for his name – or perhaps, once he has learned the convention, "POTUS" – in the same way he might have looked for someone else's name, if he wanted to find out where they would be in the early evening. If he saw that Clinton was to attend a barbecue at some rich person's house, sharing a limo with some other staff at 5:30, he realized that it means that he* was to attend the barbecue, and he* needed to get to the limo. He did not find out this fact about himself in a normally self-informative way; he found out about it in the same way any member of his staff would have, by finding the name 'Clinton' and looking at the events along the row to the right. Another example: suppose Clinton misplaced his cell phone, and decided to call himself on another phone to make his cell phone ring. If he hadn't memorized his cell number, he could have looked it up on the staff directory the same way he would have looked up anyone else's phone number. In these sorts of cases there is no use of normally self-informative methods; we find information about ourselves in the same way we find out information about others. Still, we associate this information with our self-notions. Once he learned his cell phone number, Clinton thought of it as his* cell phone number.

A second reason for having a self-buffer is when we pick up information about ourselves by observing other things like us. I see that other people are removing their shoes before going through airport security. I generalize that everyone must remove his or her shoes. I need something like a self-buffer to instantiate this generalization to myself.

So far then, the idea is that we have self-notions, which are buffers, in the sense that they are tied to an epistemic/pragmatic role (self) that a certain individual plays in our lives, and allow us to think *of* the person who plays that role in a certain way. And we also have information about ourselves that was acquired in the same way we acquire information about others, from publicly accessible sources of information, such as our names, social security numbers, telephone numbers, addresses, office numbers, and the like.

Typically, all or most of the second kind of information will also be associated with our self-notion; most of us know who we are, and recognize, at least most of the time, when we are reading about ourselves or hearing about ourselves. There are exceptions, cases of amnesia and dementia, for example. In such cases, someone might be wrong about who he is. Some people think they are Napoleon. I admire John Searle a lot; I often fantasize about being him, and approaching life and philosophy with the intelligence, confidence, and energy that he does; perhaps, as I slip into senility, these fantasies will give way to delusion, and I will come to believe I am John Searle, and start showing up for lectures he is scheduled to give. And there are other sorts of examples, where we have been assigned names, or something like names, that we do not necessarily know. A bank employee may be looking over a list of seriously overdue accounts, and see his own account number without recognizing it, and form the belief that *that* person had better pay his bill, without believing that he* was delinquent.

But most of us have it right about who we are. And herein lies a great difference between self-notions and most other buffers. Unlike most notions, self-buffers do not need to be detached from the epistemic and pragmatic roles they are associated with, as time passes and circumstances change. I can accumulate information about the person I am looking at, as I track her through a lecture; but when the lecture ends and we go our separate ways, the information in my buffer needs to be detached, either uploaded into a pre-existing notion of the person, if I recognize her, or used as the basis for a new notion. But I do not have to do that with my self-notion. It can remain tied to the epistemic/pragmatic role of *self*. Once you have the connection right, it is good for life.

In the general case, I need ways of recognizing the objects I am currently in epistemic and pragmatic relations to, in order to get the new information I pick up to the right notion, and apply the information associated with that notion to the objects. I need to have some way of getting the person I see at my office door associated with my 'John Fischer' notion rather than my 'Omar Sharif' notion. But in the case where the buffer serves the purposes of the detached notion, as a place to accumulate knowledge about the same thing, the need for such modes of recognition vanishes. This is the basis for the "immunity to misidentification" that we consider in the next section.

The self-notion is not unique in this respect. I have a buffer for the planet I live on, the one I find out about by looking around. I have a file for the Earth; I can read about it in the encyclopedia. The buffer and the file are one, and can safely remain so, until interplanetary travel becomes not only possible but also affordable. And then there is my "this universe" file, and my "this possible world file." As Ken Taylor once put it, if anything is "immune to error through misidentification," it is the actual world.

ROLE-LINKING AND IMMUNITY

In "Self-Reference and Self-Awareness" Sydney Shoemaker argues for the thesis of *immunity to error through misidentification relative to the first-person pronoun* (1968/1984). If, while wrestling, I perceive a bloody foot and think, "I am bleeding," I may be wrong, because although someone is bleeding, the someone is not me. In contrast, if I see a canary, and, on the basis of visual experience say "I see a canary," it will not turn out that I was right that someone was seeing a canary but wrong that it was me doing the seeing. In the bleeding case we do not have first-person immunity, in the seeing case we do.

On my account of self-belief, when I see a canary, I find out, in a normally self-informative way, that someone is seeing a canary, and incorporate the condition of being one who is seeing a canary into my self-notion. I do not have to figure out who is seeing the canary, in any sense that would involve matching features of the person seeing the canary with some identifying information associated with one of my notions. It is the way that I know that someone is seeing a canary, and not features I notice of that someone, that ensures that it is me.

I might think it *possible* that someone else is seeing a canary. Perhaps my visual centers have been wired to someone else's eyes, so I have the visual experiences that person has; he is the one who is seeing a canary; I am merely seeming to see a canary. In the throes of such doubts, I might restrain myself from an otherwise automatic reaction, and not believe that the someone I have discovered to be seeing a canary is me. Given such doubts, I will not use criteria of identification to look for sure signs that it is me, but rather check to see if there is any evidence of someone playing tricks on me – feel my scalp for new electrodes, perhaps.

Even if I cannot eliminate the possibility of such skulduggery, I will believe that I am *seeming* to see a canary. It seems that my experience is not simply a normally self-informative way of finding out that someone seems to see a canary, but a *necessarily* self-informative way of doing so.

We seem to have three sorts of situation. If I see someone else looking at a canary, my perception by itself only gives me a role-based way of identifying the person: the person I am now seeing. To get the information about the person associated with some detached notion, I am going to have to figure out who it is. I will need some method of identification, some criteria, in order to do this. If I figure out that it is my neighbor Dick Grote who is seeing the canary, it will be because of some set of more or less identifying conditions I associate with Dick Grote, and see exemplified by the canary seer.

In the second sort of situation, I see a canary. So I know in the normally self-informative way, that someone sees a canary. Here I do not need to identify who it is, or at least to do so I do not need anything like a set of identifying conditions to connect my notion of myself to something I notice about the canary-perceiver. The only person whose canary-seeing I can find out about in that way, at least in anything like normal circumstances, is me. If I am worried about it, I will check to see the circumstances are normal, rather than searching for some telltale sign of me.

The third sort of situation is when we have necessarily self-informative methods. If I find out that someone has a headache, or seems to see a canary, or is thinking about the futility of existence, in the normal ways that one finds out about oneself, there really seems to be no possibility that one is mistaken that it is oneself that is having the headache, or seeming to see a canary, or thinking.

In the last two cases we have something suitably called "immunity to misidentification." It is absolute in the last case and conditional in the second case. But in neither case does one need an identifying description or anything like it to assign the property to its rightful owner, oneself.

There is nothing mystical going on here. The *primary* way we identify objects is by the role or roles they play relative to us, in virtue of the fact that they affect us in ways appropriate to objects in those relations. If there is more than one object that can play that role in our lives, and if it matters to us which one it is, *then* there is an issue of further identification, and the possibility of a mistake. The chicken does not care which grain of millet it sees and pecks, and has all the information it needs in order to peck it, simply in virtue of seeing it. I care a lot about who is having the headache, but if I know about the headache in the way that people who have headaches know of them, the issue is settled. I am the only one whose headaches I can find out about in that way.

Rosenthal says,

When I assert that you are in pain, I must identify the self I ascribe pain to in some way independent of your simply being in pain. But there is no similar need, according to Shoemaker, to identify the individual I take to be in pain when I assert that I am in pain or am aware of myself as being in pain. But it is far from clear that this is so. For one thing, when I am aware of myself as being in pain, I identify the individual I take to be in pain as the individual that is aware, in a distinctively first-person way, of being in pain. Such identification is very thin, and does not take one far. But if I am aware of myself as being in pain, it does distinguish the individual I take to be in pain from you, as well as any other person. (39, this volume)

I think this is confusing in a couple of ways. First, we need to distinguish between asserting and being aware, and the relevant concepts of identification. I do not think it is part of Shoemaker's concept of immunity that I do not need to identify the individual I take to be in pain, when I assert that I am in pain; certainly in the normal case of communicating with someone I will have to do so, most often by using the word 'I.' With assertion, as Rosenthal says, I need to identify myself when I am talking about me, just as I need to identify you when I am talking about you, if I want to be understood. Here identifying means making known to my interlocutor.

Nor does Shoemaker say that when I recognize that I am in pain, I do not identify myself. The point is that the identification is immune to error, not that it does not happen. Unlike chickens, we have self-notions, and when we are in pain we usually believe that we are in pain, and not someone else. We know that the person whose pain we are aware of in a certain way is ourselves. What we do not need to do is ascertain this by checking the features of the person known to be in pain against some description or set of criteria, which would create the possibility of mistaken identity.

When I am driving, and look at the speedometer, I identify which vehicle the speedometer is telling me the speed of; that is, the car I am driving. This is a normally car-one-is-in method of ascertaining how fast some car is going. And normally, the identification is automatic; it is a nice feature of cars that the speedometers in them tell us about the speed of the cars they are in; it is a feature we are very used to, and do not need to consciously worry about. Now for certain purposes, I might need to *further* identify the car. Maybe I have a bet with my wife that my 96 Mazda Protégé cannot go over 70 miles per hour. I see from the speedometer, much to my surprise, that I am going 75. To be sure I have lost the bet, I need to double check that the car I am in is the Mazda, and not my wife's newer and perkier Hyundai.

Similarly, if you and I have a bet that the oldest person in the seminar cannot figure out the square of 37 in his head, and I somehow manage to do this, I can be sure that it is me that has done it. I might be wrong that my solution was correct, but I cannot be wrong that I was the one who arrived at it. But I will not thereby know that I have won the bet, until I check that I am the oldest. But that is why Shoemaker says, immunity to misidentification relative to the first person. My thought, "I have figured out the square of 37 in my head," is immune to an identificatory error, when its basis is being aware of just having done so, but my thought, "The oldest person in the seminar has figured it out," is not immune.

Suppose I hurt my hand and have a sensation of pain. I also have a higher-order thought, or HOT, about this sensation. Now it seems that a sensation is an event, which can be referred to in a variety of ways. Call my sensation 'SJP.' Now that I have named it and told you about it, you can think about SJP. You may wonder what caused it: Did he go to sleep? Did he hit his hand with a hammer? Just how painful was SJP? And I can also think of my sensation by this name. Maybe years from now I will read this chapter, and have some thoughts about SJP: was that the sensation I had when I accidentally drove a staple into my thumb? Or was it the time I was eating too fast and nearly bit off the end of my middle finger?

These are not the kind of HOTs that Rosenthal is thinking of, of course. There is nothing about such thoughts that could confer special status, like being conscious, on my sensation. The kind of thoughts Rosenthal has in mind are the sorts of thoughts we can have about a sensation or something else going on in our own minds at the time it occurs, and only if we are the very same person that has it. I think Rosenthal is correct, that this sort of thought is what he calls "essentially indexical," which means simply, I think, that it is what I call a "self-thought," a bit of self-belief. And I think he is correct that this requirement does not present a telling objection to his theory of HOTs. But I do not see that the account of the fact that HOTs are self-thoughts requires one to abandon Shoemaker's doctrine of immunity to misidentification.

SELF-REFERENCE

So let us go back to Clinton and the hamburgers. Perhaps the episode begins with a vague aroma of a hamburger cooking on a grill quite some way away. As he walks through the crowd shaking hands, he finds himself heading in the general direction of the grill, even though he is, in some sense, not conscious that he is smelling the hamburger, and that it is affecting him. As he approaches the grill, the aroma becomes stronger, and he becomes aware that he is sensing it, and that he has been edging closer to its source, and that he is hungry, and would like a hamburger. He says to the chef, "I would like a hamburger, please."

Here's how I see this unfolding. First, Clinton has a certain kind of sensation, appropriate to a hamburger being grilled someplace upwind, a bit off to the right of the direction he has been heading. I think it is like something for Clinton to have the sensation, even if he is not conscious of it, but some may doubt this, and think that its being like something to be in the state he is in only happens when he is conscious of the state. At any rate, the sensation, or perhaps potential sensation, has an incremental effect on him; combined with being slightly hungry, and liking hamburgers, and various other auxiliary beliefs, it causes him to change direction. Clinton, I would say, is *attuned* to the fact that this state is a sign of food in a certain direction, and changes direction without the need of conscious thought. In order for someone else's mental state, or brain state, or sensation, to affect Clinton, it seems he would have to have some sort of thought about it; Hillary's desire for a hamburger, for example, would not directly affect Bill, rather he would notice something about Hillary's behavior, or hear what she said, conclude that she would like a hamburger, and go order one for her. But his own brain states do not have to affect him by being represented elsewhere in his brain, for they are already in his brain, and can do so directly.

At some point, being conscious and reflective, Clinton has a HOT about his sensation. I am not sure that Rosenthal is right that consciousness is a matter of higher-order thought, but this does seem more plausible than thinking that he somehow has a sensation of his sensation, so let us assume that part of his account is basically correct. Clinton has a HOT about his own sensation. This is what Rosenthal calls an "essentially indexical" thought, it is one he would express with the first person; he takes himself to have the sensation, as well as the thought about the sensation.

A brief aside about the phrase "essential indexical." I doubt that I was the first to use this phrase, although my use of it seems to have put it into the philosophical vocabulary. As noted above, Castañeda had written extensively about the topic before my article, "The Problem of the Essential Indexical" appeared (Perry 1979). The term has come to be used by some people for the view that having a self-belief requires the word 'I' or some other first-person expression, most notably by Ruth Millikan, who calls this view "The Myth of the Essential Indexical" (Millikan 1990). However, that was not my view. The *problem* of the essential indexical was why indexicals *seemed* to be essential for expressing first-person thoughts, and how an account of propositional attitudes might deal with that fact. My solution then was that belief-states were more directly associated with *roles* than they were with propositions. Roles were formally analogous to the *characters* that Kaplan had shown were associated with sentences; characters only determined propositions relative to context. I did not claim, did not believe, and do not believe that first-person pronouns are essentially involved in having self-beliefs. While my theory of roles and belief-states has become quite a bit more complex, for better or worse, that is still the basic idea behind it.

Rosenthal talks about the mental analogue of the first person. I think that can be rather misleading. Self-notions are similar to uses of the word 'I,' in that self-notions are notions *of* their *possessor*, while uses of the first person are references *to* the *speaker*. But self-notions are mental structures that are components of belief-states, while utterances of 'I' are bits of purposeful activity. Self-notions are about their possessors because of their causal and informational role, not because of convention, as is the case with 'I.' 'I' is a basic tool for communication, but the self-notion is a tool for organizing information and guiding action.

Back to the main thread. While Rosenthal thinks the HOT must contain something like a descriptive identification of their possessor, in order to be about the possessor, I think that is dubious. In general, if we believe in something like the principle of sufficient reason, and do not think that aboutness and reference are built into the basic structure of the world, we must suppose that there is some relation between a mental event or structure and the object it is about, and between an utterance of a term and the object it is about. Accepting this bit of common sense is not the same as accepting a descriptive account of that relation. A descriptive account holds that the relation is mediated by some set of beliefs, and facts about who or what fits these beliefs. Attunement to the relation that our self-notions have to ourselves, or our perceptions have to the object they are of, does not require belief or thought about the relation; it requires know-how, and not knowledge-that. This is not the way that descriptions work. The relation is not mediated by our beliefs about who we are. It might be correct to say that when I see the cup, and reach out for it to get a drink, I identify the cup as being in front of *me*, and reachable by *me*. But this sort of identification is not like the case in which I identify a certain person as the oldest man in the seminar, or a certain cup as being the one I bought at the Grand Canyon. And, in particular, it seems immune to misidentification in the way Shoemaker says. If I see the cup, and take it to be me that is seeing it, I cannot be wrong about that.

To get back to Clinton. We have him now in front of the grill, having sensations of hunger and hamburgers cooking, aware of these sensations, thinking about them and what to do about them, and this all leads him to his utterance, "I'd like a hamburger." Clinton knows English, and knows that if he utters this sentence, it will be true if and only if he would like a hamburger. And, like most of us most of the time, Clinton knows how to produce the utterance. He knows that an utterance he produces intentionally will be his utterance, and that a use of 'I' in it will refer to him. Normally, he will be aware of the characteristic changes in his mind and mouth involved in producing an utterance, and know that it is his mind and his mouth that are giving rise to it. Using the first person is a normally self-effecting way of acting, and so under the control of our self-notion. So

Clinton knows how to produce an utterance, using the first person, that expresses his beliefs and desires about himself.

Why, one might ask, does he say "I would like a hamburger," rather than "Bill Clinton would like a hamburger"? According to referentialist theories of indexicals and names, the two utterances would express the same proposition, that Bill Clinton would like a hamburger. Granting this, still, the plans that he would have in mind, for getting the hamburger, would be rather different.[11] In the one case, he assumes that the chef will hear the utterance, recognize that the person in front of him is the speaker, and so the utterance is true iff the person in front of him would like a hamburger. He knows how to give a hamburger to the person in front of him, and will do so. If Clinton had said "Bill Clinton would like a hamburger," Clinton's plan would have put an additional cognitive burden on the chef: he will hear the utterance, realize it is true iff the person the speaker is referring to with "Bill Clinton" would like a hamburger, recognize that the person in front of him is the person named "Bill Clinton" that is most likely being referred to, and hand him a hamburger. This second plan is less modest than the first, in that it assumed the chef will recognize Clinton.

Of course, the chef likely will recognize Clinton. Still, it seems a bit pompous to refer to oneself with one's name, when the fact of who one is, and what one's name is, is irrelevant to one's goals, and Clinton, at least for a politician, is not very pompous.

Thus our theory enables us to account for an insight of Ellen Goodman's.[12] At a political rally in Philadelphia, while campaigning against Clinton in 1996, Bob Dole said,

If something happened along the route and you had to leave your children with Bob Dole or Bill Clinton, I think you would probably leave them with Bob Dole.

Goodman commented,

I am not at all sure that I'd want to leave my children with someone who talks about himself in the third person.

---

[11] For (a lot) more about such plans, see Korta and Perry (forthcoming) and Perry (2001b).

[12] Ellen Goodman, "Presidential race '96: The country as child, candidates as ultimate care-giver," *Boston Globe*, April 20, 1996 (http://articles.sun-sentinel.com/1996-04-20/news/9604220286_1_national-debt-bob-father).

CHAPTER 4

Ordinary self-consciousness

Lucy O'Brien

"the thinking about others thinking of us ... excites a blush"
Darwin ([1872] 1965, 325)

I. INTRODUCTION

1. Ordinary self-consciousness

When one walks into a room full of strangers one may describe oneself as "feeling self-conscious." To feel self-conscious is to be conscious of oneself as an object represented by others. It seems to me that this kind of self-consciousness is a pervasive phenomenon that is worthy of our attention. It has, however, been rather overlooked in philosophy. When philosophy has focused on self-consciousness it has been the kind of self-consciousness that characterizes our ability to think about ourselves in the first person. While that ability might be required for feeling self-conscious, the latter self-consciousness is I think a distinct and important phenomenon. In this chapter I will explore the nature of what I will call 'ordinary self-consciousness' (OSC) and offer an analysis that aims to identify its key components.

My main aim is to identify, and to look closely at the phenomenon. However, I will also raise the suggestion that the phenomenon has a crucial role to play in explaining and understanding the nature of the self-conscious emotions of guilt, shame, pride, and embarrassment. Darwin has tended to

I have given this paper as a talk on a number of occasions: "The Self and Self-Knowledge" Conference, Institute of Philosophy, London; "Workshop on the Self," Fribourg; Research Seminar, Essex University; 12th Philosophy and Psychiatry Conference, Lisbon; APIC Research Seminar, Institute Jean Nicod. I am very grateful to audiences for excellent questions and discussion that have directed how the paper was written up. My thanks for very helpful written comments to JeeLoo Liu, co-editor of this volume. I am also very grateful to Chris Peacocke for discussion on these topics and for written comments on the chapter.

be slightly mocked by psychologists of the emotions for his tendency to treat all self-conscious emotions as if they were like embarrassment, and to treat embarrassment as merely being the focus of attention of others. Surely, not all emotions that involve "the thinking about others thinking of us" excite the blush associated with embarrassment, and surely more is needed for embarrassment than just being the focus of others. Guilt, shame, pride, and hubris all involve others thinking about us, but often do not, and certainly need not, make us blush. It is of course right that not all self-conscious emotions are like embarrassment. Nevertheless, I think that Darwin might be right in thinking that a relatively simple self-conscious emotion is at the heart of the family of self-conscious emotions. It is not that the relevant emotion is an emotion of which the other self-conscious emotions are a variety. Rather it is what we might call an 'ur-self-conscious emotion' – an emotion which will enable us to understand the others, and out of which the others develop. Nor do I think the relevant emotion is embarrassment, rather it is ordinary self-consciousness. I will not, in this piece, try to account for the particular relations between ordinary self-conscious and the distinct self-conscious emotions. Rather, I will table a general hypothesis that ordinary self-consciousness is a phenomenon that has a role to play in our ability to have self-conscious emotions at all.

Before offering some quotations, which I hope will serve to fix and bring color to the notion of self-consciousness I am interested in exploring, let me distinguish between ordinary self-consciousness understood as a conscious mental attitude and ordinary self-consciousness understood as a way of acting. We talk not only about someone feeling self-conscious when, for example, she walks into a room full of strangers, but we also talk about someone acting self-consciously when in the presence of others. In this chapter I am going to take feeling self-conscious, rather than acting self-consciously, to be my focus. I take it that feeling self-conscious is the primary notion in terms of which acting self-consciously will be under-stood. However, the relation between feeling self-conscious and acting self-consciously is not straightforward. Acting self-consciously is arguably the way individuals act in paradigm cases of feeling self-conscious. But one can feel self-conscious and not act self-consciously, and act self-consciously without feeling self-conscious. Further, feeling self-conscious will lead different individuals to act differently; and a single individual will act differently on different occasions, whilst feeling self-conscious. However we are to explain the relation between the two, my interest in this piece will be with the phenomenon of feeling self-conscious, however it manifests itself in action.

2. *Some examples*

In this section I want rather to step aside and let more gifted authors do some of the work of identifying and describing the phenomenon of ordinary self-consciousness for me. In particular, I want to use some quotations from fiction, as well as a couple from philosophy, to help get a grip on the phenomenon. These quotations serve to illustrate the phenomenon both by describing what it is to be in the grip of it, and just as effectively, by describing the complete absorption in another which can push aside the feeling of self-consciousness, and which the return to self-consciousness in relation to the other breaks up. I hope I will be excused for quoting extensively here. The authors quoted (Scott Fitzgerald, Eliot, Sartre) are each clearly aiming to conjure in their readers a vivid recognition of the state of the subject being described. I hope to use this conjuring as an effective way of presenting the phenomenon before going on to analyze and dissect it.

First, let me start with a quotation from F. Scott Fitzgerald:

> Gradually he [Amory] realized that he was really walking up University Place, self-conscious about his suitcase, developing a new tendency to glare straight ahead when he passed any one. Several times he could have sworn that men turned to look at him critically. He wondered vaguely if there was something the matter with his clothes, and wished he had shaved that morning on the train. He felt unnecessarily stiff and awkward among these white-flannelled, bareheaded youths, who must be juniors and seniors, judging from the *savoir faire* with which they strolled. (Fitzgerald 2000, 34)

As we read this we can easily enough imagine the slight stiffness in the neck, the inhibition of the free flow of action, and the sense that to turn left or right would constitute a deliberate act, one that would need a definite decision. Amory walks conscious of others and conscious of how he appears to others – in particular how his external features, his clothes, his suitcase, his skin might be taken. Amory's continued self-consciousness is in contrast to Maggie's loss of self-consciousness, and its painful return, in the following scene from Eliot. In the scene, at the book club, Maggie's friend Lucy is delighted to introduce Maggie to Stephen, her fiancé. Lucy hopes that they like each other. They do, very much:

> Stephen became quite brilliant in an account of Buckland's Treatise, which he had just been reading. He was rewarded by seeing Maggie let her work fall, and gradually get so absorbed in his wonderful geological story that she sat looking at him, leaning forward with crossed arms, and with an entire absence of self-consciousness, as if he had been the snuffiest of old professors, and she a downy-lipped alumna. He was so fascinated by the clear, large gaze that at last he forgot to

look away from it occasionally toward Lucy; but she, sweet child, was only rejoicing that Stephen was proving to Maggie how clever he was, and that they would certainly be good friends after all.

"I will bring you the book, shall I, Miss Tulliver?" said Stephen, when he found the stream of his recollections running rather shallow. "There are many illustrations in it that you will like to see."

"Oh, thank you," said Maggie, blushing with returning self-consciousness at this direct address, and taking up her work again. (Eliot 1985, 489–90)

Sometimes one best captures a phenomenon, and its frequent presence, by noting the effects of its removal or institution. One notices that the radio has been on and has been distracting and aggravating when, blissfully, silence falls as someone turns it off. Or one notices that the silence was pleasant when the radio is switched on. Here it is Maggie's *unselfconscious* engagement with Stephen and his illuminating talk on the Buckland Treatise that enables us to see her sudden switch to self-consciousness and the awareness of being the object of Stephen's awareness.

Sartre is perhaps the *philosopher* who has come closest to discussing what I calling ordinary self-consciousness. He talks about '*la honte,*' generally translated as 'the shame,' which is involved in the recognition of one's being the object looked at and judged by another. He illustrates what he means in this famous passage in the section of *Being and Nothingness* called 'The Look':

Let us imagine that moved by jealousy, curiosity or vice I have just glued my ear to the door and looked through a keyhole. I am alone and on the level of non-thetic self-consciousness. This means first of all that there is no self to inhabit my consciousness, nothing therefore to which I can refer my acts in order to qualify them. They are in no way known, I am my acts and hence they carry in themselves their whole justification ... My consciousness sticks to my acts, it is my acts; and my acts are commended only by the ends to be attained and by the instruments to be employed ...

But all of a sudden I hear footsteps in the hall. Someone is looking at me. What does this mean? It means that I am suddenly affected in my being and that essential modifications appear in my structure – modifications which I can apprehend and fix conceptually by means of the reflexive cogito.

First of all, I now exist as myself for my unreflective consciousness. It is this irruption of the self which has been most often described: I see myself because somebody sees me. (Sartre 1969, 259)

And he goes on to say:

Now shame ... is shame of self; it is the recognition of the fact that I am indeed that object which the OTHER is looking at and judging. (Sartre 1969, 261)

Sartre uses shame in these discussions both to stand for the usual notion, which involves the painful sense of being judged or seen in a negative light, and also for the "pure" or "original" shame that is just the feeling of being an object to another. The latter is what I mean by ordinary self-consciousness and what I want to focus on in this chapter. However, if I am right about the relation between ordinary self-consciousness and the other self-conscious emotions, it is no accident that such self-consciousness and shame get run together. They share the same structure and one can be seen as the transformation of the other.

Finally, we see this connection between shame and the sense of being an object for others, in this case for the eye of the world, dramatically, even hysterically, expressed by Nietzsche:

Centre – The feeling "I am the mid-point of the world!" arises strongly if one is suddenly overcome with shame; one then stands there as though confused in the midst of a surging sea and feels dazzled as though by a great eye which gazes upon us and through us from all sides. (Nietzsche 1997, 166)

3. Why consider ordinary self-consciousness?

It might be asked why we should bother devoting our philosophical efforts on this rather specific and particular aspect of human life. I have at least three reasons for bothering.

First, specific and particular human phenomena can be interesting in themselves. And if our attention alights on such phenomena, there is no more reason needed to justify our perusal and attempt to analyze them than that they are interesting and human. Ordinary self-consciousness is fascinating. Although specific and particular, it is a salient and engaging feature of our conscious lives that is a prelude to pain and pleasure of a particularly human kind. It is also a complex psychological phenomenon in which a number of different facets of our consciousness of ourselves, and others, come together.

Second, ordinary self-consciousness is in my view the basis of an important source of knowledge about ourselves. It puts us in a position to gather information about ourselves both from (i) others and from (ii) our reaction to others. With respect to (i): in being conscious of others' reactions to us we can gather information about how we are presenting to the world. With respect to (ii): we can gather information about ourselves, and about what and who we in fact care about by monitoring our reaction to the reaction of others picked up when we feel self-conscious. It is not straightforward to explain how feeling self-conscious is a source for knowledge, particularly if we consider it to be an emotion. Emotions are not, in general, straightforward sources of knowledge about the world. To tackle this issue properly would take me beyond the aim of this chapter. It is enough for present purposes to note that ordinary self-consciousness seems to put one in a state of receptiveness that is epistemologically significant, however precisely it does so.

Third, I want to contend that a consideration of ordinary self-consciousness may enable us to understand better the self-conscious emotions of hubris, pride, shame, guilt, and embarrassment. I will suggest that ordinary self-consciousness has a nature and structure that makes it a candidate to be a kind of *ur*-self-conscious emotion, an emotion suited to adaptation and transformation into the more familiar self-conscious emotions.

However, within the confines of this discussion, I will not be able, and will not try, to make good this claim. To do so would need a case-by-case treatment of the relations between ordinary self-consciousness and shame, or guilt, or pride and such a treatment is not feasible here. Nevertheless I hope I will say enough to give one reason to think that the attempt to do the latter may not be a vain one.

II. THE CHARACTER OF ORDINARY SELF-CONSCIOUSNESS

In this section I want to try to do a bit more in the way of identifying the particular character of ordinary self-consciousness.

First, in central cases, ordinary self-consciousness seems to involve particular phenomenological and bodily features. There is a heightened awareness of one's skin, clothes etc. – an awareness of one's physical externalities. There is an externalized awareness of one's speech and other actions – an awareness about how our sayings and doings come across to others. There are sensational and physical reactions: prickles in the back of the neck and elsewhere, blushing, turning the head away from a gaze. These phenomenological and bodily features vary in nature and intensity. Nevertheless, they are the natural concomitants of the phenomenon of ordinary self-consciousness.

Second, and essentially, OSC seems to involve a subject taking two perspectives on herself: an *observer's perspective* and a *subject's perspective*. It is my thinking about others' thinking about me. However, it is important to note that it is *not* that these perspectives oscillate within ordinary self-consciousness, as we might oscillate between self-consciousness and absorption. We do not capture the phenomenon if we think of it as shifting in serial between an observer's perspective on us and a subject's perspective on the observer – flik-flaking back and forth between a focus from the inside out, to one of outside in. That would not capture what is so central to the phenomenon, and that is that it is an awareness of others' awareness of me. Rather what we have is the two perspectives held at one and the same time. It is this simultaneous awareness that it is me, as I appear to others, that gives rise to the particular pleasures and pains of self-consciousness. If in ordinary self-consciousness we inhabited the observer's perspective only, and fully, we would look on ourselves only as another, and be displaced from our selves.

Consider, for example, sitting in front of an interview panel – suppose one experiences a kind of hyper-awareness of oneself from the outside. This would not be such an intense state if one fully occupied the position of the observer. One is not the observer who is thinking: "She might have polished her shoes," "I wonder why she is blushing," etc. One is the subject of perusal who is conscious of her scuffed shoes and her blushed face as presenting themselves to others. It is the self-perusal from the perspective of the other, knowing at the same time that it is oneself that is the object of perusal, which gives the state the character it has. Thus, rather than oscillating between awareness of oneself from the inside and from the outside, it is that the two perspectives are held Janus-faced together.

Third, it is a crucial feature of ordinary self-consciousness that it seems to involve an evaluative component, without there needing to be a particular evaluation. And connectedly it is a state that *need* be neither pleasurable nor painful. I can be conscious of myself as the object of a possible evaluation from others without having any view about whether a particular evaluation – good, bad, or indifferent – has been or will be reached. There are two parts to this claim. The first is that there is an evaluative component, and the second that there need be no particular evaluation. Let me start with the second. It seems clear that one can be aware of oneself as being under the inquisitive gaze of another without taking the other to have reached one or other evaluation. One is self-conscious to just the same degree when one is aware of others' awareness of one's bristly chin – I imagine – even if one has no idea whether it will present as shoddy or designer stubble. Consider the interview case that was raised earlier – I might be quite comfortable, even though highly conscious, of the way in which I appear to the panel. It may be that I am waiting, ready for the first question from the interview panel, with no particular hopes or anxieties about how I come across. However, that is perfectly compatible with my being self-conscious in the sense of being highly conscious that I am the object of attention of others. And what of the first part of the claim: that there is an evaluative component? In the state I have in mind it is not just that I am aware of myself being the object of attention from others – it is an awareness that I might please or displease, be praised or criticized. I am *up for evaluation* even though no specific evaluation need have come in.

Fourth, ordinary self-consciousness seems to involve the idea of an evaluator without there needing to be a concrete evaluator. In the sorts of cases mentioned so far, there have tended to be particular evaluators. Maggie is self-conscious with respect to Stephen and the assembled group, Sartre is self-conscious with respect to the person seeing him look through the keyhole, and in the interview case, the evaluators are the interviewers on the panel.

However, note that in the Fitzgerald quotation the self-consciousness precedes the thought that others are turning to look. The observer in this case seems to be an imagined one, or perhaps to be the agent himself catching himself from the outside. Consider a slightly different version of the interview case. Imagine that I am shown into the room, asked to sit down, and left on my own to await the arrival of the panel. While waiting, I may feel self-conscious in my sense, while having no idea who, and how many, will constitute the panel. There is more to say about the identity and nature of the evaluator, and I will come back to the issue. However, I hope enough has been done to put a recognizable phenomenon before us.

III. HOW SHOULD WE CLASSIFY OSC?

How should we classify ordinary self-consciousness? It is a state that involves a number of distinct kinds of self-awareness, awareness from the observer's perspective and from the subject's perspective, and has an evaluative dimension without necessarily involving an actual evaluation. Is it an emotion?

It is standard in philosophy and psychology to distinguish between the "simple emotions" and the "self-conscious emotions." The "simple emotions" of joy, anger, fear, sadness, etc. are supposed to be more or less universal, culture independent and are thought to characterize the mental lives of even very young babies and non-human animals. In contrast, the "self-conscious emotions" of guilt, shame, pride, hubris, and embarrassment, while marked by certain universal forms of expression, are supposed to be more sensitive to cultural differences and to characterize the lives only of somewhat older human beings and perhaps some adult primates. Human beings are generally not thought to be capable of these self-conscious emotions until they reach the age of three – although embarrassment may come earlier.

It seems clear that if OSC is an emotion, it is not a simple emotion. It will require cognitive capacities beyond those required for joy, anger, and fear. The nature and complexity of structure involved in feeling self-conscious – in particular in the capacity to be aware of others' awareness of oneself – is more like that involved in the self-conscious emotions. Perhaps having OSC is a matter of experiencing an emotion like pride, embarrassment, guilt, or shame.

There seem to be a number of options here that we need to consider separately. There are different ways we might view the relations between OSC and the more familiar self-conscious emotions. Roughly, we might think of it as no more than a specific type of self-conscious emotion or we might think it has generality and is in some way involved in all or most of the other self-conscious emotions. Let me identify seven options:

(Option A) Pride, guilt, shame, etc. are feelings of self-consciousness and we should take OSC to be a genus under which such emotions fall as species.

(Option B) OSC is in fact only what others have called embarrassment, and it has no special generality or claim to basicness.

(Option C) OSC is in fact only what others have called embarrassment, but it has special generality and a claim to basicness.

(Option D) OSC is not just embarrassment, rather it is a specie of "self-conscious emotion" distinct from the more familiar ones. It has, however, no special generality or claim to basicness.

(Option E) OSC is not just embarrassment, and is a specie of "self-conscious emotion" distinct from the more familiar ones. Moreover, it does have some special generality or claim to basicness.

(Option F) OSC is not itself an emotion at all, but does have some special generality or claim to basicness with respect to the self-conscious emotions.

(Option G) OSC is not itself an emotion at all, and it has no special generality or claim to basicness with respect to the self-conscious emotions.

Option A seems quite implausible. The phenomenon I have tried to identify is a concrete one, not an abstract structure that can be thought of as genus. One can feel self-conscious in a particular situation at a particular time, and such self-consciousness can fade, or perhaps morph into shame, embarrassment, or pride. OSC may, I will suggest, have a role to play in explaining any such consequent emotions but they are not varieties of OSC.

According to options B and C, OSC just is embarrassment. But that cannot be right – you can be self-conscious without it being painful, or in any way uncomfortable. You can be self-conscious while standing at the front of a lecture hall waiting for the audience to settle without being embarrassed. Embarrassment seems, necessarily, to be at least a bit uncomfortable, and to involve some sense of misfit or inappropriateness, to involve the desire to turn or hide. Like the other self-conscious emotions, it seems to involve a positive or negative evaluative element. Ordinary self-consciousness may very quickly involve discomfort, or a desire to shy away from the eyes of others. But it need not. It can also come to involve a feeling of pleasure, and a sense of well-being, or holding one's own under the circumspection of others. And it can, just occasionally, be neutral, characterizing a stable feeling of being up for the perusal of others without fear or hope. I say "just occasionally," because more often than not, given the creatures that we are and the nature of ordinary self-consciousness, we fear or expect evaluation to go a certain way, or we pick up information about how that perusal of others is going: are we too much a focus or too little, are we disappointing or are we pleasing? Once we come to be aware of the particular reactions of others we may become embarrassed, or proud or shameful, but it seems that we can be self-conscious without being in those states. What is less clear is whether one could be embarrassed without also being self-conscious, or having been self-conscious. I think probably not – when one is embarrassed one is reacting to the feeling of oneself being the object of perusal by others.

Options D and E agree that the feeling of self-consciousness is distinct from embarrassment and agree that it needs to be treated alongside the other self-conscious emotions. However, they disagree about its importance in understanding the other self-conscious emotions. Establishing which option is right will ultimately depend upon more detailed work in analyzing OSC and its connection with the other self-conscious emotions. Even though a complete account cannot be given here, I do aim to do enough in a subsequent analysis of the elements involved in OSC to make it seem plausible that it may play a useful role in understanding the self-conscious emotions, thereby giving us reason to prefer option E to option D.

What about options F and G? The standard self-conscious emotions seem to be characterized along a dimension of success or failure with respect to some standard, or by some measure of pleasure or pain. They split into roughly two groups: the ones that involve a negative evaluation or a painful character (embarrassment, shame, guilt) and the ones that involve a positive evaluation or pleasurable character (hubris, pride). If we take some such determination of a value – positive or negative – as a *necessary* mark of emotions, then OSC cannot unproblematically be classified as an emotion. On such an understanding of an emotion we would be forced to choose between options F and G.

I cannot hope to settle here whether we should think of emotions as, of necessity, requiring either a negative or positive character, so cannot hope to settle properly whether we should count all cases of OSC as cases of a self-conscious *emotion*. However, OSC does emerge as a feeling, with a complex structure, that naturally takes its place in the category of self-conscious emotions. It is true that it need not be evaluative or be characterized along a dimension of success or failure: one can be OSC without suffering a painful sense of misfit, or without thinking that one has offended the rules or mores of one's peers, or transgressed some moral standard. However, while OSC need not involve an *actual* evaluation, it is wrong to say that it involves no evaluative dimension at all. OSC involves a focus on ourselves on which we are, as I will put it, *up for evaluation*. By "up for evaluation" I mean that in feeling self-conscious we are aware of others – others who are aware of us – as potential evaluators, as subjects capable of judging us fitting or unfitting, well dressed or badly dressed, foolish or sensible, or merely as capable of giving us an undetermined evaluative thumbs up or thumbs down with respect to some standard. Note, however, that unlike shame and guilt, one can feel self-conscious without having any grasp of what standards or rules are in operation, and relative to which one may be evaluated; and further, one need have no evidence that one is actually being evaluated one way rather than another. Rather, in feeling self-conscious, one is aware of being the subject of a potential evaluation of some kind or other. Given the nature of feeling self-conscious, I see no obvious reason to deny that it is a self-conscious emotion, and therefore am inclined to option E. However, if it were to be established, for independent taxonomic reasons, that all emotions, and the self-conscious emotions in particular, *must* be determinate in value – positive or negative – then instances of OSC on my account may not be emotions, and I would have to countenance option F.

IV. THE STRUCTURE OF OSC

Let me now turn to the job of trying to analyze ordinary self-consciousness to understand better its structure and component elements. OSC seems to involve at least the following elements:

1. OSC involves *focus on oneself from a third-person perspective*. That is, we have reflexive consciousness from the perspective of another. Thus, OSC involves the capacity to think of another as minded and to think of one as the object from the perspective of that other. So, if X is our subject,

   [OSC-1]   X is conscious of X from a third-person perspective.

2. OSC involves focus on oneself from a third-person perspective while *knowing it is 'me' I focus on*. That is, one does not just have consciousness of oneself as an object from the outside, from over there. The consciousness has a *duality*, which means I am at the same time conscious that it is *me* that is the focus of others' awareness. This is the double perspective mentioned earlier and involves not only the capacity to think of what is in fact myself from "over there" but also the capacity to think of the object of awareness *as myself*. We can say,

   [OSC-2]   X is conscious of X from a third-person perspective, aware that *she herself* is X.

3. OSC involves focus on oneself from a third-person perspective, knowing it is 'me' I focus on *with an evaluative question*. This element points to the idea that in feeling self-conscious, the subject feels *up for evaluation* from the third-person perspective, aware of having she, herself, in their gaze. There does not have to be a fixed standard for evaluation nor a fixed evaluation. It is rather that the self-conscious subject is aware of herself as up for evaluation in some way or other. So we have:

   [OSC-3]   X is conscious of X from a third-person perspective, aware that she, herself is X, and an object of a potential evaluation.

4. OSC involves focus on oneself from a third-person perspective, knowing it is 'me' I focus on, with an evaluative question, and *with an evaluator assigned*. In the central case the evaluator or evaluators involved in OSC are the person or people looking at you as you look at them: the people on the interview panel, or at the party where you do not know anybody, or the audience in front of which you give a paper. However, they need not be. Imagine you are dancing on your own in your study. You could suddenly disengage from your leaping, seeing yourself from the outside, and thereby coming to feel self-conscious about what you are doing, quietly sitting back to finish writing that paper. In this case there is not an actual external evaluator – unlike the case when you realize that the guy in the building opposite is glued to his window staring at your antics. Rather, in this case one seems to function as one's own evaluator, or one has imagined an evaluator. Note also that there are other cases in which one might have a particular other assigned as an evaluator, but the other person's presence, and indeed identity, may be imagined rather than

actual. For example, I might suddenly think of my mother watching me dancing when I was supposed to be working, or imagine Anne Elliot (of Austen's *Persuasion*) disapproving of my frivolity. So we now have:

[OSC-4]   X is conscious of X from a third-person perspective, aware that she, herself is X, and an object of potential evaluation, by Y.

5. OSC involves focus on oneself from a third-person perspective knowing it is 'me' I focus on with an evaluative question, with an evaluator assigned, and *sometimes* with *an evaluative schema*. A final element often in play in OSC is the evaluative schema/schemas of the evaluator. If anything substantial is meant by 'schema,' this element seems not to be essential. One could feel self-conscious with no more than the presence of another and the sense that one might please or fail to please, may elicit a smile, or a frown from the evaluator with no more sophisticated schema in play. One might know in the interview case, for example, that one is likely to be judged relative to the demands of the job for which one is being interviewed. There are other cases where the subject might suppose that there are evaluative schemas in play, but know almost nothing about what they are and so not know, and perhaps worry about, how and on what basis one is likely to be judged by the evaluator. For example, one can feel self-conscious when one walks into a room of strangers not knowing anything much at all about what standards are in play. So, finally we have:

[OSC-5]   X is conscious of X from a third-person perspective, knowing she, herself is X, and up for evaluation, by Y, using Y's evaluative schema(s).

If we identify OSC using the above five elements we can see that it allows for variation along at least the following dimensions:

1. Identity of the evaluator.
2. Presence of the evaluator (actual, imagined, expected).
3. Knowledge of the evaluator.
4. Degrees of weight given to the evaluator.
5. Nature of evaluative schema.
6. Degrees of knowledge of the evaluative schema.
7. Degrees of weight given to the evaluative schema.

Let me say something about these in turn.

As we have seen, the identity of the evaluator can vary. The central case involves others – strangers, acquaintances, friends – looking at one. But we can, as mentioned, also function as our own evaluator. In the interview case when we are sitting alone in the room waiting for the panel we can feel self-conscious, seeing ourselves from the outside, and feeling self-conscious as a result. Perhaps even the beady eye of a pet or portrait can trigger a feeling of self-consciousness. We can also have an imagined evaluator – a fictional character we admire, for example. The identity of the evaluator is fixed by whomever, or whatever, is supposed by the subject to be at the external viewpoint from which she takes an observer's perspective on herself.

We need also to distinguish between the *identity* of the evaluator and the *presence* of the evaluator. Standardly, the evaluator is the person standing in front of you. But it may not be. Obviously, if the evaluator is a fictional character then both the evaluator and her presence are only imagined. However, the evaluator's identity may be real enough with only her presence imagined, as in the case where I imagine being seen by my mother, or father, or some admired teacher. Or it may not be that their presence is purely imagined; rather, it may be that the evaluator is *expected*. In the interview case, where I feel self-conscious sitting alone, the relevant evaluator may be myself, but may also be the expected interviewers.

Additionally, our knowledge of the evaluator can vary from the case where we know almost nothing at all – the evaluator is a stranger – to the case where the evaluator is well known to us – our mother, our colleague. There are then of course many cases in between.

Perhaps the dimension that has the most effect on the consequences and nature of our feeling self-conscious is the *weight* we put on the evaluator. OSC does not just involve focus on oneself from a third-person perspective knowing it is 'me' I focus on with an evaluative question, with an evaluator assigned; it also tends to involve *a weighting given to the evaluator*. The more we care about how that person takes us when we are aware of being the object of attention, the more anxious we are likely to be and so the more likely will our self-consciousness tip into embarrassment or discomfort, or perhaps into hubris and attempts to show ourselves off.

I have distinguished between the evaluator and the evaluative schema. It is clear that the identity and our knowledge of our evaluator(s) and the nature and knowledge of the evaluative schema(s) in place will be linked. The better I know someone the more I am likely to know about the schemas she is likely to be operating with, and the less I know generally the less I will know about how I am likely to be judged. But note that there are circumstances and situations in which I will know little about the evaluator personally but will know, or have a good idea about, what schema will be in place and by means of which I will be evaluated. The interview situation is obviously one such case. Or suppose I am asked to give a talk on women's dress codes in philosophy at the London Fashion Show – this might seem an unpromising topic, but would in fact be a rich seam. Whatever else I know when I stand ready to speak, I know that my appearance will be up for evaluation.

Furthermore, just as I can weight the evaluator and just as that weighting will make a significant difference to the likelihood of feeling self-conscious and to the consequences of feeling self-conscious, so too I can weight the evaluative schema. OSC involves focus on oneself from a third-person perspective knowing it is 'me' I focus on with an evaluative question, with an evaluator and evaluative schema assigned, a weighting given to the evaluator, and a *weighting given to the evaluative schema in play*. Importantly, my weighting of the evaluator and the evaluative schema may not run together. I may not care a jot about my clothing and appearance, but I may nevertheless care about the audience and their engagement and interest at my talk on women's dress codes in philosophy. This weighting given to the evaluator might lead me to become self-conscious about the aspects of me the evaluator is concerned about, even though I do not independently weight their evaluative schema.

Consider the following case: Suppose I have a much-admired and loved grandfather: a career soldier in the British Army, retiring as a colonel, after a significant number of years of active service, earning one or two medals for bravery. I trust his judgment on many matters, think he is a decent and good man, and find him to have a pretty unerring eye for nonsense. I care very much that he thinks well of me, care that I do not disappoint him. I might nevertheless think his views about when and when not military intervention is justified are quite mistaken. Thus, I weigh his status as an evaluator very highly, even though I might put little weight on the evaluative schema he is likely to be operating with in certain contexts and conversations. And putting little weight on the relevant evaluative schema does not mean that I will not become highly conscious of saying something that contradicts his views on the matter. I am likely to refrain from expressing a view contrary to his, to try to get the conversation away from the interventionist wars on to other matters. And if I do this, it is not, in the case I am imagining, because I do not want to hurt him, or argue with him, or think I do not have the arguments to convince him if I tried hard enough. It is because I do not want him to see me in a certain way; I do not want to disappoint him. I become self-conscious of my contrary views in his presence.

In the grandfather case we have a dislocation between the weight given to the evaluator and the evaluative schema in play. It can, of course, happen the other way around. You can weight someone's evaluative schema within a given context or situation without caring much about the evaluator himself. The main point to note is that variation along the dimensions identified within the basic structure of OSC allows for a level of complexity and structure in the phenomenon. It will explain the different ways in which one can feel self-conscious and different things one can feel self-conscious about.

V. RELATION BETWEEN OSC AND THE OTHER SELF-CONSCIOUS EMOTIONS

Having tabled some ideas about the structure and dimensions involved in ordinary self-consciousness, I return very briefly to the question as to what the relation is between ordinary self-consciousness and the more discussed self-conscious emotions of embarrassment, shame, guilt, and pride.

I have suggested that we treat ordinary self-consciousness as a distinct self-conscious emotion, but also suggested that aside from being another self-conscious emotion, ordinary self-consciousness may have a claim to being the core self-conscious emotion in relation to which the others can be better understood.

The general idea is that the familiar self-conscious emotions, and indeed self-conscious emotions that are distinct from familiar ones and for which we do not have fixed names, will develop out of the different ways the elements identified in the analysis of OSC get filled in. In particular, a consequence of feeling self-conscious may be that the potential evaluations to which the subject is sensitive get fixed. One feels self-conscious, on my account, when one is aware of the awareness of others' awareness of oneself and takes oneself to be up for evaluation by an evaluator. So, to feel self-conscious is to be in a receptive state. It is to read others' reactions and one's own reaction to others' reactions. This means that as we feel self-conscious the evaluations will be fixed – as negative or positive or mixed. The subject will come to form hypotheses, beliefs, or knowledge of the reactions of others. A further dimension of the analysis is the distinct weighting given to the evaluator, and the evaluative schema, that the subject might be using. Therefore, the subject can tip into a number of different possible states depending on how she weights the evaluator and how she weights the evaluation that has been fixed.

My suggestion is that in being a receptive state, with the structure I have outlined, ordinary self-consciousness can tip over into embarrassment, humiliation, shame, or hubris. If, for example, I come to judge that I, as a person, am failing to meet the approval of the evaluator and care sufficiently about the evaluator (whether I also weight their evaluative schema or not), I may feel shame. I may come to feel either, what we can call, *identifying shame* – shame in which I identify with the values by which I am judged or *non-identifying shame* – shame in which I do not identify with the values by which I am judged. If, however, I were to judge that I was meeting the standards I might come to feel socially comfortable or feel social pride, but if I were too hasty or secure in my judgments I might be suffering from hubris. (And, again, there is scope to distinguish between identifying and non-identifying cases.) But, what of guilt and personal pride? They do not seem to share quite the social dimension of the other self-conscious emotions. I have suggested that in some cases the subject herself, perhaps an imagined "better self," can be identified as the evaluator under whose gaze the subject is up for evaluation. It is these cases that will be important if we are to explain guilt or personal pride in terms of ordinary self-consciousness.

I have not said enough properly to show that the standard self-conscious emotions might at least partly be understood in terms of OSC, but I hope I have said enough to suggest it might be worth pursuing the idea. But now, finally, to some problems that might seem to trouble the account of OSC offered.

VI. PROBLEMS

The first worry with the analysis of ordinary self-conciousness offered is that it may seem to contradict the developmental facts. Michael Lewis (in Lewis and Brooks-Gunn 1979, and in his 1993 and 1995) places the age of development of a capacity for embarrassment pretty early – at around eighteen months to two years. This is roughly when children also start to pass the mirror test, which we can take as a marker of the capacity to be aware of ourselves as objects (Gallup 1970, 1979). However, Lewis (1993, 1995) places the age of development of evaluative standards, and the capacity to evaluate by of them, at about three years. He argues that prior to that subjects are unable to have the evaluative emotions of guilt, shame, and pride. Lewis understands the development of a capacity for evaluation in terms of what he calls SRGs ('Standards, Rules, and Goals'). SRGs, for an individual, are for Lewis, a unique set of beliefs about what actions, thoughts, and feelings are acceptable for others and for herself. He takes the set of beliefs to be constituted by information acquired through "culturalization in a particular society" (Lewis 1995, 567). Thus SRGs vary across societies, across times, and between groups within societies at a time.

Lewis divides the self-consciousness emotions into those he calls "exposed emotions" and those he calls "evaluative emotions" (Lewis 1995, 207). Embarrassment, of the kind exhibited by young children who hide their faces or hide behind their mothers, is his central example of an exposed emotion. Guilt, shame, and pride are the central evaluative emotions. The exposed emotions do not, thinks Lewis, require mastery of SRGs, but the evaluative emotions do.

Now, if we were to place ordinary self-consciousness into this schema, it would surely fall on the side of being an exposed emotion. Indeed, we might think that it is the exposed emotion par excellence – it is the feeling of oneself being available to view by others. If I am right, then embarrassment is what happens when a feeling of self-consciousness gets filled in a certain way. It is uncomfortable because it is when we suspect or fear that we are not or may not be viewed well.

However, it may be objected that if the analysis of ordinary self-consciousness is right, and if the supposed relation to embarrassment is right, then a subject must have the capacity to operate SRGs in order to feel self-conscious or embarrassed. The reason is that the analysis of self-consciousness offered here involves the subject's being aware of herself being *up for evaluation* by others, and may in some cases involve knowledge of the evaluative schema with which others operate.

The first thing to say is that what it takes to think of something as having a value, or what it is to take oneself as up for or being evaluated by another is likely to be a complex matter admitting of many gradations. (Indeed, Lewis acknowledges that the process of incorporating the SRGs operating around one starts early in life.) In particular, there seem to be three distinctions that may give us the materials to show that one could meet the conditions set out in the analysis of OSC offered before one is in a position to be attributed the capacity to master Lewis' SRGs.

First, we need to distinguish between a subject's being aware of being 'up' for evaluation and the subject's knowledge of, or beliefs about, the evaluation. We have already talked about the possibility of feeling self-conscious under the eye of another even though we know nothing much of the identity of the other, or of her evaluator schema. In most cases of ordinary self-consciousness – as opposed to some forms of embarrassment, and to shame and guilt – the subject only suspects, hopes, fears, guesses at how the other is evaluating her. It is a fluid, information gathering state, and the more developed the subject is, the more complex her suppositions, hopes, etc. will be. She does not need to be able to settle on a view about how she is viewed. The subject needs to be able to look for an answer to the question about how she is being viewed – with pleasure or displeasure – but she does not need to be able to answer the question with reference to SRGs in order to count as having ordinary self-consciousness.

Second, we need to distinguish between the capacity for being aware of an evaluation by another and the capacity for self-evaluation. We do not have a capacity for guilt, or pride, or perhaps for shame or hubris, unless we have a capacity for self-evaluation as well as a capacity to be sensitive to the evaluations of others. Since guilt and pride just are self-evaluations – they are evaluations by the self of herself, or of her actions – this is obvious in their case. Shame and hubris may seem slightly different: they seem to be more closely linked to a subject's judging that others have judged her as failing the norms of the group. However, on most accounts of shame, shame is also an evaluation of the self – it is an evaluation of the self as bad, or failing. One of the reasons shame seems to be so damaging is that it involves the subject drawing into herself the perceived judgments of the group; moreover, it involves the subject, as a result, forming an attitude to her *whole* self, and not just to one of her actions or character traits. It is not clear that feeling self-conscious need involve a corresponding capacity for self-evaluation. It is a sensitivity to the power to elicit certain evaluative responses in others, and a sensitivity that it is *oneself* that is the object of a potential response. But it need not result in a self-evaluation and may not require the subject to have the capacity to judge herself.

Third, and most importantly, given our explanatory needs, we need to distinguish between the development of particular SRGs and the development of the idea of an evaluator. At its simplest, a subject can be aware of being up for evaluation even if she can be aware only that she can please or displease, elicit a smile or frown, or a behavioral thumbs up or down. The subject need have no grasp or capacity to grasp the standards, rules, or goals of the evaluator; she needs no grasp of the particular nature of the evaluation, just the fact that there is one.

These distinctions, I think, leave room for the possibility that young children before the age of three can take someone to be an evaluator, and take themselves as up for evaluation, even though they have not yet developed the capacity to master SRGs. They may not need to be able to know the particular SRGs that the evaluator is operating with in order to be self-conscious. They may not need to be able to grasp a particular evaluation, and need not be able to apply the evaluation of another to themselves.

A second worry about the analysis of OSC offered was suggested to me by Christopher Peacocke: does the characterization of OSC not need, over and above the consciousness by a subject that *she, herself* is the object of an evaluator's evaluation, also the supposition by the subject that the evaluator represents her *as conscious*, and indeed *as self-conscious*? There are three forms of awareness that one might think could be involved in OSC: awareness of oneself as the object of an evaluator; awareness of oneself, represented as conscious, by the evaluator; and awareness of oneself, represented as self-conscious, by the evaluator's evaluation. There is a further complication that comes when we ask: must the subject take her evaluator also to be conscious and self-conscious? In the analysis above I have offered the most minimal characterization: the subject must be conscious of she, herself as the object of awareness of another, whom she takes to be an evaluator – whatever that requires. I have not committed myself to whether in feeling self-conscious a subject *must* think of the other as self-conscious, nor whether she *must* think of the other as thinking about *her* as a self-conscious object. I am inclined to think that most cases of OSC *will* involve the more committed forms of self-consciousness, and that a full explanation of the relation between OSC and certain forms of the other self-conscious emotions *will* require us to appeal to the more committed forms of self consciousness. And, there is nothing in the analysis offered that prohibits additions that will capture such extra elements. However, there are some advantages to keeping as basic the more minimal formulation offered here. In particular, we may not want to rule out certain cases as cases of OSC, even though they are cases in which the subject does not take the evaluator to represent her as a self-conscious subject. Consider Hermione in Shakespeare's *Winter's Tale*. She stands, at the end of the play, taken to be a statue by those around her. Leontes, her husband who falsely accused her of infidelity years before, comments on the statue saying "Hermione was not so much wrinkled, nothing so aged as this seems" (Act v, Scene 3). Hermione might surely feel self-conscious at his perusal, and embarrassed by his remark. It is true that were she to feel self-conscious and embarrassed by his earlier accusations of adultery she may have to think of him as thinking of her as self-consciously wanton. We would then need to appeal to a subject's awareness of herself as the self-conscious object of an evaluator's evaluation in order properly to capture the emotion. But for the simpler case, where only her wrinkles are the focus, the more minimal analysis will do.

I want to consider a third objection, really only to set it aside as a pointer to future work. We might wonder how promising the suggestion that OSC is a kind of *ur*-emotion, with respect to the other self-conscious emotions, can be, given that the phenomenology and bodily feeling associated with ordinary self-consciousness – the awareness of one's skin and posture, the feeling at the back of one's neck, the heightened awareness of one's voice, etc. – is so different from those associated with guilt, shame, and pride. It might be objected that, if the latter emotions of guilt, shame, and pride were indeed transformations of ordinary self-consciousness, we would get more continuity in the phenomenological features of feeling self-conscious and feeling shame, guilt, or pride, than we do.

It is true that there seems little in common between the phenomenology of guilt and OSC. However, the suggestion that the bodily feelings of shame and the bodily feelings of pride are quite separate from those of OSC is less obvious. Shame is associated with heightened awareness of one's body and the desire to hide or shrink it away from the gaze of others. Hubris is also associated with an awareness of one's body, but in contrast to shame, with a comfort with one's body taking up space under the gaze of others – there is a puffing up, rather than shrinking away. It makes sense to think that if the elements of one's self-conscious awareness of others get filled in in a certain way – if one is criticized, mocked, or sneered at – one's feeling of self-consciousness may tip over into a sense of shame. What was a neutral, but enhanced, awareness of one's externalities may become painful and uncomfortable and one may, as a result, want to screen oneself from the gaze of others. If, in contrast, we are praised or lauded, in a way that results in us feeling hubristic, we may enjoy the gaze of our evaluators and relax, allowing our body to take its full space, in full view. Although more work is required to meet the anxiety expressed in the objection, it does seem to me that we can expect ways of explaining the transformation from OSC to other emotions which will make the transformations in phenomenology involved plausible also. As earlier acknowledged, guilt and personal pride are perhaps not so clearly characterized by a distinctive phenomenology, and the affinities are not so clearly available. I do, however, think that they are there. The right place to start in linking OSC with guilt and personal pride is, I think, to consider feeling self-conscious by oneself, where oneself is the supposed evaluator having internalized the evaluations of others. However, it is clear that a development of this suggestion *really* is the job of another paper.

Finally, it has been suggested to me – often – that the concern with feeling self-conscious is a product of being *British*. I am assured that other nationalities do not tend to suffer in this way: it is only the British that suffer to any extent from the feeling of others thinking about them, that shift around nervously when in groups, rather than getting on with the business of connecting and enjoying their fellow human beings. So is OSC, therefore, too parochial an emotion for more than parochial interest?

I do not think so. It may be that the British find more occasions for feeling self-conscious – that they more often, and in more situations, take themselves as up for evaluation, and it may be that the British find self-consciousness more often more painful, because they tend to read the evaluations as unfavorable, and therefore more salient, than others. But surely ordinary self-consciousness is quite universal. One only has to look at teenagers across the globe, whether carefully observing, withering, or strutting, to see the pains and pleasures of feeling self-conscious.

CHAPTER 5

Waiting for the self

Jesse Prinz

I. HUME'S THESIS

In one of his most famous passages, Hume writes:

[W]hen I enter most intimately into what I call myself, I always stumble on some particular perception or other, of heat or cold, light or shade, love or hatred, pain or pleasure. I never can catch myself at any time without a perception, and never can observe any thing but the perception. (Hume 1739, 252)

This remark admits of various interpretations: metaphysical and phenomenal, strong and weak. Here I want to defend a strong phenomenal version of Hume's view. I want to argue that there is no phenomenal quality corresponding to the subject of experience – no phenomenal I.

This topic has been much discussed by philosophers, and, like Hume, most tend to rely on intuitions, introspective reports, and contestable transcendental arguments. My review will begin with Descartes, but I will be more interested in assessing lines of research that treat the phenomenal I as a topic for empirical inquiry. There have been a number of recent attempts to identify a subject of experience using the techniques of contemporary brain science. I will consider some of the more promising proposals and argue that they come up short in important ways.

Let me begin with some clarifications. Hume offers his introspective report in a discussion of personal identity, which is traditionally regarded as a metaphysical issue. Thus, one can interpret him as addressing the question of what it is to be a self and how a single self can endure changes over time. Hume's so-called "bundle theory" identifies the self with collections of perceptions, and, elsewhere, Hume despairs of ever finding an adequate theory of endurance if this is right (Hume 1739, 635f.). My concern here is not metaphysical. Perhaps selves exist, and perhaps they endure. My concern is with the phenomenal thesis that Hume advances in the course of addressing the metaphysical question.

I take the phenomenal thesis to be this: among the various phenomenal qualities that make up an experience, there is none that can be characterized as an experience of the self or subject in addition to the qualities found in perceived features of the world, sensations, and emotions. Though we might convey the content of our experience using a sentence of the form, "I am experiencing X," the actual qualities that make up the experience can be exhaustively surveyed by enumerating the qualities that constitute the experience of X. There is no remainder corresponding to the word "I" in the subject position of the sentence.

This interpretation remains ambiguous on a crucial point, however. The claim that there are no I-qualia *in addition* to the qualities of perception, sensation, and emotion might be understood in two ways. On a weak reading, there are qualia corresponding to the I, but these are nothing above and beyond the qualities of perception, sensation, and emotion. That is to say, I-qualia exist but are reducible to other kinds of qualia. I feel myself *as* a bundle of perceptions. When I say, "I experience X," there is an experience of the I, but it is to be found in the experience of X. Call this the reductive reading of Hume's thesis. On a stronger reading, Hume's thesis says that there are no I-qualia, whether reducible or not. On this reading, we cannot save the phenomenal I by equating it with the qualia that correspond to something that the I would be described as experiencing. Call this the eliminativist reading of Hume's thesis. I will be defending a version of this stronger interpretation.

Now it is important to get a little clearer about what the eliminativist is denying. There is an obvious sense in which conscious experience of a self is incontrovertible. Many of my experiences are experiences of things that take place inside my body. A sensation on my skin or an emotion is in me. If the body is part of the self, then surely I can experience myself. So the eliminativist about the phenomenal I cannot deny that the self (or part of the self) can be an *object* of conscious experience. There is a phenomenal *me*. The issue concerns the subject of conscious experience. When I experience a sensation in my body, there is an experience of me, but is there also an I – a subject who is having that experience? Is there any experience that corresponds to the "I" when I say, "I am experiencing X"? The eliminativist will say no. One might put this by saying that the eliminativist denies any consciousness of a self *as a self*, that is, serving as the subject of an experience, thought, or action. More precisely, the eliminativist says there is no component of an experience that has a special claim to being the experience of self such that *that* component is playing something like a subject role for the experience. There is nothing phenomenal that corresponds to the "I" in states that we would express using that word.

Those who believe in the phenomenal I, whether reductive or not, claim otherwise. They claim that we can find an I in experience. Reductionists claim that the I is there in Hume's bundle, and non-reductionists say that the I is something above and beyond the bundle. Some believers say the I comes and goes and others say it is always there in every experience. I reject both claims.

To be clear, the eliminativist about the phenomenal I need not be an eliminativist about the I in a metaphysical sense. The eliminativist is not necessarily what Strawson calls a no-subject theorist, nor a defender of Wittgenstein and Anscombe's semantic thesis that "I" is not a referring expression. Perhaps "I" refers. Nor is the eliminativist committed to the view that we cannot find anything in experience on the basis of which an I can be inferred. Perhaps we are indirectly or inferentially aware of an I. Indeed, there may be an implicit I in every experience. In the concluding section, I will discuss several ways in which this might be true.

2. NON-REDUCTIVE THEORIES OF THE PHENOMENAL SELF

2.1 *The Cartesian I*

Philosophical thinking about self-consciousness got a major boost when Descartes formulated his *cogito*. In saying "I think" in the first person, and declaring that this is indubitable, Descartes implies that there is an I, which is directly accessed in consciousness. He then went on to speculate on the nature of this I, noting that it can be accessed with greater certainty than any thing in the physical world and, implying too, that it exists independently from any existing thought. I am a thing that thinks, he concluded, a *res cogitans*.

Descartes' account is a paradigm case of a non-reductive theory of the phenomenal self because it implies that the self is present in experience but not reducible to anything else. Unfortunately, however, Descartes does not say much to back up this claim, and he has been accused, most famously by Lichtenberg (1765–99, 190), of smuggling in the I. It may be indubitable that there is thought, quips Lichtenberg, but not that there is a thinker. The I is not given in the experience of thought; we just experience whatever it is that we are thinking about.

Lichtenberg's critique is damaging if we interpret Descartes's *cogito* as a deductive argument. If Descartes thinks that the existence of thought logically entails a thinker, he is mistaken. Or rather, the logical entailment here is just an empty fact about grammar. It is true that Latin requires verb conjugation and English requires a grammatical subject. So sentences using the verb "to think" will always allow quantification into the subject position. But this point of logic does not carry ontological weight. We could always swap out verbs for nouns and say: an episode of thinking is occurring now.

A Cartesian might try to avoid this reliance on grammar by appeal to introspection. Perhaps we find an I in experience whenever we think. This strategy is unpromising. To see why, consider the kind of thoughts that lead up to Descartes's *cogito*. Consider the thought we might express as, "I doubt that the table in front of me really exists." In consciousness, this thought might present itself as a combination of verbal imagery (saying "this table may be a dream"), visual imagery (seeing the table and perhaps imagining it vanish suddenly), and emotions (a feeling of uncertainty or withered confidence). Now the question for Descartes is: can we find a phenomenal I in this conscious episode? If so, it certainly is not obvious. It seems I can have all these experiences without any experience as of an I.

One might think the I appears when introspection turns inward, and I recognize my own doubt. I move from doubting the reality of the table to judging that I have such a doubt. But this shift can be explained without bringing in any phenomenal I. To recognize my own attitude toward the table, I need only have a capacity to notice and label my feeling of doubt. Imagine that this is achieved the way ordinary perceptual object recognition is achieved: I match a current experience against stored, labeled records of prior states. When I turn inward, I am able to classify my feelings of uncertainty as such. In so doing, I do not seem to require any kind of conscious experience of a self. I just need to experience an emotional state. Indeed, phenomenologically, the experience of doubting that a table is real and the experience of recognizing such a doubt in myself may be extremely similar. In both cases, there is an experience of an emotion, some verbal narrative, and a table. An inward focus on the emotion may lead to an intensification of that feeling, which is what happens when we focus on any perceived feature, and the verbal narrative might change from "the table may not be real" to "I am having doubts about the table's reality." But these changes, including the addition of the word "I" in my subvocal report, do not bring in an experience of a subject; just the doubt itself, a particular feeling, comes into sharper view.

I do not intend this introspective sketch as a powerful argument. My point, on the contrary, is that introspection is not especially reliable here.

The Cartesian who is certain that there is an experience of a thinker as an add-on to every thought will clash with Lichtenberg, who introspects and finds no such thing. Given the clash in introspective reports, it seems the debate is at best a stalemate.

Concerns about the limits of introspection are not limited to Descartes. We find contemporary thinkers falling into the same trap. One example is Kriegel (2005) who claims that it is introspectively apparent that every phenomenal experience contains an element of me-ness. It is usually not the focus of experience, he concedes, but it is there in the periphery, in the way one might be aware of a canvas while looking at what a painting depicts. He uses this introspective intuition to ground a self-referential theory of consciousness according to which consciousness arises when mental states represent themselves. Self-referential states have the requisite duality, according to Kriegel: they represent features of the world, and they represent representing, which imparts a sense of me-ness (notice that this theory is reductive, unlike Descartes').

There are some problems with Kriegel's account, which I will no more than flag here. One issue concerns the biological plausibility of the claim that perceptual states represent themselves. Neurons are said to represent perceptual features in virtue of their response-profiles: edge detectors fire when edges are present. There is nothing about these neurons in virtue of which we should say they also represent themselves: they do not cause themselves to fire, and when perceptual cells fire unconsciously, they do not change their dynamics in any way that could be plausibly interpreted as a loss of a self-representing function. Another concerns the claim that self-reference would impart a sense of me-ness. Self-reference is cheap. The word "word" refers to itself; this sentence refers to itself; a concave mirror represents itself infinitely. None of these things can be said to have a sense of me-ness as a result. It is not clear why a perceptual state that also represents itself would give rise to a phenomenal I. Finally, and most importantly, Kriegel's theory rests on an introspective datum that might be challenged. When I introspect, I do not find the me-ness that Kriegel describes. I find only the world. Which one of us is introspecting more accurately? Who knows! Clashing reports of this kind are notoriously difficult to resolve. That is precisely why introspectionist psychology failed.

In summary, the long and distinguished tradition of arguing for a phenomenal I by appeal to intuition may be a blind alley. Of course, Hume's argument rests on introspection as well. He says he finds no I when he looks inward. But Hume is at a slight advantage. He does find other things that everyone can agree on: perceptual, sensory, and emotional qualia. Given the obviousness of these, one might wonder why the phenomenal I is not obvious to everyone. That asymmetry gets his position off the ground. But, it does not settle the case, because there is always a chance that Hume and his followers are not introspecting well. So we need to look for other kinds of evidence.

In making these remarks, I do not mean to be suggesting that we should do without introspection entirely. Studies of consciousness often depend heavily on first-person reports. Rather the claim is that introspection on its own may not suffice. Those who claim to find an I in experience would do well to find some non-introspective convergent evidence. Perhaps a substantive theory of what the phenomenal I consists in, backed up by non-introspective evidence for whatever the theory postulates, can help the Humeans see that there is an I in experience, after all.

2.2 Self, lost and found

Descartes supposes that the I is always present. There is no experience without an experiencer. For some, this does not ring true phenomenologically. There is a common phenomenon that we refer to as "losing yourself" in experience. Sometimes we become so absorbed in an activity that we seem to lose awareness of everything else, including, it is said, one's own self. Taken at face value, this phenomenon would be hard to square with the Cartesian perspective on the topic. When we lose our selves, we do not stop thinking, as a Cartesian might suppose, and we do not lose conscious unity. More importantly, the phenomenon suggests that the consciously experienced self can come and go. If that is right, there is a clear strategy for trying to find out what the conscious self consists in: we can compare what happens when we lose ourselves to what happens when the self reappears.

This is exactly the strategy that has been pursued by a group of researchers in contemporary neuroscience. Goldberg *et al.* (2006) used fMRI to test brain activation while subjects listened to brief musical recordings or looked at pictures. In one condition, they had to say whether the pictures depicted animals and whether the recordings contained a trumpet. They were given ample time to reflect on their choices. In another condition, they had the same instructions, but the recordings and pictures were presented very quickly. The authors reasoned that when subjects are forced to answer quickly they would tend to lose themselves in the task. Finally, there was a condition in which subjects were asked to decide whether they liked recordings and pictures, a task that requires introspection, and is thus maximally self-involving. They found that the introspection condition showed greater activation in the superior frontal gyrus (SFG) than the other two conditions, and SFG was actually suppressed in the rapid task, suggesting that self-awareness was actively being suppressed. In another pair of studies, they also found that SFG was highly active when people read a word list and decided whether each was true of themselves, as compared to when people read a word list and decided whether each word is a noun or a verb. The word list included a wide range of objects and activities, which are not especially emotional in nature, unlike the picture preference task (e.g. study, run, coffee, and bus). Here again, SFG seems to correlate with the degree of self-involvement. One of the authors of this work was also involved in a further study that showed minimal SFG activation (along with other frontal structures) during passive watching of a movie, suggesting that viewers lose themselves in the film. All this evidence suggests that SFG is active in self-related tasks, and inactive when people lose themselves. The authors conclude that it is a neural correlate of self-awareness.

Interestingly, the authors also imply that SFG is not reducible to any other aspect of experience. It is an area associated with perception (it is active with both sounds and pictures) or emotion (it is active when we reflect on emotional preferences but also on the applicability of any words pertaining to the self). This might be taken to suggest that it is the neural correlate of a pure sense of self. In this respect the work differs from research that will be summarized below, which attempts to reduce self experience to some kind of bodily experience.

To assess this research, it is important to have some perspective on SFG. We cannot conclude that this is the neural correlate of the self without knowing what other roles it might play in cognition. The answer that emerges from other areas of cognitive neuroscience is that SFG plays a role in working memory, especially when working memory tasks are highly demanding (du Boisgueheneuc *et al.*, 2006). That is interesting for two reasons. First, Goldberg *et al.* predict that SFG should diminish with task difficulty, because we tend to lose ourselves when cognitive load increases. But the research on working memory shows just the opposite. Second, the fact that SFG is involved in working memory can explain the Goldberg results without assuming that it is a correlate of self-awareness. In order to decide whether a picture or a song is appealing one has to focus attention on the song *as well as* one's reactions to the song. Holding two things in mind at once requires more use of working memory than mere perceptual classification. And searching memory to see whether words apply to one's self requires more working memory effort than deciding whether they are nouns or verbs. In both cases, the authors are comparing a relatively passive bottom-up classification task to one that requires reflection. In their high-speed task, reflection would slow down performance, so working memory is inhibited. And, when we watch movies, we often absorb the content without reflecting. Thus, all the results are consistent with the view that SFG is a structure whose function is to play a role in demanding forms of working memory – the kind that are characteristic of reflection. There is little pressure to say it is the neural seat of the self.

Goldberg *et al.* might object that this deflationary reading is *ad hoc*. After all, they explicitly ask subjects to introspect by giving them questions about their preferences and traits. Isn't it obvious that the tasks require self-awareness? I do not think so. Or, rather, I do not think the tasks require any special phenomenal character that corresponds to the experience of oneself as a subject. The picture/music preference task involves emotional responses to stimuli. These emotions exist within the minds of the experimental participants, of course, but there is a difference between feeling an emotion and feeling a phenomenal I. If you introspect and discover delight in a piece of music, your experience contains delight and the music. You might describe it by saying "I like this music," but you could equally well say, "there is a delight response happening along with the music," without using a first-person pronoun. Likewise, when you decide whether a word applies to you ("Do I run?" "Do I take a bus?"), you may call up memories of your morning jog or your morning commute, but there need be no experience of a self in these. The recollection may be relived from a particular point of view (running from this perspective), but points of view need have nothing especially self-like. Notice that a movie camera presents the world from a point of view. To assume that such *memories* involve a phenomenal I begs the question against those who think the recalled activities do not involve a phenomenal I. When I board a bus, I experience the bus, but not a subject of that experience.

Goldberg *et al.* might still object. They might say that the phenomenon of "losing yourself" is commonplace, and that it is clearly a case of losing a phenomenal experience of one's self as a subject of experience. I think we may be misled by language here. The phrase "losing yourself" implies that there is an experience of one's self that comes and goes. But, in reality, that phrase is characteristically used to refer to situations where we focus attention narrowly on an activity and stop experiencing other things, whether they are self-involving or not. If you lose yourself watching a movie, that means you stopped thinking about the day's events, that overdue paper you need to get done, and perhaps even the people sitting in the theater all around you. Losing yourself is just temporal absorption. It is true that when you stop thinking about your to-do list, you have thereby stopped thinking about yourself in some sense, but that is only because the items on the list are things *you* need to do. Phenomenologically, your experience does not lose an explicit sense of me-ness; it just loses the usual rumination about activities or events that happen to involve you.

These lines of reply might be summarized by saying that the Goldberg *et al.* study can at best be regarded as an investigation of the self as object, rather than the self as subject. In their tasks, we report things about ourselves, but, in so doing, we are treating the self as just another thing in the world with certain describable features. We are not experiencing ourselves acting as the subject of thought or experience – this not elusive self as I. They do not establish that some thoughts have a qualitative component that occupies the position that the word "I" occupies in self-ascriptions, such as "I like this music." As Lichtenberg might say, they establish the liking, not the liker.

3. REDUCTIVE THEORIES OF THE PHENOMENAL SELF

3.1 *Feelings*

The theories I have been considering are non-reductive. They suppose that the phenomenal I is something above and beyond the things experienced by that I. Such theories incur a heavy burden because it is difficult to find anything in experience above and beyond the items delivered to our senses. All contents of consciousness seem to be perceptual. If we were to list each perceptual feature that we were experiencing at a given moment, including sensations of our own bodies, mental imagery, and subvocal speech, there would seem to be no remainder. This is the central insight behind Hume's thesis, and it is very hard to deny. We have just seen two efforts to locate a self that transcends mere perceptual qualia, but none is convincing. This suggests that Hume was right. But, recall that Hume's thesis has two versions. The weaker version says there is no self *over and above* the items we perceive. The stronger version says there is no phenomenal self at all. One could try to challenge the stronger version by offering a reductive account, on which the phenomenal I gets equated with some subset of the many things we happen to be perceiving in any given moment. Some privileged subset of conscious perceptions may qualify as the perceiver – the subject of experience. As Damasio (1999) puts it, the I may not be the viewer of an internal movie, but rather an object in the movie. This is the kind of approach I want to consider now, and Damasio will be the first example.

Damasio came into widespread recognition because of his (1994) work on emotions. Here he resuscitated a theory that originates with William James and a Danish physician, Carl Lange. On the James–Lange theory emotions are not the things that cause us to laugh, or cry, or flee, or fight. Rather, they are perceptions of patterned bodily changes that include such characteristic responses. When an emotionally significant stimulus is encountered, it triggers a bodily change that prepares us for a behavioral response, and then the mind perceives this change, and our experience of that bodily perception is the emotion. Damasio argues that contemporary research in psychology and neuroscience (including his own field, neurology) supports the James–Lange theory, and I have argued at great length elsewhere that he is right (Prinz 2004). But, Damasio also thinks that this story can help provide an account of self-consciousness, and here we part company.

Damasio's (1999) story goes like this. Emotions are short-lived events that arise in response to specific elicitors, but emotions are not the only mental events in which we perceive changes in our bodies. In reality, we are perceiving our bodies all the time, and emotions are just one special case of this broader phenomenon. Damasio (1994) calls such perceptions "background feelings" and, despite the term, he thinks these can go on unconsciously. In his (1999) book, he says we can think of these background feelings as a "proto-self" for reasons that will become clear in a moment. Background feelings are not constant over time, but rather change incessantly as objects in our environment impinge on our senses. When we see something or hear something or smell something, the body reacts. Damasio speculates that the nervous system must keep track of these changes; it must monitor how the world is affecting the body at all times. To do this, there must be "second-order maps" – representations of the first-order bodily representations as they undergo changes. Damasio thinks these second-order representations are conscious, and he thinks they constitute a basic form of self-consciousness shared by humans and other animals. To experience the feelings constituted by fluctuations in your body is, according to Damasio, to experience yourself. Damasio calls this the "core-self" and he distinguishes it from the "autobiographical self" which involves the reliving of episodic memories. The autobiographical self is not found in all animals, and can be absent in people with anterograde amnesia. Its status as a form of self-consciousness depends, in part, on the fact that when we relive memories, we experience the core-self acting in events from the past. The core-self is essential for self-experience. As I understand him, Damasio thinks the core-self is necessary and sufficient for having an experience of one's self as a subject.

Damasio's account of self-consciousness echoes themes in William James' discussion of that topic. James is interested in how we feel like the same self from moment to moment – the qualitative counterpart of personal identity – and he suggests that continuity of bodily experiences plays an important role: "*Resemblance among the parts of a continuum of feelings* (especially bodily feelings) experienced along with things widely different in all other regards, *thus constitutes the real and verifiable 'personal identity' which we feel*" (James 1890, 336, original italics).

The bodily feeling proposal has some intuitive plausibility. First of all, the body is part of the person, so an experience of the body, unlike an experience of some object out there in the environment, is an experience of the self, in some sense. Second, changes in the body reflect a person's subjective responses to the world, including emotional responses, as well as the myriad unnamed responses we have to everything we encounter. Everything makes us feel some way, and tracking those feelings is, to that extent, tracking subjectivity. Third, there may be repeatable or predictable bodily responses that correspond to enduring aspects of the self such as values and personality traits, which are part of personal identity. The way my body reacts reflects something about who I am as a person, and I can recognize those reactions as such. I can also notice that, on some days, I do not "feel myself" because my reactions are different than they normally are. Here again, we find something very self-like in the experience of the body.

Given all this, it is very tempting to adopt the Damasio–James approach and identify the phenomenal I with the experience of bodily feelings, associated with second-order bodily maps in the brain. But I think this temptation should be resisted. I think the experience of our bodily feelings is neither necessary nor sufficient for a phenomenal experience of one's self as a subject.

Let us begin with necessity. The intuition that bodily feelings contribute to self-awareness is strongest when we imagine encounters with physical objects that matter to us. If a loud noise startles me, for instance, I will feel a strong sudden response in my body. Attention is drawn inward as I feel my body reacting to the sound. But there are many other cases where the experience of the body is less pronounced without any loss in the impression that I am the subject of my experiences. Consider intellectual exercises such as reflecting on philosophy, answering crossword puzzle questions, or performing calculations in your head. Such activities might engage the body but, intuitively, they need not. To take one simple case, imagine counting backwards from 100. It seems very plausible that, while doing this, one periodically loses conscious experience of the body for brief moments. Indeed, there is evidence that tasks involving working memory tend to suppress activity in brain structures associated with emotion and bodily experience (Yun *et al.* 2010). But, when that happens, the task seems no less agentic, no less self-involving. I am not claiming that there is some phenomenal I present in counting backwards, which is preserved when we stop experiencing the body. I think there is no experience of an I in either case. My present point is that Damasio's theory predicts that a phenomenal I should disappear when body awareness does, and this seems implausible. Body awareness does not seem necessary at all.

Nor does body awareness seem sufficient for a sense of self. To see this, consider the phenomenon of emotional contagion (Hatfield *et al.* 1993). Emotions are catching. If I see you grimace in anger, I will undergo the corresponding bodily change, and feel a flash of anger too. It turns out that this capacity may play a crucial role in emotion attribution. My ability to know what you are feeling depends to some degree on my ability to catch your emotions. We use our own bodily switchboard to attribute feelings to others. This is confirmed in many neuroimaging studies, showing that the same brain structures are used to both experience emotions and to recognize them in others, and injuries to these structures result in deficits of both experience and attribution (Adolphs 2002). Now, imagine a case where I recognize an emotion in you. Perhaps I see that you are mad. The science suggests that I do this by first mirroring your bodily expression in my own body and then feeling that change in me. Still, there is no temptation for me to say, I am mad. I might not be. I feel madness, but I do not feel like it is mine. The madness I feel is, in some sense, yours. I feel through myself; but it does not feel like myself that I am feeling. There is no subjective ownership of the felt state. This suggests to me that we can feel patterns of change in our own bodies without that feeling constituting a phenomenal I. This may sound paradoxical (how can I feel my body as you?), but perplexity subsides when you recall that a bodily feeling is just an inner state that registers basic physiological facts: a heart is racing, muscles are tensed, breathing is constrained, and so on. It seems plausible that one could become aware of those facts without thereby experiencing them as facts about me. For example, if my brain could get wired to your heart, I could feel your heartbeat, just as I do when I put a stethoscope to your chest.

Finally, it should be pointed out that, if bodily feelings were the basis of self-consciousness we should find a correlation between these feelings and the degree to which one experiences a sense of self. But that does not seem to be the case. The sense of self neither increases or decreases with felt bodily changes. For example, consider very intense emotions. These do not seem to engender a greater phenomenal sense of self than mild emotions do. Terror after hearing an intruder enter your house does not feel more self-like than does mild delight while strolling on the beach. Indeed, with intense emotions focus is often more outward than inward: the terror makes you forget yourself for a moment and focus intensely on the sounds coming from the intruder. Conversely, a sense of self can increase without a change in the intensity of bodily experience. Emotions, again, can illustrate. Consider a familiar contrast between shame and guilt. With guilt we focus on some offending act, and, with shame, we focus on the self. When ashamed, one feels like a bad person. Both emotions can be equally intense, and hence the bodily feelings are equally vivid, but one seems to involve a greater degree of self-awareness. I am not suggesting that there is a phenomenal I in either of these emotions (I am skeptical about the phenomenal I), but if there is anything at all to the idea that experiences can relate to the self, shame seems to be a better case than guilt. The difference may involve the thoughts and actions that come to mind when shame is experienced: there is a desire to conceal one's self, a feeling of being impure, and a self-conceptualization as a bad person. These specific contents, not the degree of bodily involvement, add up to a pattern of behavior and judgment that can be characterized as self-focused. The intuition that some mental states involve a greater degree of self-awareness seems to track the degree to which those states lead us to think about ourselves, not anything about their bodily character.

This leaves us with just one question. Why do we use locutions such as, "I don't feel like myself today" when our bodily responses depart from their usual pattern? Doesn't this suggest that feeling one's self is a matter of feeling one's body? I do not think so. When one says, "I don't feel like myself today," one is comparing a current experience to the past. It does not require a feeling that is feeling myself in the past, but rather the knowledge that certain feelings are typical for me, and the judgment that those typical feelings are not arising in the present. Recognizing variation in feelings is no more self-involving than recognition of variation in behavioral performance. Suppose I am a good ping-pong player and have an off day. I can say "I'm not playing like myself today." And, in saying this, I am not implying that there is subjective feeling of self-ness present on most days but absent on this one. I am saying that my response patterns are diverting from the statistical norm. By analogy, if I am normally giddy but feel depressed today, I might say, "I don't have those feelings I usually feel." In saying this,

I am not saying I have lost my phenomenal I. Perhaps there was never one to lose.

3.2 Ownership

One difficulty with identifying the phenomenal I with feelings and emotions is that there seems to be nothing paradoxical about an unfeeling self. Another difficulty is that the mere presence of feelings does not yet decide between self and other: we need a story about what makes feelings count as mine. Both of these concerns are addressed by another approach to the phenomenal I, which has been gaining momentum in cognitive science. It is the view that the experience of a self can be reduced to a feeling of body ownership. The phenomenal I emerges when we feel our own bodies and feel them as belonging to ourselves.

This view bears a resemblance to the view advocated by James and Damasio, because it places emphasis on the body, but it shifts from inner feelings and emotions, which are associated primarily with visceral changes, and focuses on bodily position and location. Here, the most relevant sensory qualities are proprioception and kinesthesia, which help us determine the configuration of our limbs and torso in space. By shifting away from the viscera, the view avoids an implausible commitment to the view that emotions and feelings are essential to the experience of selfhood. Perception of body position can be present even when experience of emotions and feelings is not.

That said, a mere feeling of a body in space is not sufficient for a sense of selfhood. Just as you can feel emotions without feeling them as yours, you can feel a body without feeling it as yours, even if it happens to be your own body. This may seem paradoxical, but the possibility is brought out clearly in some pathological cases. Consider, for example, alien hand syndrome in which a person comes to believe that one of his or her own hands belongs to someone else. For example, Moro et al. (2004) describe patients with right brain injuries who suffer from a lack of feeling in their left arms (a syndrome often co-morbid with unilateral visual neglect); when these patients cross their arms, some feeling is restored, but they continue to insist that the affected limb does not belong to them. Healthy people may also be capable of experiencing bodily sensations without feeling a sense of self. Indeed, this may be commonplace in social cognition. Just as we use our own emotion systems when perceiving emotions in others, we use our own capacity for bodily sensation when perceiving the bodies of others. For example, Keysers et al. (2004) found activation in somatosensory cortex when individuals watched another person's leg being touched. Thus, any theory that identifies the phenomenal I with perception of bodily position needs a further element: an account of how the body feels like it is mine. This is often called a sense of ownership.

Body ownership has been intensively studied in recent cognitive neuroscience. One popular strategy is to investigate cases where the ordinary sense of ownership breaks down. Consider out-of-body experiences, in which one seems to occupy a ghostly imaginary body that hovers in the air or stands beside one's real body. This may sound dubiously mystical, but actually such experiences are relatively common. Moreover, they can be induced in the laboratory, and they can also arise with high prevalence after certain brain injuries. Blanke and Metzinger (2009) review this literature, and they argue that research on out-of-body experiences can help us identify brain structures associated with body ownership. Normally, people feel as if they own their real bodies, but in these exotic cases, ownership shifts to a new imagined body. Blanke and Metzinger reason that the underlying mechanism may be the neural correlate of felt body ownership, which they regard as a minimal form of the phenomenal self. (More elaborate forms of phenomenal selfhood arise when this minimal self is integrated into a global workspace.) To find the mechanism, we can look for the brain area that is active when people have out-of-body experiences and that leads to such experiences when damaged. Here, all signs point to the right temporoparietal junction (de Ridder *et al.* 2007). This, Blanke and Metzinger surmise, is the neural correlate of the phenomenal I.

There is a problem with this inference, however, and it has to do with what we know about the right temporoparietal junction. This region is also known to be active in mental-state attribution (Saxe and Powell 2006), and when subjects imagine another person performing an action (Ruby and Decety 2001). Such findings suggest that the region has more to do with a sense *of the other* than a sense of the self. And, indeed, this makes sense in the case of out-of-body experiences. Such experiences typically involve seeing one's real body (or sometimes the imaginary body) as if it were another person. So the temporoparietal junction may not be the seat of body ownership after all. To find the mechanism, we must consult other research.

The most promising line of investigation involves a class of perceptual illusions that are, in a way, the inverse of out-of-body experiences. When people have out-of-body experiences, they can see their real bodies without a sense of ownership. But there are also cases in which persons experience artificial bodies or body parts as their own. Under certain conditions, we can be made to feel like we are located in the body of a mannequin, a virtual avatar, or even a block of wood. The most studied demonstration of this phenomenon is the rubber hand illusion (Botvinick and Cohen 1998). Here, a rubber hand is placed in front of a person while that person's real hand is hidden from view. Then both the real and the rubber hand are stroked using a paintbrush at the same time. After a short time, many people begin to experience the rubber hand as if it were their own. They even misremember the location of their real hand after the procedure is finished, locating it closer to the rubber hand than it actually was. The rubber hand illusion is well suited to study the sense of body ownership because it involves both a feeling of the body in space and an impression that the body belongs to the self.

Tsakiris *et al.* (2007) set out to identify the neural correlates of body ownership by inducing the rubber hand illusion inside an fMRI scanner. In comparison to a control condition in which the rubber and real hand are stroked out of sync, the illusory sense of ownership was associated with activity in the right posterior insula and the right frontal operculum. The frontal operculum has been associated with motor planning in a TMS study (Tunik *et al.* 2008), and the insula is associated with body perception and control (Critchley *et al.* 2004). Indeed, the right posterior insula has been directly implicated in other research as a basis of ownership. Farrer *et al.* (2003) found that activation in this region correlates with a sense of control in a task involving a virtual hand. Karnath *et al.* (2005) found that injuries here are associated with anosagnosia for paralyzed limbs, suggesting that an inability to monitor limb ownership results in a failure to recognize when an owned limb is not responsive.

To understand the role of the right posterior insula, it is helpful to understand how the rubber hand illusion works. We can experience our bodies using a number of senses: we can see a limb, feel something touching a limb, and experience position through proprioception. Normally such experiences converge on a single location in space, but, in illusory cases, that fails to happen. Seeing a rubber hand while feeling a paintbrush shifts the proprioceptive sense of location into the region occupied by the rubber hand. The visual representation of location dominates the proprioceptive, causing the shift. Against this background, it is reasonable to speculate that the right posterior insula plays a role in sensory integration. It brings the different sources of information together and facilitates the proprioceptive shift. The feeling of ownership may arise when senses are brought together. I can feel a hand without it feeling like mine (as in alien hand syndrome), but if the hand I feel is integrated with the hand I see in the right way then it feels like mine.

The results of the Tsakiris *et al.* (2007) experiment may seem somewhat puzzling at first. The authors found *more* activation in the right posterior insula when subjects experience the rubber hand illusion than in the control condition when there is no illusion. But, in both conditions, subjects presumably have a sense of ownership; the difference concerns only the accuracy of that sense. Moreover, in the control condition, there is greater activation in somatosensory cortex than in the illusion condition, even though both conditions involve a tactile feeling on the hand. Perhaps what is going on here is a shift in attention. In the control condition, subjects may be focused on the sensation in the hand, and then in the illusion condition they focus on the sense of ownership because they are surprised to feel the rubber hand as their own. In addition, the increased insula activation may reflect the extra neural work that is involved in forcing visual and proprioceptive information to come into alignment, despite the initial mismatch.

In summary, then, it does seem that the right posterior insula is playing a role in sensory integration and that integration of bodily representations supports judgments of ownership. Tsakiris *et al.* regard this as a kind of self-consciousness, and surely, in some sense, they are right. When I experience a body (real or otherwise) as mine, I am experiencing something as relating to myself. But things get a little bit thorny when we try to unpack that relation. Ownership is normally thought of as a two-place relation. Body ownership is a relation between a body and a self. It cannot be, however, that the phenomenal experience of body ownership involves two relata: a feeling of the body and a feeling of a self. Those interested in the feeling of ownership want to explain the latter in terms of the former. Thus, the feeling of ownership has to be understood in a non-relational way, if that makes any sense. Or rather, it is experienced in the integration of multiple experiences as of a body. Thus, there is an *n*-place relation here but no component is privileged as owner of the other components.

Once we see this, we can see a problem for any attempt to explain the phenomenal I in terms of body ownership. For the question arises, where is the I in experience? The I cannot be identified with any part, because each bodily perception on its own can be had without a sense of it belonging to the self. So the I must be experienced in the relation or, more plausibly, in the various components as they are related to one another. But what is it to experience two bodily perceptions as related in this way? It will not do to say we experience them as belonging to the same self, because then we need to experience a separate self to which they are related. Instead, we must just experience them as bound together like two features of an object. Perhaps we achieve this using a map strategy – perhaps visual, tactile, and proprioceptive experiences can be linked to a shared unconscious body map. This analysis treats bodily unity in the same way unity is explained more broadly. Body perceptions are bound together the way color is bound to shape. If this is right, it may cast doubt on the view that the experience of body ownership can be accurately described as a phenomenal experience of the self. Instead, it seems to be an experience of a bound whole, with no more claim to being me than my polysensory experience of your body when I simultaneously see you and shake your hand. In other words, what began as a theory of ownership turns out to be no such thing. It is just another case of polysensory binding and does nothing to bring anything especially self-like into experience.

Now hold on, you might object, surely when you unify the sensory components of your own body it feels more like yourself than when you unify the sensory components of someone else's body. After all, I do not confuse myself for you. True enough, but this objection only serves to highlight the deeper concern. The question is, why don't I confuse myself for you? One might think that the answer has to do with the specific qualities that get bound together. Proprioceptive and tactile sensations, in particular, seem to be uniquely self-involving. But this possibility has already been rejected. I can experience these qualities without experiencing them as me. Indeed, it may well be that when I form an integrated representation of someone else's body, I do so by generating an integrated mental image using my own proprioceptive and tactile mechanisms. I may simulate what it is like to be the other. If so, when I encounter another I may have two tactile-proprioceptive unities in mind, and there may be nothing in those polysensory bundles as such that determines which one is me. This problem comes out all too vividly in the case of out-of-body experiences. The person who drifts outside of her own body will experience two polysensory somatic bundles. The fact that they are unified is not what makes her identify with one of these bundles as opposed to the other. She might feel both bundles simultaneously, but only identify with one. Thus, identification cannot simply be a matter of sensory integration. Something else must be going on.

I am arguing, in effect, that the phenomenal sense of ownership cannot simply be a matter of integrating multiple bodily representations. More pointedly, I think it is misleading to ever talk about phenomenal ownership of the body, because there is nothing like an experience of an owner bearing a relation to bodily perceptions. I am not denying that we can form *judgments* about ownership. I know that my limbs belong to me. But there may be no *experience* of ownership. There may be an experience on the basis of which we *infer* ownership, but the experience must involve more than an integrated body-representation. Such a representation is not sufficient.

Moreover, even if an integrated bundle of bodily perceptions were sufficient for a sense of ownership, it is far from obvious that it would be sufficient for having a sense of one's self as a subject, as opposed to an object. If I feel a pain in the foot, I might be able to perceive that the affected foot is mine, but it does not follow that I experience the foot as a subject of thought, experience, and action. The foot does not correspond to the "I" in the ascription "I have a pain in my foot." There is a gulf between "my" and "I." The thesis of this chapter is that there is no phenomenal I, and integrated bodily representations do not allay that skepticism. If there were a phenomenal sense of ownership (which I doubt), it would not qualify as a phenomenal experience of being a subject.

I would add that having integrated bodily representations is also not necessary for having a sense of self. It seems perfectly possible to have one kind of bodily perception in the absence of others. An anesthetized person may lose the sense of touch, a severely dizzy person may lose coherent proprioceptive information, and a blind person will have no visual experiences of the body. Yet none of these conditions prevents a person from using the intact faculties to identify the self. This point is poignantly illustrated in the case of Ian Waterman, who lacks proprioception and touch (Cole 1995). Waterman locates his body using vision, and has as much claim to knowing where he is and how his body is positioned as someone with a more diverse sensory repertoire. He faces challenges in the dark, of course, but, when vision is available, he can recognize that his limbs are his own.

In summary, I see several serious hurdles for those who want to find the phenomenal I in the experience of body ownership. First, a sense of ownership would not be sufficient for a sense of self as subject. Second, the leading theory of body ownership – integration of bodily perceptions – is not sufficient for explaining how we judge that a given bundle of bodily experiences are mine. Third, integration of bodily perceptions is not necessary for making such judgments. Fourth, there may not even be such a thing as the phenomenology of ownership.

3.3 *Authorship*

The notion of ownership has been contrasted in cognitive neuroscience with the notion of authorship. Ownership is the feeling associated with a mental state belonging to me. Authorship, also called "agency," is the feeling associated with being the author of physical and mental acts. It is identified with a feeling of control. I experience some thoughts and actions as issuing from me. Like ownership, agency involves a kind of possession: the acts I control are mine. But it is an active form of possession, and this, one might think, introduces an entry point for the self. With passive perception, the world can pass by the senses without any sense of being a subject, but with active agency, the self seems to come in essentially. Perhaps the phenomenal I is an experience of oneself as the author.

This proposal overcomes the four problems adduced in response to the suggestion that the phenomenal I derives from a sense of ownership. First, I said that ownership is not sufficient for a sense of oneself as subject, but, as just intimated, authorship is a form of subjectivity *par excellence*; to experience oneself as author is to experience oneself as the subject of an act – as the *I*, as opposed to the *me*. Second, I said the leading theory of ownership could not explain how a bundle of experiences feel like they are mine. Authorship may provide the solution. If I experience two separate bundles of bodily perceptions, I can figure out which one is mine by figuring out which one I control. A sense of control can provide a greater sense of mineness than mere *sensory* integration because it brings in a motor element that provides for a robust sense of possession; my body is the one that obeys my intentions in predictable ways. The element of control may help explain why the frontal operculum, a motor control structure, is active in the rubber hand studies. We imagine owning the rubber hand, in part, by preparing to issue action commands. Third, I said that sensory integration is too demanding, because people with just one bodily sense have no difficulty judging which body is theirs. Authorship handles this easily, because one can recognize one's control over a single dimension of bodily perception, without reference to any others. Ian Waterman can confirm his bodily control using vision to see that his limbs obey his movements. Finally, I raised doubts about whether there even can be a phenomenology of ownership, because ownership requires an owner. With authorship, things are easier, because there is a functional and anatomical separation between the intentions or commands we issue and their subsequent effects.

One might try to argue against this approach by maintaining that authorship is never directly experienced but only inferred. One such argument can be distilled from Wegner's (2002) critique of the conscious will. Wegner argues that we derive a sense of control when we experience a conscious intention that meets three conditions: it occurs just before an observed effect (priority), it is consistent with the observed effect (consistency), and it is the only salient event that meets these first two conditions (exclusivity). Wegner's main point is that the sense of control can be an illusion, because these three conditions can occur even when there is no causal link between intention and effect. Suppose, for example, that my limbs are controlled by unconscious motor commands, but those commands also generate conscious intentions to move – intentions that dangle idly without having any impact on my behavior. The intentions occur before the movement, are consistent with it, and are the only conscious precursor, so I conclude that my intentions are efficacious. Wegner's theory can also be adapted to raise a skeptical worry about the phenomenology of authorship. If he is right, control might not be something we experience; it may be something that we simply infer from conscious intentions and conscious bodily movements. This would spell trouble for defenders of the phenomenal I, because one can surely experience an intention or a movement without feeling any quality that corresponds to being a subject. Indeed, as Wegner points out, in some cases we experience intentions and actions without inferring control because alternative explanations become available. In one experiment, he asks subjects to press True or False on a keyboard in response to questions, but subjects are instructed to provide answers on behalf of another person by feeling minute muscle movements in that person's hand, rather than providing their own answers. In actuality, the other person cannot even hear the questions, so the answers derive entirely from the subjects, but they nevertheless believe that the other person is selecting the answers. Intention and action are both experienced but subjects infer a lack of control (Wegner and Wheatley 1999). This experiment shows that control is not part of the phenomenology, but is only inferred by an argument to the best explanation.

The Wegner story gives us reason to be cautious in assuming that there is a phenomenal experience corresponding to authorship. It is possible that, in many cases, authorship is merely inferred. But Wegner's theory is not the only game in town. In cognitive neuroscience there has been an active campaign to find the neural correlates of authorship, and the people conducting this research think that authorship can be phenomenologically experienced and they even have an explanation of how this occurs. The leading story stems from research on motor control. According to prevailing theories of motor control, intentional action begins when an intention is converted into a motor command by a mechanism called a "controller" (or sometimes an "inverse model"). The controller outputs motor commands, and it also sends "efference copies" of those commands to a mechanism called a "forward model" which uses the copy of a command to generate a prediction of how the body will move when the command is carried out. Meanwhile, the body carries out the command, and sensory transducers register the resultant changes, which are called reafferent signals. The reafferent signals are compared to the predicted outcomes by means of a comparator – a mechanism that determines whether predicted and actual movements arc alike. This account has been adapted to explain the phenomenology of authorship (Wolpert *et al.* 1995). We experience actions as our own when a predicted action and a perceived action match. If our bodies move in unpredictable ways, we lose the sense of agency. This happens, for example, when something pushes into us, causing the body to move without a prior motor command.

The comparator model explains a number of interesting phenomena. It explains why it is so hard to tickle yourself (Blakemore *et al.* 2000). Tickling seems to depend crucially on unpredictability. If you try to tickle yourself, your motor system will accurately predict the hand movements, and you will lose the crucial element of surprise. The comparator model also explains some striking pathologies in the phenomenology of agency. There arc cases of alien and anarchic hand syndrome where patients feel that an appendage is not in their control even though they can feel its movements (Biran and Chatterjee 2004). These patients characteristically describe the disobedient hand in the third person, as if it did not belong to them. The syndrome is typically associated with damage to the corpus callosum, which allows for communication between the hemispheres. That damage may prevent one hemisphere from predicting actions controlled by the other, giving rise to the experience of alien control.

So far, the cases I have been discussing involve motor behavior. A nice feature of the comparator model is that it can be adapted to explain the experience of authorship in cognitive processes as well (Frith *et al.* 2000; Hohwy 2007; though see Vosgerau and Newen 2007). One can explain the sense that a thought is my own by supposing that prior to generating a conscious experience of the thought, we anticipate what that experience will be like. The two are then compared, and if the thought is as predicted, it seems to belong to us. If not, it seems to come unbidden. Frith *et al.* (2000) use this model to explain the experience of thought insertion in schizophrenia. A thought that comes without being predicted may seem to come from some external source, as if it has been planted in the head. People with schizophrenia may experience their own thoughts this way because of a malfunction in their comparator mechanisms.

The extension of the comparator account to thought is a big advantage. One problem with the ownership theory discussed in the last section, as well as Damasio's account of self-awareness in terms of feelings, is they place too much emphasis on the body. If there is a phenomenal I, it would be extremely surprising that it could manifest itself only through the body (see also Strawson 1999). After all, we are subjects of thought just as much as we are subjects of physical actions. There may even be conditions under which all bodily phenomenology is lost (sensory deprivation tanks? locked-in syndrome?), but there is no reason to think that such conditions essentially involve any less sense of selfhood than we find in the case of physical actions. For those who think the body is inessential to the sense of selfhood, the comparator model is surely attractive.

In sum, the comparator model provides an elegant and unified account of authorship. It locates the experience of authorship in a process that is well motivated by theories of motor control, and it extends nicely to cases of cognitive ownership as well. It also offers a tidy explanation of cases in which authorship seems to be lost. All this is very good news for those who want a reductive account of the phenomenal I. In authorship, unlike mere ownership, the self functions as the subject of a thought or act. Thus, authorship gives us an I rather than a mere me. It is, therefore, tempting to equate the phenomenal I with the phenomenology of authorship, which, in turn, can be equated with the experience of a successful matching process in an output/input comparator.

This account of agency differs from Wegner's in that it treats authorship as an experience, rather than as a mere inference. But it can be easily reconciled with Wegner's experimental findings and his skeptical hypothesis about free will. The comparator model does not presuppose the causal efficacy of conscious intentions, because it is consistent with the view that motor commands are initiated unconsciously. Wegner may be right that conscious intentions lack efficacy and are linked to actions through an inferential, rather than phenomenological process. Wegner's experiments on erroneous lack of control may appear to conflict with the comparator model, but this appearance can be explained away by a more careful look at the findings. In Wegner's true-or-false study, subjects judge that they did not choose which answer to type into the keyboard, but, if asked, they probably would not deny feeling a sense of control when pressing the keys. They feel like the initial choice of which key to press has an external source, but once that choice is registered, the subjects press the keys themselves and might experience a sense of authorship in doing so. In other words, these studies do not show that authorship is inferential, rather than phenomenal; they merely show that we can have false beliefs about the factors that lead us to carry out the controlled actions that we experience.

It may look like we have found the phenomenal I at last. Appearances, however, can be deceiving. I think the comparator model does offer a plausible theory of the processes by which we recognize agency and disruptions to agency, but I do not think it gives us the coveted I-qualia. I have two reasons for this disheartening assessment. First, I think that the comparator model cannot, in the end, give us a phenomenology of subjectivity in the required sense; it continues to present the self as object rather than subject. To see this, we need to consider the neural correlates of the comparison process (focusing here on the case of physical actions, as opposed to thoughts). One might think that comparison involves a conscious experience of a motor command being matched against a perceived movement. This would be something like an experience of authorship, because one would be experiencing the command *that created* an action together with the action caused. The command could stand proxy for the self, in an act of agentic control. But, in reality, the experience cannot be an experience of a motor command. For one thing, there is no evidence that we have motor phenomenology. The best theories of phenomenology are theories of sensory phenomenology, and every experience associated with motor response can be chalked up to a sensory experience of the corresponding movements. For another thing, the motor command cannot be directly matched against a perceived action, because motor command and action perceptions are couched in different neural codes; to make a match, we need to generate an anticipatory image of what the action will feel like perceptually and then compare that to the actual perception. And finally, neuroscientific research on comparator models using fMRI and cell recordings in animals suggests that the comparison takes place in the posterior parietal cortex – a somatosensory area – rather than motor cortex. If this is right, the feelings associated with authorship are really not experiences of an author and an authored act; rather, they are experiences of an anticipated act and a real act. To experience the body acting, whether through perception or anticipatory imagination, is to experience the self as object rather than as subject. Such an experience is not a phenomenal correlate of the "I" in first-person reports. It is a correlate of the *me*. When I say, "I feel myself act," what I report is an action, not an actor. Put more pointedly, there is no experience of authorship. To suppose otherwise is to mistake a feeling that occurs when we are the authors of our actions for a feeling of authorship itself. It is to mistake the effect for the cause. When we use the experience generated by the comparator to judge that we are in control, the judgment is inferential, rather than a direct report of the phenomenology.

The second complaint I want to advance against the comparator theory of phenomenal authorship is that its defenders give the erroneous impression that the comparison process itself has a phenomenal character. If authorship had a phenomenology and the comparator theory of that phenomenology were true, then we might expect to find, in controlled action, a phenomenal experience of an anticipatory image being compared with a perceptual input from the body. But when we act, we find no such thing. We experience only our bodies in action. There is one experience, not two. It is a single unified perceptual experience of action, not a comparison between image and percept. It is the same for the phenomenology of thought. When we experience subvocal speech, for example, we do not experience an anticipation of this silent narrative, followed by the narrative itself – much less a matching between two verbal streams. We just experience one stream of speech. This suggests either that the comparison process is entirely unconscious, or that the anticipated act and the experienced act blend into each other seamlessly in experience. Either way, there is no hook to hang the selfy hat on. There is no item or process in experience that we can label the I. There is an experience of the action, but not the actor.

Against this deflationary reading, one might object that we *must* be able to experience ourselves as actors because, otherwise, we would not be able to consciously distinguish cases of control from cases where others act upon us. It does seem that we can tell the difference between lifting an arm and having an arm lifted by another, but, if my arguments succeed both should be alike; in both we just experience the movement. It will not help here to say that our own actions are accompanied by feelings of effort while externally caused actions come accompanied by resistance, for some self-controlled actions are effortless and some other-controlled actions meet with no resistance. The puzzle can be put like this: the distinction between internally and externally generated actions seems to be phenomenologically available, and the comparator model offers a good explanation, but on my account of the phenomenology of the comparator model, internally and externally generated actions should be phenomenologically alike because the matching process is unconscious.

I think we can solve the puzzle by considering what happens when the unconscious comparison process fails to find a match between anticipated acts and perceived acts. Presumably, the experience of an uncaused action sets off a kind of alarm signal that tells the body it has come under external influence. To cope with this fact effectively, the source of that influence must be identified. So, if your body moves in an unpredictable way, your mind goes searching for the cause. You may find the cause – perhaps something or someone is forcing your body to move – and you may not – perhaps you had a spasm or a twitch. Either way there may be a conscious experience associated with the recognition that an external source caused a movement. And there is no special puzzle about having a phenomenal experience of external causes. You can experience someone or something acting on you, even if you cannot experience yourself acting. Thus, there is a fundamental asymmetry here. We cannot be conscious of ourselves as agents, but we can be conscious of others as agents. There is no phenomenology of being a controller, but there is a phenomenology of being controlled. Ironically, we can feel the absence of the self (or rather, the presence of some external cause), but not the presence of the self.

4. CONCLUDING REMARKS: IS EXPERIENCE SELFLESS?

The foregoing has been an extended defense of Hume's thesis against recent developments in cognitive neuroscience. Hume says that when he looks for a self in the flow of experience, he does not find one. He can find perceptions of the world and the body, but no subject. On a weak reading, Hume thinks there is no subject above and beyond the flow of perceptions, and, on a strong reading, he thinks none of our perceptions qualifies as an experience of one's self as a subject. Both of these assertions have been challenged, and recent work in cognitive neuroscience has offered several theories, both reductive and non-reductive of the phenomenal I. It has been my contention that these theories fail. Some of them may point to ways we can experience ourselves as objects, but that we can do so has never been in dispute. Some may also provide some of the mechanisms and experiences on the basis of which we can infer that we are acting as subjects of our actions and thoughts, but they do not bring the self-qua-subject into phenomenal view. Thus, Hume seems to be right, even on a strong reading. There is no phenomenal I. If I wait for myself to appear in experience, I will never arrive. I might believe that I exist as a subject through inference and philosophical speculation, but I have never been acquainted with myself. I see indirect signs or, more strikingly, recognize my own agency at just those moments when agency is lost.

Fortunately, we do not need to end on this gloomy existential note. Perhaps the search for the self, like the wait for Godot, is a pointless exercise, but there may be a sense in which the I is present *in virtue of* its absence. To see this, consider three ways in which the self enters implicitly into experience. First, the self is present in the fact that we always experience the world from a perspective. It is a striking feature of consciousness that conscious states are always from a point of view. After all, sensory systems do encode information in vantage-point invariant ways as well, but these representations are unconscious. Consciousness is perspectival. Second, consciousness cannot present what lies beyond our senses; objects too far in the periphery or distance escape our field of view. Consciousness may fill in missing details, but it always presents the world as seriously bounded – bounded by the I. Third, the qualities of experience are dependent on our sensory apparatus. The colors and even the shapes we see are, in some sense, not given to us by the world. Shapes are out there, to be sure, but only at one level of analysis. The ladders that feel so solid under our feet are really swarms of atoms. So the senses do not simply pick up the world as it is; they select from a vast range of possible joints and impose order that would be invisible if we were different kinds of selves. Our goals, interests, and histories can contribute to this process of selection and construction, and, in that way, the contents of experience are not a transparent window onto the mind-external world, but are always instead filtered through the self. In these three ways, the self is always present in the perceptions given to us in consciousness. It is present, not as an item of experience, but as a kind of constraint. To echo Wittgenstein, echoing Schopenhauer, the self is the limit of my world. I cannot see the eye that sees, but seeing is constrained by the eye, and hence the I. For this reason, consciousness is not selfless; it is thoroughly permeated by the self. The self is absent if we look for it, but is always already there in each act of looking.[1]

---

[1] My heartfelt thanks to JeeLoo Liu and Kelsey Fernandez for their extensive and helpful comments.

CHAPTER 6

I think I think, therefore I am – I think: skeptical doubts about self-knowledge

Fred Dretske

Valid arguments – even those with true premises – do not take you very far if you do not know whether the premises are true. The fact that I am in Heidelberg does not give me a reason to believe I am in Germany unless I know (or at least have reason to believe) I am in Heidelberg. So why does everyone believe the *Cogito* – I think, therefore I am – is such a terrific argument? Because, I suppose, everyone thinks he knows the premise is true. Everyone who thinks he thinks thinks he *knows* he thinks. So everyone thinks his existence – at least his existence as a thinking being – is the conclusion of an irresistible argument.

The Cartesian inference is certainly valid, no doubt about that. And the premise is clearly true – at least it is for everyone who thinks it is true. I am not questioning either of these claims. I do, however, think it worth pondering the question of whether – and if so, how – one knows that the premise is true. What reason do thinkers have for thinking they think? If you are going to demonstrate, *à la* Descartes, that you exist, you need a premise you *know* to be true. Merely *thinking* you think is not good enough to generate *knowledge* you exist anymore than (merely) *thinking* you are in Heidelberg can generate *knowledge* that you are in Germany. As my title is intended to suggest, the most it will generate is a *belief* – perhaps (depending on whether you have any reasons for thinking you think) an altogether *groundless* belief – that you exist. In epistemology you cannot manufacture A+ conclusions from C- premises. Garbage in, garbage out.

I am not interested, though, in proofs that I (or you) exist. I suspect no one – not even the most fanatical philosopher – has a real problem about his

My thanks to the Alexander von Humboldt Foundation for their support of this research and to Andreas Kemmerling, Heidelberg, for the many things he did during my visits to Germany to help me think more clearly about this problem. Also special thanks to JeeLoo Liu, a thoroughly responsible editor, for gently nudging this chapter into better shape than it was originally.

or her own existence. But I am interested in the epistemological status of Descartes' premise – interested, that is, in how we know, or what reason we have for thinking, that we think. I suspect that no one has serious worries about *this* question either since, as suggested above, everyone who thinks he thinks is already convinced he *knows* he thinks. This is not, therefore, a burning issue. Nonetheless, despite the absence of active debate about, or even interest in, the topic, I have reached a stage in my thinking about this question in which it is no longer clear to me *how* we know we think, what *reasons* we have for believing it. What follows, therefore, is my effort to infect others with my own bewilderment about this problem.

I. REASONS FOR THINKING YOU THINK

So let me begin by asking what reason you have for thinking you think. Is it simply the fact that you think? You might also have cancer, but the mere fact that you have cancer does not give you a reason, all by itself, to believe you have cancer. If you have a reason to believe you have cancer, you have been talking to doctors. Or you have been made aware of some sign or symptom of the cancer, something that indicates or increases the chances that you have cancer. If this is true of cancer, why isn't it also true of thought? Why should the fact that you think give you a reason to think you think? Just as with any other fact about yourself (e.g. that you are hungry), to have a reason to think you are in this condition you must, it would seem (given the nature of reasons), be aware of something that indicates (or at least increases the likelihood) that you are in this condition. In the case of hunger, it is pretty clear what this is. You *feel* hungry. You are aware of something, if not the hunger itself (is that what one feels when one feels hungry?), then something that indicates you are hungry. In the case of thought, what is it? Is it the thought itself? Is it your awareness of your own thoughts that gives you a reason to believe you have them?

Those who have cancer (as opposed to the doctors attending them) are seldom if ever visually aware of (i.e. see) the cancer itself. So if the victims, the ones who have the cancer, are to have a reason to believe they have it, they either have to be told they have it, examine (with some degree of expertise) X-rays for themselves, or feel the unmistakable symptoms of the disease. But thoughts (I expect to be told) are completely different. Unlike cancer victims, thinkers need not rely on the symptoms of thought, the observable results or manifestations of thought. They need not rely on these outward indicators because they, as the person doing the thinking, *are* aware of the thoughts themselves – thus giving them the best possible reason for thinking they have them. Other people have to rely on the external indicators, but the thinker does not have to. He or she has direct – indeed, privileged – access to his or her own thoughts.

I do not believe this is true. I believe it is *half* true, and the half that is true encourages one to think the other half is true. Thinkers *are* aware of their thoughts, yes, and this awareness gives them a unique authority about what they are thinking (this is the half that is true), but that does not provide them a reason, much less the best possible reason, for thinking that they have thoughts. That is the false half. As far as I can determine, thinkers have *no* reason – no reason, that is, to which they have privileged access – for thinking they think. If thinkers have a reason to think they think, it is a reason their family, friends and neighbors have equal access to. In this respect thinking is just like having cancer.

Before I explain why I believe this, a few remarks on the very special kind of thought we are dealing with – the thought that one thinks. Maybe, after all, one does not need reasons to qualify this very special thought as knowledge. Maybe reasons are beside the point, extraneous, irrelevant, to knowing you (as opposed to others) think. You know it simply in virtue of believing it. As some of my friends tell me, we know we think, but there is no *way* we know it. We just know it. So forget about reasons.

2. SELF-VERIFYING THOUGHTS

One can think one has cancer and be wrong, but one cannot think one thinks and be wrong. Thinking one thinks is, as philosophers now like to put it (although Descartes expressed it differently), a self-verifying thought. Unlike the thought that one has cancer or a thought about almost any other topic, the thought that one thinks has to be true. If *I* think I think I have to be right. If *you* think I think you can be wrong. So *my* thought is special. Infallible. Yours is not. That is why I know (in a way my friends and neighbors cannot) that I think. And they know in a way I cannot that *they* think.

The thought that one thinks is self-verifying – no doubt about that – but having this self-verifying thought does not provide one with a reason to think one thinks unless one has reasons to think one has this self-verifying thought. Remember, the question is: what reason do you have for thinking you think? It is no answer to say that you cannot be wrong in thinking you think. That just leaves the question: what reason do you have for thinking you think you think? We are back to where we started – maybe even (epistemologically speaking) a little *behind* where we started.

It is important to stress this point. One does *not* have a reason to think one thinks merely in virtue of having a self-verifying thought that one thinks. One also needs a reason to think one is having this self-verifying thought. But that, of course, is exactly what we are looking for: a reason to think one has thoughts. One cannot give as a reason to think one has thoughts the fact that some of one's thoughts – the thought that one has thoughts – have to be true. That would be like giving as a reason for thinking I said something, the fact that saying I said something is self-verifying. So it is, but what reason do I have for thinking I said I said something?

I expect impatient readers to remind me, though, that we are now considering the possibility that having reasons to think you think (or to think you think you think) is beside the point. You do not need them. The fact that this thought (the thought that one thinks) is self-verifying means one *knows* one thinks merely by believing one thinks whether or not one has reasons for believing one has this self-verifying thought. Beliefs that are perfectly reliable, beliefs that have to be true, qualify as knowledge even if one has absolutely no reason to think one has such beliefs.

If you, the reader, subscribe to this conception of knowledge – a lean (I would say emaciated) version of reliability theory – you may as well stop reading now because nothing I am going to say will convince you, nothing I say is *intended* to convince you, that you are wrong. I simply assume you are wrong. Or, if you are not wrong, if it turns out that there are things one knows to be true simply in virtue of the fact that one cannot be wrong about them (whether or not one has any reasons to believe them true or any reason to believe one cannot be wrong), I hereby declare that I am looking for something quite different, something more satisfying. I am asking whether we are *reasonable* in thinking we think and, if we are, what our reasons are.

We do enjoy a special kind of authority about *what* we think, yes, but that should not be confused with authority about, or knowledge of, the fact that we think it. John Heil (1988) and Tyler Burge (1988) have argued – persuasively to my mind – that with respect to a certain limited class of thoughts (conscious current thoughts), we think whatever we think we think. We enjoy a kind of infallibility. This is so because in thinking that I am thinking *P* I (thereby) think *P*. It is something like an exasperated mother saying to her misbehaving son, "I am telling you, Billy, stop pestering your sister." Mother cannot really be wrong about what she says to her son. She tells him whatever she says she tells him because in saying what she is telling him to do she (thereby) tells him to do it.[1] Even if the words Mother utters ("Stop pestering your sister") mean by prior agreement between Mother and Son that he should get ready for bed, Mother is still entirely correct in using the words, "Stop pestering your sister," to say what she is telling her son to do. She *is*, as she says she is, telling him to get ready for bed. So she cannot be wrong no matter what the words she uses mean. The same is true for thought. There is no room for mistake at the second-level no matter what one at the first-level happens to think or how (in what form or with what "words" in the language of thought) one thinks it.

If this is the way thoughts about (currently conscious) thoughts work, then we all enjoy a kind of authority in our thoughts and statements about our currently conscious thoughts. But even if things do work this way, it does not help us understand what reasons we have for thinking we have thoughts, much less such infallible thoughts about what we think.[2] If I think I am thinking that there is water in the glass, then according to this view, that must be what I am thinking. And if I think I am thinking, that too must be what I am thinking. But what tells me, what reason do I have to think, I have these foolproof thoughts about what I am now thinking? The answer is not to be found in the infallible nature of higher-order thoughts about our own thoughts. Mother does not have a reason to think she told her son to do X just because she knows that *if* what she said to him was "I am telling you to do X," she certainly *did* tell him to do X. Infallibility about what you think you are thinking and what you say you are saying does not, by itself, give you a reason to think you are thinking or saying anything at all.

3. PRIVILEGED ACCESS

First, a reminder of just what we are looking for. We are looking for reasons S has for thinking S thinks that are not available to others. We are looking for conditions that S has exclusive, and therefore privileged, access to that indicate or constitute evidence that S thinks. If S is a normal human being, we *all* have reasons to believe he thinks. He has a

---

[1] Katia Saporiti in her comments on this paper in Heidelberg suggested that Mother cannot be wrong for the same reason she cannot be wrong, for example, in saying to Billy, "I promise to give you a cookie if you stop pestering your sister." These are performative utterances. In using the words, "I am telling you . . .," Mother is not describing herself as telling her son to stop pestering his sister. She is, rather, verbally executing the telling. I think this is probably right, but the same might be said of one who thinks to himself: this (*P*) is what I think. That is a way of thinking that *P*.

[2] I am not suggesting here that Burge thinks it gives us such reasons. See Burge (1996) for his account of the role of critical thinking in self-knowledge.

Ph.D. in physics, forty-three publications, and he runs rings around us at the bridge table. Of course he thinks – probably better than we do – and there is no shortage of reasons for believing this to be so. S, of course, also has these reasons. Anything *we* can point to as accomplishments symptomatic of S's intellectual powers are also available to S. If we have reasons for thinking S thinks – and we clearly do – so does S: the same facts we have.

This is not in question. Of course we, and therefore S, have reasons to think S is a thinking being. What is in question is whether there are any facts that indicate this to be so that S has *exclusive* or *private* access to, facts or conditions that S is aware of that we cannot be aware of – at least not in the direct and authoritative way that S is. Is there anything S is privy to that others cannot be aware of that gives S an epistemic advantage on questions about whether S has thoughts?

Like Descartes, I mean to be pretty inclusive about what is to count as a thought. I focus on current conscious thoughts, and I include as a thought (that P) any attitude having P as its propositional content in which the truth of P is accepted by, but not required for, those having this attitude toward P. So believing and judging as well as thinking (in an everyday sense) that P are ways of thinking that P in my somewhat enlarged sense. Knowing, seeing, and remembering that P – since requiring the truth of P – are not. Neither are wanting, hoping, and doubting that P since the truth of P is not thereby accepted. I believe the skeptical point I am trying to make here can be generalized to other mental states (including experiences and feelings), but the effort to make the general case would entangle me in too many troublesome details (for an early attempt to deal with some of these details see Dretske 2003). So I here limit myself to current conscious *thoughts* in my slightly enlarged sense of "thought."

4. THINKING WITHOUT KNOWING YOU THINK

One way to proceed in a project of this sort is to look at how we learned we think. We all think before we ever discover what thinking is, before we were able to think we (and others) think. So at some point in time, during some phase of childhood, we learned that we (and others) think. How did we learn this? Who taught us? Parents? Did we take their word for it? Were we already aware of our own thoughts as we were of the television and dishwasher and merely had to learn (as we did with ordinary household items) what to call them?

Imagine a normal three-year-old, Sarah, who thinks but has not yet learned she thinks. That one thinks is something (psychologists tell us[3]) that one only comes to fully understand around the age of three or four years. Sarah is not quite there. She thinks Daddy is home. That is what she tells Mommy. That is why she runs to the door to greet him when she hears a car pull in the driveway. What Sarah tells Mommy is (what else?) what she thinks (knows, hears): that her father is home. She does not, however, think she thinks it. She may use the word "think" ("know" or "hear") in describing herself, but if she does, she does not yet fully understand that what she is giving expression to is a fact about herself, a subjective condition having a content (what she thinks) that may be false. She will, however, soon acquire this knowledge. How and from whom? No doubt from parents, teachers, older siblings, and friends. If one does not actually teach children this, if they merely absorb it the way children acquire their native language, it is nonetheless from others, or at least with the help of others, that Sarah will learn that what she has been telling them is what she has been thinking, what she believes, what she (sometimes) even knows. It is from (or with the help of) other people (and, perhaps, a few disappointed expectations) that she will learn that she has thoughts that usually accord with the way things actually are, but that sometimes fail to correspond to the facts. In the process she will learn that her behavior and, of course, the behavior of others can be explained not only by the fact that her father is home (Sarah already understands this), but also by the fact that she *thinks* he is home – something she will learn that can exist in her, and can explain her rush to the door, without her father actually being home. As Jonathan Bennett (1991, 97) once put it in describing what psychologists have learned about child development, a two-year-old predicts and explains another person's behavior on the basis of what she, *the child*, thinks is true; a four-year-old does so on the basis of what *the other* person thinks is true (or at least what the child thinks the other person thinks is true). To reach this level of sophistication one has to understand, as two-year-olds do not, what it means to think something is true. That is why normal two-year-olds do not understand the behavior of someone who chooses *this* box when she (the child) knows the candy is in *that* box. A four-year-old will understand this: the person chose

---

[3] I rely here on Astington (1993); Flavell *et al.* (1993); Gopnik (1993); Bartsch and Wellman (1995); Flavell (2003); Carpendale and Lewis (2006). I am not really interested in exactly when children acquire a theory of mind, exactly when they acquire the capacity to think they (and others) think. I simply assume it is somewhere around the age of three or four. All that is important for my argument is that children think *before* they (are able to) think they think. This much seems incontestable.

this box because *the person* (but maybe not the four-year-old) *thought* (mistakenly) the candy was in this box.

To understand what kind of access we, those of us who think we have thoughts, have to our own thoughts, and thus what kind of reasons we have for thinking we have them, it is instructive to consider the kind of access Sarah, a person who does not think she has them (she does not think she doesn't have them either), has to her thoughts. I said above that Sarah told her mother that her father was home and rushed to open the door because she *thought* he was home. It might not have been her father she heard pulling into the driveway, of course, but Sarah thought it was, and the fact that she thought so explains why she behaved that way. If she had thought, instead, that it was the mailman she would not have told her mother that her father was home and she would not have rushed to open the door. Sarah's thoughts and desires explain her behavior (verbal and otherwise) in the same way our thoughts and desires explain ours. The only difference is that Sarah does not understand that her behavior can be explained by the fact that (whether or not her father is home) she *thinks* he is home. We do.

If Sarah's behavior is to be explained by what she thinks even when she does not realize she thinks it, and the behavior in question is a deliberate, purposeful act (Sarah has and is prepared to give *reasons* for what she does, and these reasons are, in part, what she thinks), there is a sense in which Sarah is aware of what she thinks – that her father is home – without being aware (of the fact[4]) that *this* (that Daddy is home) is what she thinks. Call this form of awareness *acquaintance*. Sarah is acquainted with what she thinks. Although this word has a troubled philosophical history, I use it in its ordinary sense, the sense in which one can be acquainted with – in fact, good friends with – a philosopher (a concrete object) and not know she is a philosopher. One can also be acquainted with abstract objects. I might, for example, be aware of what was reported on the radio – that it is snowing in Miami – without knowing it was reported on the radio.[5] This is an epistemically neutral form of awareness: one can be aware of X (e.g. see or hear X) in this way without knowing it is X. One *might* know it is X, but one

---

[4] It will become increasingly important to distinguish awareness of facts (e.g. that Daddy is home) from awareness of objects – both concrete objects (e.g. Daddy) and (as we shall see) abstract objects (e.g. what Sarah thinks). When there is danger of confusion, I will try to indicate which I mean by a parenthetical "the fact that."

[5] I assume here that if you tell me it is snowing in Miami and this (that it is snowing in Miami) is what was reported on the radio, then I am aware of what was reported on the radio without (necessarily) knowing that it was reported on the radio. Note: what was reported on the radio need not be true. So what was reported on the radio need not be a fact. So awareness of what was reported on the radio is not (necessarily) fact-awareness.

need not. It is in this sense that Sarah is aware of, acquainted with, what she thinks – that her father is home. She is aware (conscious) of what she thinks in a way that does not require her to know (or even think) it is something she is thinking in order to be aware of it. If Sarah had thought, instead, that it was the mailman she heard outside, she would have been acquainted with (aware of) something quite different. Something different would have been going through her mind – her *conscious* mind – at the time she spoke to her mother. She would not have said what she did nor would she have rushed to greet her father at the door.

5. AWARENESS OF PROPOSITIONS

What is it that Sarah is acquainted with (aware of) when she thinks her father is home? Although we commonly speak of ourselves as being aware of facts that we use to explain the behavior of ourselves and others (I was aware that it was late so I took a shortcut, she looked away when she became aware that I was watching her), there does not seem to be any relevant *fact* that Sarah is aware of that explains her behavior. We cannot say that she is aware (of the fact) that her father is home because her father need not be home for her to think he is home and to behave (and to give the same reasons for behaving) in exactly the same way. Whatever she is acquainted with when she thinks he is home must, therefore, be (logically) independent of her father's actual whereabouts in the same way her thought that he is home is (logically) independent of his actual whereabouts. So it is not the *fact* that her father is home that Sarah is aware of. There may be no such fact. Nor can we say that what Sarah is acquainted with is the fact that *she thinks* her father is home because although this (unlike her father's being home) must be a fact, it is not a fact that Sarah, lacking the concept of thought, is aware of. She is not aware that she thinks this. What, then, is Sarah aware of when she mistakenly thinks her father is home if it is not: (1) the fact that her father is home, nor (2) the fact that she thinks he is home? It is what philosophers call a *proposition* – the proposition that her father is home. Propositions are the (abstract) objects of thought. In thinking that her father is home, Sarah is acquainted with a proposition, the proposition that her father is home. Propositions are the meanings of those declarative sentences we use to express what one thinks. Unlike facts, they can be false. So what Sarah is acquainted with when she mistakenly thinks her father is home is neither the fact that her father is home nor the fact that she thinks her father is home, but the proposition (in this case, *false* proposition) that he is home.[6] Given the way we are understanding 'acquaintance,' Sarah can be acquainted with this proposition without knowing it is a proposition.

If acquaintance with propositions sounds strange, like some piece of philosophical hocus pocus, one has to remember that it is merely my way of saying that one can be aware (conscious) of what one thinks in the same way that *we* (who know we think) are aware of what we think without knowing it is (merely) something one thinks. One way to describe the development of children is to say that what they learn around the age of four is that what they had been taking to be (what philosophers call) a fact about the world (the fact that Daddy is home) is really (what philosophers call) a proposition – an item that (unlike a fact) can be false. Awareness of the proposition that her father is home does not mean, of course, that Sarah cannot (also) be aware of the fact that her father is home, but awareness of the fact requires more than awareness of the proposition (see footnote 6).[7]

So there is a sense, a perfectly straightforward sense, in which one has a privileged awareness of one's own present conscious thoughts even *before* one knows one has them, before one knows what they are. Sarah is aware of what she thinks – that her father is home – without knowing she thinks it in the same way you might be aware of what they reported on the radio – that it is snowing in Miami – without realizing it was reported on the radio. In describing Sarah's awareness of what she is thinking as a *privileged* awareness I do not mean that *only* she is aware of what she thinks. We, too, can be aware of what she is thinking (that her father is home) by thinking it ourselves. No, her awareness is privileged in the sense that although we *can* be aware of what she is thinking (the proposition she is aware of), Sarah *has to be* aware of it. That is what it is for *her* to think it. It is the fact that she has to be aware of it that makes her an authority on what she thinks despite not knowing she is thinking it. She is an authority on what she thinks in the sense that if we want to find out what Sarah thinks, we have to "consult" her. We cannot, of course, do so by asking Sarah what she thinks. She will not (we are assuming) understand what we are talking about. But there are other ways of getting this information. Given a cooperative child, we can ask Sarah whether her father is home. Or why she is rushing to open the door.

---

[6] Of course if Sarah's father *is* home, and his being home is appropriately related (causally and otherwise) with her belief that he is home, we can speak of her as knowing (seeing or hearing that) he is home and, therefore, in this sense, aware (of the fact) that he is home.

[7] See Feit (2008) for a thorough description of the problems with talking about propositions as the content of thought – especially the problem of *de se* thoughts (thoughts about oneself). Feit defends a property theory of mental content. I will, for convenience, continue to speak of propositions as the object of thought since (as far as I can see) these metaphysical niceties (the difference between propositions and properties) do not affect the epistemological point I am (and will be) making.

The answers will reveal, reliably enough for us to know what she is thinking, what Sarah thinks. If Sarah was not aware of what she thinks as she rushes to the door, how could she (not her mother or anyone else) be the authority on *why* she is running to the door?

This is not to say that Sarah *knows* what she thinks. She does not. She does not know she thinks anything at all. But she does not have to *know* what she thinks to be *aware* of what she thinks. You do not have to *know* what was reported on the radio – that it is snowing in Miami, for instance – to be *aware of* (in our non-epistemic sense of being acquainted with) what was reported on the radio. And if you, but not I, know that everything I say is reported on the radio, I will be the person you will consult, I will be the authority, when you want to know (without listening to the radio) what is being reported on the radio. You will learn what is being reported on the radio from me, a person who does not himself know (but is nonetheless aware of) what is being reported on the radio. I will have the kind of authority Sarah has about what she is thinking. This is why Mother can learn what Sarah thinks, and she can learn it from Sarah, despite Sarah not *knowing* that it (what she tells her Mother) is what she thinks.

6. PROPOSITIONS AS REASONS?

Well, if this is our mode of access to our own thoughts, doesn't this provide us with an answer to the question we have been struggling with – the question of what reason we have for thinking we think? Everyone who thinks has a reason to believe he thinks because he is acquainted with a proposition, the content of his own thought, which indicates the presence of the thought for which it is the content. Since you cannot have a thought-content without a thought, awareness of a thought-content is awareness of something that is the surest possible sign of a thought. Even Sarah has a reason to think she thinks. She just has to learn to recognize these reasons as reasons by learning to recognize *as* propositions, as the contents of thought, the propositions she is (and has been) acquainted with. It is like learning – also at an early age – that what one has been feeling when hungry is called hunger.

Unfortunately, though, thinking is not like hunger. When you are hungry there is (often enough, anyway) something you are aware of, something you feel, that indicates you are hungry. You *feel* hungry even if you do not know it is hunger you feel. When you think, though, there is nothing you are aware of, nothing you feel, that indicates you are thinking. What you are aware of when you are thinking is a proposition, and propositions, unlike the things you feel, do not indicate anything. Unlike facts, propositions can be false, and false propositions (unlike the fact that they are false) do not increase the probability that anything else is true. False propositions are a dime a dozen, epistemically worthless. The proposition that pigs have wings, for example, a perfectly respectable proposition – something a person might actually think – has absolutely no probative value. It certainly is not a reason to think pigs can fly. If it were, we would all have reasons to think that pigs can fly. What would be a reason to think pigs can fly is if it were *true* that pigs have wings, if it were a *fact* that pigs have wings. Propositions, though, do not have to be true. They are not facts. So awareness of what one thinks – the proposition that pigs have wings – does not give one a reason to believe that pigs can fly. It does not give one a reason to believe anything. It certainly does not give a person who thinks pigs have wings and who is thereby aware of this proposition a reason to think that he *thinks* pigs have wings. If it did, you and I (also aware of this proposition in a different mode) would have a reason to think pigs can fly.

The same is true when *what* one thinks is *that* one thinks. What one thinks, in this case, is that one thinks, but, once again, *this*, the proposition that one thinks, is not a reason to think the proposition is true. It is not a reason to think one thinks. What would be a reason to think one thinks is something that indicated this proposition was true (or that one was thinking it true). But neither of these facts are facts one is acquainted with in thinking or in thinking one thinks.[8]

What this means is that there is nothing we are aware of in thinking that indicates we are thinking. We enjoy a necessary and privileged awareness of our own thoughts (our own thought-contents, that is), yes, but what we are aware of is evidentially worthless. Privileged awareness of it makes one an authority on *what* one thinks, but it does so in the same way it makes Sarah an authority on what she thinks. It does not make one an authority on the fact that one is thinking it.

7. SAYING AND THINKING

As the discussion of Sarah illustrates, our access to our own thoughts is through their content: *what* it is we are thinking. That is the aspect of one's thought one is aware of even when one does not know what it is one is aware

---

[8] If one knows one thinks, then, of course, one is aware (of the fact) that one thinks. But this does not count as a reason to think one thinks since it is merely a restatement of that knowledge (that one thinks) for which we are looking for reasons.

of. This mode of access to our own thoughts gives us awareness of them via an aspect (their content) that not only makes the thought a thought, but also makes it the particular thought it is – the thought, say, that Daddy is home. One would suppose, therefore, that it would surely be awareness of *this* aspect of the thought as opposed to other aspects of the thought that would reveal most clearly and definitively to those aware of it exactly what it was an aspect of – viz., a thought. It doesn't. It reveals absolutely nothing. So if those who believe in a "phenomenology of thought" (where this phenomenology derives from aspects of the thought other than its content) want to say that it is these *other* aspects of thought (aspects other than the thought's content) that reveal to the person having the thought the fact that it is a thought, they have an obligation to tell us what these other (epistemically significant!) aspects are. When I introspect (as best I know how) I do not find them. But I confess that I have no argument that they do not exist. I therefore await instructions from others on where to look for them.

In this regard, though, it may be useful to compare our mode of awareness of our own thoughts with our awareness of our verbal declarations. People think things and they say things, and, often enough, what they say is what they think. Nonetheless, one's access to what a person (including oneself) says is through the act of saying it – an acoustic or observable event of some sort. We hear the person *say* he has a dental appointment, and then, if we understand the language, we come to know, become aware of, what that person said, the proposition expressed. We go from the saying to what-is-said, from *act* to *content*. We first become aware of the act, then (if we know the language) the content. If we do not know the language, we nonetheless remain aware of (hear) the speech act, the verbal action, while remaining unaware of (failing to learn) what is being said (the proposition expressed). When we are the speaker we (typically) know the language, of course, but awareness of the utterance, the act of saying it, still comes first.[9] We hear *what* we said (content) by hearing ourselves *say* it (act). Sometimes we say things we do not intend (mean) to say: "Oops, I am sorry, I didn't mean to say that." If I do not hear myself utter the words, "My, you've gained a lot of weight" (I am listening to deafening music on my Ipod), I will never know (for certain) what I said. I could not hear myself. Even if I am certain I would never say such a thing (at least not to her face), others, those who did hear me utter the words, know better than I do what I said. They heard me say it. I did not.

---

[9] I here ignore the possibility of becoming aware of the locutionary act in some indirect way (e.g. by reading a simultaneous translation of what I say).

In the case of thought, however, the route of access is reversed. Our point of access to our own thoughts is through the content. We are, like Sarah, first made aware of what we think (that Daddy is home) and then, around the age of four, we become aware of the fact that we are thinking it. There is first awareness of content and then awareness (fact-awareness) of the act. Unlike a person saying, "Daddy is home," a verbal action one can be aware of without being aware of what is being said (the proposition that is being expressed), one can be (and at two years one *is*) acquainted with what one is thinking (the proposition associated with the act of thought) while having no awareness or understanding of the act of thought itself. The mode of access is completely reversed.

s *SAYS* THAT p: S achieves awareness of what he said (content) via awareness of his saying it (an act)

s *THINKS* THAT p: S achieves awareness of what he thinks (content) *directly* and only later becomes aware of (the fact that there is) an act – a thinking – that has this content.

If one happened to confuse or conflate these two modes of access to one's own representational efforts (mental in the one case, verbal in the other), or if one merely used *saying that P* as one's model for *thinking that P* (e.g. thinking that *P* is internally saying that *P*) one might, confusedly, be led to suppose that we are aware of, and come to know about, our own thoughts in something like the way we are aware of, and come to know about, our own verbal declarations. I know what I think (and *that* I think) in the same way I know what I said (and *that* I said it): by awareness of the act itself – awareness, that is, of my thinking (internally saying) it. The mode of access is the same: act (saying, thinking) first, next (if we are lucky) content: what is said and thought. I become aware of what I think via awareness of my (act of) thinking it.

This, as I say, is a confusion. Or, if it is not a confusion, one needs reasons to think it is not. One needs reasons to believe that our awareness of what we think (and that we think it) is appropriately modeled by our awareness of what we say (and that we said it). I have been arguing it is not. I have been assuming that Sarah, although aware of what she thinks (but *not* that she thinks it), is not also aware of some internal event or condition – her own act of thinking her father is home. Nor are we. Neither Sarah nor we have an internal sense that makes us aware of our own act of thinking (a mental event) in the way our auditory sense makes us aware of our own act of speaking (an acoustic event). We adults, unlike Sarah, are, of course, aware of certain facts that Sarah is not aware of. We are aware, we know, that we have thoughts, and we are aware that these thoughts have content that (in the case of current conscious thoughts) we are directly aware of. But we are not aware of our thinking so-and-so in the way we are aware of (i.e. hear) ourselves saying so-and-so.

8. CONCLUSION

I am left, then, with the following conclusion: our mode of contact with our own thoughts, a mode of contact (direct awareness of content) that gives us a certain authority about *what* we think, does not give us a reason to think we are having these thoughts. I am willing to concede that we have reasons – in fact, overwhelming reasons – to think we think, but these reasons are the same reasons our family, friends, and neighbors have for thinking we think. What we do not have is some cache of evidence, some body of fact, to which we have access that promotes our thoughts that we think to a certainty not obtainable by others. If we hanker after Cartesian certainty, then,

COGITAS: You think, therefore you are
is as good as
COGITO: I think, therefore I am.

CHAPTER 7

Knowing what I want

Alex Byrne

As it is silly to ask somebody, 'How do you know you are in pain?' it is equally foolish to ask, 'How do you know that you want to go to the movies?'

Vendler (1972, 50)

Knowing that one wants to go to the movies is an example of self-knowledge, knowledge of one's mental states. It may be foolish to ask the man on the Clapham Omnibus how he knows what he wants, but the question is nonetheless important – albeit neglected by epistemologists. This chapter attempts an answer.

Before getting to that, the familiar claim that we enjoy "privileged access" to our mental states needs untwining (section 1). A sketch of a theory of knowledge of one's beliefs that has received some attention in the recent literature (section 2), and the case for extending that account to self-knowledge in general (section 3), sets the stage for our answer to the main question (section 4).

I. A "TWOFOLD PRIVILEGED ACCESS"

The term "privileged access" is due to Gilbert Ryle; on the Cartesian view that he is concerned to attack, "[a] mind has a twofold Privileged Access to its own doings" (Ryle 1949, 148). The first kind of privileged access is that:

(1) . . . a mind cannot help being constantly aware of all the supposed occupants of its private stage, and (2) . . . it can also deliberately scrutinize by a species of non-sensuous perception at least some of its own states and operations. (Ryle 1949, 148)

Thanks to audiences at the University of Oxford and Cal State Fullerton, and to Lauren Ashwell, Caspar Hare, Richard Holton, Rae Langton, JeeLoo Liu, Julia Markovits, Eric Schwitzgebel, Ralph Wedgwood, Tim Williamson, and Steve Yablo.

And the second kind is that:

both this constant awareness (generally called 'consciousness'), and this non-sensuous inner perception (generally called 'introspection') [are] exempt from error. (Ryle 1949, 149)

(1) in the first quotation together with the first conjunct of the second quotation basically amount to the claim that one's mental states are *self-intimating*: if one is in a mental state M, one knows (or believes) that one is in M.

Self-intimation is extremely implausible, at least with respect to the mental states that will be under discussion in what follows. Here is a perfectly ordinary *prima facie* example of believing that *p* (and possessing the relevant concepts) without knowing, or even being in a position to know, that one believes that *p*. Pam is now not in a position to retrieve the name of her new officemate (it is on 'the tip of her tongue,' say) and so is not in a position to verbally self-ascribe the belief that her officemate's name is 'Andy.' Nothing else in her behavior, we may suppose, indicates that she believes that she has this belief. But she nonetheless does believe now that her officemate's name is 'Andy,' because otherwise there would be no explanation of why she recalls the name later when taking the train home.[1]

Of more interest is (2) in the first quotation, the claim that one employs a kind of "non-sensuous perception" to find out about one's own mental life. Non-sensuous perception is supposed to work only in one's own case: according to Ryle's opponent, "I cannot introspectively observe … the workings of your mind" (Ryle 1949, 149). A more general version of (2), then, is the claim that one knows about one's mental life in a way that one cannot know about another's mental life. That is, one has a special method or way of knowing that one believes that *The Searchers* is playing at the Orpheum, that one wants to go to the movies, and so on, which one cannot use to discover the mental states of someone *else*. Since such a first-person method need not be epistemically privileged or authoritative, 'privileged access' is not ideal terminology. Instead, let us put the generalized (2) by saying that we have *peculiar* access to our mental states.

Ryle's second kind of "Privileged Access," "exemption from error," is evidently better-named. Infallibility sets the bar too high, though: a weaker and more useful claim is that our beliefs about our own mental states, arrived at by typical means, are more likely to amount to knowledge than

---

[1] And if Pam *does* believe that she believes that her officemate's name is 'Andy,' the question whether she believes *that* arises, and so on through progressively more iterations. This regress stops somewhere, presumably.

the corresponding beliefs about others' mental states and the corresponding beliefs about one's environment. (The latter comparison has clear application only for some mental states, paradigmatically belief.) Retaining Ryle's terminology, let us put this weaker claim by saying that we have *privileged* access to our mental states.

A number of authors (for instance, Alston 1971; McKinsey 1991; Moran 2001, 12–13), presumably following Ryle, use 'privileged access' for what is described in our preferred terminology as privileged *and* peculiar access. Whatever the labels, it is important to keep the two sorts of access separate.

The distinction between privileged and peculiar access is one thing; the claim that we actually have one or both sorts of access is another. Let us briefly review some evidence.

1.1 Privileged access

Consider Jim, sitting in his office cubicle. Jim believes that his pen looks black to him; that he wants a cup of tea; that he feels a dull pain in his knee; that he intends to answer all his emails today; that he is thinking about paperclips; that he believes that it is raining. Jim also has various equally humdrum beliefs about his environment: that it is raining, that his pen is black, and so on. Furthermore, he has some opinions about the psychology of his officemate Pam. He believes that her pen looks green to her; that she wants a cup of coffee; that her elbow feels itchy; that she is thinking about him; that she believes that it is raining.

In an ordinary situation of this kind, it is natural to think that Jim's beliefs about his current mental states are, by and large, more epistemically secure than his corresponding beliefs about his officemate Pam and his corresponding beliefs about his environment.

Take Jim's belief that he believes that it is raining, for example. It is easy to add details to the story so that Jim fails to know *that it is raining*; it is not so clear how to add details so that Jim fails to know that he *believes* that it is raining. Perhaps Jim believes that it is raining because Pam came in carrying a wet umbrella, but the rain stopped an hour ago. Jim is wrong about the rain, but he still knows that he *believes* that it is raining – this knowledge will be manifest from what he says and does.

Now contrast Jim's belief that he believes that it is raining with his belief that Pam believes that it is raining. Again, it is easy to add details to the story so that Jim fails to know that Pam believes that it is raining. Perhaps Jim believes that Pam believes that it is raining because he entered the office wearing a visibly wet raincoat. Yet Pam might well not have noticed that the raincoat was wet, or she might have noticed it but failed to draw the obvious conclusion.

Similar remarks go for Jim's belief that he wants a cup of tea, which can be contrasted with Jim's belief that Pam wants a cup of coffee. Now it may well be that, in general, beliefs about one's own desires are somewhat less secure than beliefs about one's own beliefs, or beliefs about how things look. This is more plausible with other examples, say Jim's belief that he wants to be the CEO of Dunder Mifflin Paper Company, Inc., or wants to forever remain single – it would not be particularly unusual to question whether Jim really has these particular ambitions. And perhaps, in the ordinary circumstances of the office, Jim might even be wrong about his desire for tea. Still, Jim's claim that he wants tea would usually be treated as pretty much unimpeachable, whereas his claim that Pam wants coffee is obviously fallible. (Jim's evidence points in that direction: Pam normally has coffee at this time, and is heading to the office kitchen. However, she drank her coffee earlier, and now wants a chocolate biscuit.) And treating Jim as authoritative about his own desires has nothing, or not much, to do with politeness or convention. Jim earns his authority by his subsequent behavior: Jim will drink an available cup of tea and be visibly satisfied.

The precise extent and strength of privileged access is disputable; the fact of it can hardly be denied.[2]

1.2 *Peculiar access*

Peculiar access is equally apparent. The importance of "third-person" evidence about one's mental life can easily be overlooked, but it is clear that one does not rely on such sources alone. Quietly sitting in his cubicle, Jim can know that he believes that it is raining and that he wants a cup of tea. No third-person or behavioral evidence is needed. To know that Pam wants a coffee requires a different sort of investigation – asking her, observing what she does, and so forth.

It is often claimed that one knows one's mind "directly," or "without evidence." (For the former see, e.g., Ayer 1959, 58; for the latter, see, e.g., Davidson 1991, 205.) If that is right, and if one knows others' minds

---

[2] Schwitzgebel (2011) argues that there is much about our own mental lives that we don't know, or that is difficult for us to find out, for instance the vividness of one's mental imagery, whether one has sexist attitudes, and so forth. His treatment of individual examples may be questioned, but his overall argument is an important corrective to the tendency to think of the mind as an internal stage entirely open to the subject's view. However, too much emphasis on this point can lead to the opposite vice, of thinking that self-knowledge poses no especially challenging set of epistemological problems.

"indirectly," or "with evidence," then this is what peculiar access consists in – at least in part. But such claims should be made at the end of inquiry, not at the beginning.

Sometimes peculiar access is glossed by saying that self-knowledge is "a priori" (e.g. McKinsey 1991; Boghossian 1997). This should be resisted – certainly at the beginning of inquiry, and probably at the end. One leading theory of self-knowledge classifies it as a variety of *perceptual* knowledge, in many respects like our perceptual knowledge of our environment. "The *Perception of the Operations of our own Minds* within us," according to Locke, "is very like [the perception of "External Material things"], and might properly enough be call'd internal Sense" (Locke [1689] 1975, 105). On this *inner-sense theory* (Armstrong 1968, 95; see also Lycan 1987, ch. 6; Nichols and Stich 2003, 160–4), we have an internal "scanner" specialized for the detection of our mental states. No doubt the hypothesized inner sense is not much like our outer senses – recall that Ryle characterizes it as "non-sensuous perception" – but it is surely unhelpful to classify its deliverances with our knowledge of mathematics and logic.[3]

1.3 The independence of privileged and peculiar access

It is important to distinguish privileged and peculiar access because they can come apart in both directions. Hence one can find theorists who deny that we have one kind of access while affirming that we have the other (for examples, see Byrne 2005, 81). As the previous two sections suggest, this extreme claim is not credible, but a more restricted version is actually correct. Privileged and peculiar access do not perfectly coincide: in particular, there are many ordinary cases of the latter without the former.

For instance, the epistemic security of self-ascriptions of certain emotions or moods is at the very least nothing to write home about. One may have peculiar access to the fact that one is depressed or anxious, but here the behaviorist greeting – "You're fine! How am I?" – is not much of a joke, being closer to ordinary wisdom.

Factive mental states, like *knowing that Ford directed The Searchers* and *remembering that the Orpheum closed down last week*, provide further examples.[4] Since knowing that Ford directed *The Searchers* entails that Ford

---

[3] See McFetridge (1990, 221–2); Davies (1998, 323). The classification of (much) self-knowledge as *a priori* has its roots in Kant's definition of *a priori* knowledge as "knowledge absolutely independent of all experience" (Kant [1787] 1933, B3); see McFetridge (1990, 225) and McGinn (1975/6, 203).

[4] For a defense of the claim that knowing is a mental state, see Williamson (1995).

directed *The Searchers*, but not conversely, it is easier to know the latter fact than to know that one knows it.[5] The belief that one knows that Ford directed *The Searchers* is *less* likely to amount to knowledge than the belief that Ford directed *The Searchers*. Yet one has peculiar access to the fact that one knows that Ford directed *The Searchers*, just as one has peculiar access to the fact that one believes this proposition. Jim knows that Pam knows that Ford directed *The Searchers* because (say) he knows she is a movie buff and such people generally know basic facts about John Ford. But in order to know that he knows that Ford directed *The Searchers*, Jim need not appeal to this kind of evidence about himself.

2. BELIEF AND BEL

How does one know what one believes? Evans suggested an answer: "in making a self-ascription of belief, one's eyes are, so to speak, or occasionally literally, directed outward – upon the world" (1982a, 225). Different ways of elaborating Evans' telegraphic remarks have been proposed by Gordon (1995), Gallois (1996), Moran (2001), Byrne (2005), and Fernández (2005). In brief, here is the proposal in Byrne (2005).

First, a small amount of technical apparatus. Say that an *epistemic rule* is a conditional of the following form:

R If conditions C obtain, believe that *p*.

An example is:

WEATHER If the clouds are dark gray, believe that it will rain soon.

One *follows* WEATHER on a particular occasion iff one believes that it will rain soon because one recognizes that the clouds are dark gray, where the 'because' is intended to mark the kind of causal connection characteristic of inference or reasoning. In general, S follows rule R on a particular occasion iff on that occasion S believes that *p* because she recognizes that conditions C obtain, which implies (a) S knows that conditions C obtain, which in turn implies (b) conditions C obtain, and (c) S believes that *p*.

Following WEATHER in typical circumstances tends to produce knowledge about impending rain; rules that are knowledge-conducive are *good* rules.

Now we can put an Evans-inspired proposal for the epistemology of belief as follows. Knowledge of one's beliefs can be obtained by following the rule:

---

[5] With the assumption that the "KK principle" (if one knows that *p*, one knows that one knows that *p*) is false.

BEL If *p*, believe that you believe that *p*.[6]

But is BEL a *good* rule, as the proposal implies? It might seem not, because its third-person counterpart is plainly a *bad* rule:

BEL-3 If *p*, believe that Pam believes that *p*.

It would be quite a stretch, for instance, to reason from the fact that I have a quarter in my pocket, or that the Philadelphia Phillies were originally known as the 'Quakers,' to the conclusion that Pam believes these things – most likely she does not. Following BEL-3 will thus tend to produce false and unjustified beliefs. Isn't BEL just as dodgy?

Fortunately not. BEL, unlike BEL-3, is *self-verifying*: if one follows it one's second-order belief is true.[7] In this respect it is an even better rule than WEATHER – that rule is good, but following it does not guarantee that one will have a true belief about the rain.

The virtues of BEL do not stop there. Say that S *tries* to follow R iff S believes that *p* because she *believes* that conditions C obtain; hence *trying to follow R* is weaker than *following R*.[8] Trying to follow WEATHER is not truth-conducive, hence not knowledge-conducive. In contrast, trying to follow BEL is maximally truth-conducive: if one tries to follow it, one's second-order belief is true. We can put this by saying that BEL is *strongly* self-verifying. (Self-verification is thus weaker than strong self-verification.)

The Evans-inspired proposal of a few paragraphs back only covers cases where one's belief that *p* amounts to knowledge, but of course one may know that one believes that *p* even though one's belief that *p* is false, or anyway does not amount to knowledge. In the terminology just introduced, the fully general proposal for the epistemology of belief is this:

BELIEF Knowledge of one's beliefs can be, and typically is, obtained by trying to follow BEL.

BELIEF implies that *trying* to follow BEL is knowledge-conducive – that BEL is a *very* good rule.

Now true beliefs, or even true beliefs that could not easily have been false, are not thereby knowledge. So the fact that BEL is strongly self-verifying does not *entail* that it is a very good rule. It does, however, rebut an obvious

---

[6] 'You' refers to the rule-follower; tenses are to be interpreted so that the time the rule is followed counts as the present.

[7] A qualification: since inference takes time, it is not impossible that one's belief in the premise vanishes when one reaches the conclusion. Since the inference is as simple and as short at they come, this qualification is of little significance.

[8] Assuming that '. . . because S knows P' entails '. . . because S believes P.'

objection. And given the intuitive plausibility of Evans' claim that we know what we believe by "directing our eyes outward," the burden of proof is on the critics. BELIEF is at least a defensible working hypothesis.

BELIEF, if true, offers a satisfying explanation of both privileged and peculiar access. Privileged access is explained because BEL is strongly self-verifying. Peculiar access is explained because the method involved only works in one's own case: third-person rules like BEL-3 are bad.

For the sake of the argument, assume that BELIEF is true. Is there any need to press on, and try to force all self-knowledge – *a fortiori*, knowledge of one's desires – into this rough mold?

3. ECONOMY AND UNIFICATION

In answering that question, two distinctions will be helpful. To introduce the first, consider our knowledge of metaphysical modality. On one (popular) view, it requires a special epistemic capacity of modal intuition. On the alternative Williamsonian picture, it requires nothing more than our "general cognitive ability to handle counterfactual conditionals" (Williamson 2004, 13), such as "If it had rained I would have taken my umbrella." The Williamsonian view is an *economical* account of our knowledge of metaphysical modality: all it takes are epistemic capacities required for other domains. The popular view, on the other hand, is *extravagant*: knowledge of metaphysical modality needs something extra.

A similar "economical–extravagant" distinction can be drawn for self-knowledge. Let us say that a theory of self-knowledge is *economical* just in case it purports to explain self-knowledge solely in terms of epistemic capacities and abilities that are needed for knowledge of other subject matters; otherwise it is *extravagant*. A behaviorist account of self-knowledge is economical: the capacities for *self*-knowledge are precisely the capacities for knowledge of the minds of *others*. The theory defended in Shoemaker 1994 is also economical: here the relevant capacities are "normal intelligence, rationality, and conceptual capacity" (Shoemaker 1994, 236). On the other hand, the inner-sense theory (see section 1.2 above) is *extravagant*: the organs of outer perception, our general rational capacity, and so forth, do not account for all our self-knowledge. For that, an additional mechanism, an "internal scanner," is needed.

The second distinction is between *unified* and *disunified* theories of self-knowledge. Simple versions of the behaviorist and inner-sense theories are unified: for any mental state M, the account of how one knows one is in M is broadly the same – by observing one's behavior, or by deploying one's "internal scanner." But some philosophers adopt a divide-and-conquer strategy, resulting in more-or-less disunified theories. For instance, Davidson (1984) and Moran (2001) offer accounts chiefly of our knowledge of the propositional attitudes, in particular, belief. Knowledge of one's sensations, on the other hand, is taken to require a quite different theory, which neither of them pretends to supply. "[T]he case of sensations," Moran writes, "raises issues for self-knowledge quite different from the case of attitudes of various kinds" (Moran 2001, 10). Similar divisions, although less sharply emphasized, are present in the theories of self-knowledge defended in Goldman (1993) and Nichols and Stich (2003).

There is a case for unification. Suppose that the epistemic capacities one employs to know one's sensations are quite different from the capacities employed to know what one believes. As an illustration, suppose that the account just sketched for belief is correct, and that one knows one's sensations by employing (in part) a dedicated mechanism of inner-sense. Then dissociations are to be expected. In particular, a person's internal scanner could be inoperable, sparing her capacity to find out via BEL what she believes. Such a person would exhibit pain behavior like the rest of us. But does she *feel* an itch in her shin? "Well, probably, since I just caught myself scratching it."

Since such dissociations never seem to occur, this indicates that the epistemology of mental states draws on fundamentally the same capacity, in the sense that individual capacities to know that one is in particular kinds of mental state are a package deal. The capacity to know what one believes, for example, brings in its train the capacity to know that one sees a tomato, feels an itch, and wants a beer.

And since the capacity to know what one believes merely involves our general cognitive capacity for reasoning or inference from (typically) worldly premises to mental conclusions (as BELIEF implies), that capacity should also allow one knowledge of one's other mental states. And if it does, then the correct theory of self-knowledge is economical. Roughly put, our general capacity for reasoning about the world suffices for knowledge of our own minds.

But how can the account for belief be extended to desire? According to Nichols and Stich, it clearly cannot:

we can answer ... questions about current desires, intentions, and imaginings, questions like: 'What do you want to do?'; 'What are you going to do?'; 'What are you imagining?' Our ability to answer these questions suggests that the ascent routine strategy [i.e. the Evans-style procedure[9]] simply cannot accommodate

---

[9] "Ascent routine strategy" is a phrase of Gordon's (1996), whom Nichols and Stich are specifically criticizing.

many central cases of self-awareness. There is no plausible way of recasting these questions so that they are questions about the world rather than about one's mental state. As a result, the ascent routine strategy strikes us as clearly inadequate as a general theory of self-awareness. (Nichols and Stich 2003, 194)

Finkelstein agrees:

[I]t is difficult to claim that the self-ascription of belief [à la Evans] provides a model of self-knowledge that can be used in order to understand our awareness of our own, say, desires because there seems to be no "outward-directed" question that bears the kind of relation to "Do I want X?" that the question "Is it the case that *p*?" bears to "Do I believe that *p*?"(Finkelstein 2003, 161)[10]

If these philosophers are right, and the world-to-mind account that seems so promising for belief is hopeless for desire, then the account for belief should be rejected too. (Nichols and Stich, at least, reject it.) Contrariwise, if the world-to-mind account for belief is right, then there must be a similar account that works for desire. The next section takes up the challenge of finding it.

4. DESIRE[11]

In fact, the previous two quotations are far too pessimistic. Although it might superficially appear that "there is no plausible way of recasting" a question about one's desires as a "question about the world," a second glance suggests otherwise. The issue of where to dine arises, say. My accommodating companion asks me whether I want to go to the sushi bar across town or the Indian restaurant across the street.[12] In answering that question, I attend to the advantages and drawbacks of the two options: the tastiness of Japanese and Indian food, the cool Zen aesthetic of the sushi bar compared to the busy garish décor of the Indian restaurant, the bother of getting across town compared to the convenience of walking across the street, and so on. In other words, I weigh the *reasons* for the two options – the "considerations that count in favor," as Scanlon puts it (1998, 17), of going to either place. These reasons are not facts about my present psychological states; indeed, many of them are not psychological facts at all.[13]

---

[10] See also Goldman (2000, 182–83); Bar-On (2004, 114–18).

[11] For accounts related to the one defended in this section (itself an elaboration of the last few pages of Byrne 2005), see Shoemaker (1988, 47–48), Moran (2001, especially 114–16), and Fernández (2007). Ashwell (2009) has a critical discussion of Fernández's proposal and the present one.

[12] Although there are differences of usage between 'desire' and 'want,' in this chapter the two are treated as equivalent. The semantics and pragmatics of these verbs are relevant to the argument of this chapter, but are not discussed for reasons of space.

[13] On reasons as facts see, e.g., Thomson (2008, 127–28).

Suppose I determine that the Indian option is the best – that there is most reason to go to the Indian restaurant. (This might be the result of agonized deliberation; more typically, it will be a snap judgment.) Once I have this result in hand, which is not (at least on the face of it), a fact about my present desires, I then reply that I want to go to the Indian restaurant.

This example is one in which I "make up my mind" and form a new desire: prior to being asked, I lacked the desire to go to the Indian restaurant. But the Evans-style point about looking "outward – upon the world" still holds when I have wanted to go to the Indian restaurant for some time. Of course, often when in such a condition, I can recall that I want to go. But on other occasions the process seems less direct. What immediately comes to mind is the non-psychological fact that the Indian restaurant is the best option; and (apparently) it is by recalling this that I conclude I want to go there.[14]

An initial stab at the relevant rule for desire – specifically, the desire to act in a certain way[15] – is therefore this:

DES* If φing is the best option, believe that you want to φ.

This is not a bad fit for a restricted range of cases, but the general hypothesis that we typically know what we want by following (or trying to follow) DES* has some obvious problems. In particular, the hypothesis both under-generates, failing to account for much knowledge of our desires, and over-generates, predicting judgments that we do not make.

To illustrate under-generation, suppose that I am in the happy condition of also wanting to eat at the sushi bar. Eating at either place would be delightful, although on balance I prefer the Indian option. In such a situation, I can easily know that I want to eat at the sushi bar, despite not judging it to be the best option.[16]

To illustrate over-generation, suppose that I really dislike both Japanese and Indian cuisine, and I do not much care for my companion's company either. Still, he would be terribly offended if I bailed out of dinner, and would refuse to publish my poetry. I do not *want* to eat at the Indian restaurant but – as children are often told – sometimes you have to do

---

[14] Compare the discussion of Moran (2001) in Byrne (2005, 82–85).

[15] Many desires are for other things, of course, some involving oneself and some not: one may want to be awarded the Nobel Prize, or want Pam to get promoted, or want global warming to end, and so forth. These other sorts of desires do not raise any intractable difficulties of their own, and so for simplicity only desires to act in a certain way will be explicitly treated.

[16] As this case illustrates, to want something is not to prefer it over all other options. For reasons of space, this chapter concentrates on the epistemology of desire, not the (closely related) epistemology of preference.

something you do not want to do. The Indian is the best of a bad bunch of options, and I accordingly choose it. Despite knowing that eating at the Indian restaurant is the best course of action, I do not follow DES* and judge that I want to eat there. Later, in between mouthfuls of unpleasantly spicy curry, I hear my companion droning on about his golf swing, and I think to myself that I really do not want to be doing this.

The description of this example might raise eyebrows, since it is something of a philosophical dogma that intentional action invariably involves desire – on this view, if I slouch to the Indian restaurant, resigned to a miserable evening, I nonetheless must have wanted to go there. Whether this is anything more than dogma can be set aside, because (wearing my Plain Man hat) I will not agree that I want to go to the Indian restaurant. So, even if I do want to go to the Indian restaurant, I am ignorant of this fact, and what primarily needs explaining is the Plain Man's self-knowledge, not the self-knowledge of sophisticated theorists.[17]

In the under-generation example, why do I think I want to go to the sushi bar? Going there is not the *best* option, all things considered, but it is a *good* option, or (much better) a *desirable* one, in the *Oxford English Dictionary* sense of having "the qualities which cause a thing to be desired: Pleasant, delectable, choice, excellent, goodly." Going to the sushi bar is not merely desirable *in some respects*, but desirable *tout court*. The sushi bar is a short cab ride away, the saba is delicious, an agreeable time is assured, and so on. If the Indian restaurant turns out to be closed, that is no cause to investigate other alternatives: going home and heating up some leftovers, getting takeaway pizza, and so on. The sushi bar is a more than adequate alternative. In the over-generation example, by contrast, the Indian option is not desirable, despite being the best.

---

[17] One of the main contemporary sources for the philosophical dogma is Nagel:

whatever may be the motivation for someone's intentional pursuit of a goal, it becomes in virtue of his pursuit *ipso facto* appropriate to ascribe to him a desire for that goal . . . Therefore it may be admitted as trivial that, for example, considerations about my future welfare or about the interests of others cannot motivate me to act without a desire being present at the time of action. That I have the appropriate desire simply *follows from* the fact that these considerations motivate me . . .(Nagel 1970, 29)

But Nagel gives no actual argument. His conclusion does not follow from the fact that "someone's intentional pursuit of a goal" requires *more than belief*, because there are many candidates other than desire that can take up the slack, for instance intention.

A charitable interpretation is that Nagel is using 'desire' in the technical Davidsonian sense, to mean something like "pro-attitude" (cf. Dancy 2000, 11). That appears to be true of some other philosophers who follow him, such as Smith (1994, ch. 4), although not of Schueler (1995). According to Schueler, Nagel's claim is false in one sense of 'desire,' and true in another "perfectly good sense" of the word (29). However, he provides little reason to think that 'desire' is ambiguous in this way.

So these two problems can both apparently be solved simply by replacing 'best' in DES* by 'desirable,' yielding the rule:

DES If ϕing is a desirable option, believe that you want to ϕ.

And the hypothesis corresponding to BELIEF (section 2) is:

DESIRE Knowledge of one's desires is typically obtained by trying to follow DES.[18]

If DESIRE is true, then DES is a *good* (knowledge-conducive) rule. So let us now examine whether it is – if it is not, other objections are moot.

The rule BEL, recall, is:

BEL If *p*, believe that you believe that *p*.

As noted in section 2, BEL is *self-verifying*: if one follows it one's second-order belief is true. As argued in that section, this observation defuses the objection that following BEL cannot yield knowledge because the fact that *p* is not a reliable indication that one believes that *p*.

A similar objection applies to DES: that ϕing is a desirable option is not a reliable indication that one wants to ϕ. Pam's walking three miles to work tomorrow is desirable, because she'll then avoid hours in an unexpected traffic jam, and get promoted for her foresight and dedication, yet (not knowing these facts) Pam wants only to drive.

Unfortunately, a similar reply does not work: DES is *not* self-verifying. Cases of accidie are compelling examples. Lying on the sofa, wallowing in my own misery, I know that going for a bike ride by the river is a desirable option. The sun is shining, the birds are twittering, the exercise and the scenery will cheer me up; these facts are easy for me to know, and my torpor does not prevent me from knowing them. If I concluded that I want to go cycling, I would be wrong. If I really did want to go, why am I still lying on this sofa? It is not that I have a stronger desire to stay put – I couldn't care less, one way or the other.

Still, this example is atypical. One's desires tend to line up with one's knowledge of the desirability of the options; that is, known desirable options tend to be desired. (Whether this is a contingent fact, or a constitutive fact about desire or rationality, can for present purposes be left unexamined.) What's more, even though there arguably are cases where one knows that ϕing is desirable and mistakenly follows DES, ending up with a false belief about what one wants, the case just described is not one of them.

---

[18] Note that DESIRE does *not* imply that there are no other ways of gaining knowledge of one's desires (a similar remark applies to BELIEF, in section 2 above).

I know that cycling is desirable yet fail to want to go cycling, but I do not follow DES and falsely believe that I want to go cycling. Lying on the sofa, it is perfectly clear to me that I do not want to go cycling. (Just why this is so will be examined later, in section 4.2.)

Thus, although DES is not self-verifying, it is (what we can call) *practically* self-verifying: for the most part, if Pam follows DES, her belief about what she wants will be true. And that is enough to rebut the parallel objection that following DES cannot yield knowledge because the fact that φing is a desirable option is not a reliable indication that one wants to φ. Again, this does not *entail* that DES is a good rule, but the burden of proof should be on those who think it is not.

As also noted in section 2, BEL is *strongly* self-verifying. That is, if one *tries* to follow it – if one believes that one believes that p because one believes that p – then one's second-order belief is true. That feature of BEL is the key to explaining privileged access for belief. Similarly, since one's desires tend to line up with one's *beliefs* about the desirability of the options, whether or not those beliefs are actually true, DES is *strongly* practically self-verifying. Privileged access to one's beliefs and desires can therefore be explained in basically the same way.

At this point a worry about circularity might arise: perhaps, in order to find out that something is desirable, one has to have some prior knowledge of one's desires. If that is right, then at the very least a significant amount of one's knowledge of one's desires remains unexplained. The next section examines some variations on this theme.

4.1 Desirable and Desired

According to the *circularity objection*, in order to follow DES, one has to have some knowledge of one's desires beforehand. (The difference between *following* DES and *trying* to follow it only complicates matters while leaving the basic objection intact, so let us focus exclusively on the former.[19])

In its crudest form, the objection is simply that the relevant sense of "desirable option" can only mean *desired* option. If that is so, then DES is certainly a good rule, but only in a trivial limiting sense. Unpacked, it is simply the rule: if you want to φ, believe that you want to φ. And to say that

---

[19] A quick way of seeing that the distinction is of no help is just to consider someone who always knows which options are desirable. She always follows DES, and never merely tries to. If the circularity objection applies here, then only desperate measures can save the account elsewhere.

one follows *this* rule in order to gain knowledge of one's desire to φ is to say that one comes to know that one wants to φ because one recognizes that one wants to φ. True enough, but hardly helpful.

However, this version of the circularity objection is a little *too* crude, leaving no room for any other features to count towards the desirability of an option. (Recall examples of such features quoted from the *OED*: "pleasant, delectable, choice, excellent, goodly.") A slightly less crude version admits that other features are relevant, but insists that a necessary condition for an option's being desirable is that one desire it. Is this at all plausible?

No. As many examples in the recent literature on "reasons" bring out, desires rarely figure as considerations for or against an action, even the restricted set of considerations that bear on whether an action is desirable. The Indian restaurant example is a case in point. Here is another. Suppose I see that an interesting discussion about the mind–body problem has started in the department lounge, and I am deciding whether to join in and sort out the conceptual confusion. I wonder whether the participants would applaud my incisive remarks, or whether I might commit some terrible fallacy and be overcome with embarrassment, but I do not wonder whether I *want* to join in. Suppose I want to attend a meeting which is starting soon, and that this desire will be frustrated if I stop to join the discussion in the lounge. I do not take *this* to be a consideration in favor of not joining in, but rather (say) the fact that turning up late to the meeting will be thought very rude.

The force of these sorts of examples can be obscured by conflating two senses of 'reason.' Suppose I want to join the discussion, and that is what I do. So *a reason why* I joined in was that I wanted to. Doesn't that show, after all, that my wanting to join in *was* a reason, namely a *reason for* joining in? No, it does not. That I wanted to join the discussion is a reason in the *explanatory* sense, as in "The failure of the blow-out preventer was the reason why the Deep Water Horizon exploded." But it does not follow that this fact is a reason in the (operative) *normative* sense, the "consideration in favor" sense of 'reason.'

There is no straightforward connection between an option's being desirable and its actually being desired that would support a version of the circularity objection. Could a connection between desirability and one's *counterfactual* desires do any better?

As an illustration, consider the claim that φing is desirable iff if conditions were "ideal," the agent would want to φ. All such analyses have well-known problems; for the sake of the argument let us suppose that this one is correct.[20] (Since the right-hand side is surely not *synonymous* with the left, take the biconditional merely to state a necessary equivalence.) Does this analysis of desirability suggest that sometimes one needs prior knowledge of one's desires to find out that φing is desirable?

First, take a case where one is not in ideal conditions. To return to the example at the end of the previous section, suppose I am lying miserably on the sofa. I know that cycling is desirable; I also know, let us grant, the supposed equivalent counterfactual, that if conditions were ideal, I would want to go cycling. In order for circularity to be a worry here, it would have to be established that (a) I know that cycling is desirable by inferring it from the counterfactual, and (b) I need to know something about my present desires in order to know the counterfactual. Now whatever "ideal conditions" are exactly, they are intended to remove the barriers to desiring the desirable – drunkenness, depression, ignorance, and so on. And, although I do not actually want to get on my bike, the enjoyment and invigorating effects of cycling are apparent to me. Regarding (b), it is quite unclear why I need to know anything about my present desires to know that if the scales of listlessness were to fall from my eyes I would desire the manifestly desirable. And regarding (a), the most natural direction of inference is from left to right, rather than vice versa: my knowledge of the desirability of cycling – specifically, its enjoyment and invigorating effects – come first, not my knowledge of the counterfactual.

Second, take a case where one is in ideal conditions. I am lying on the sofa, not at all miserable. I know that cycling is desirable, and I know that I want to go cycling. I also know, we may grant, that conditions are ideal. Given the equivalence, do I know that cycling is desirable by inferring it from the counterfactual, which I infer in turn from truth of both the antecedent and the consequent? If so, then there is a clear problem of circularity. But how do I know that the antecedent is true, that conditions *are* ideal? Since the chief purchase I have on "ideal conditions" is that they allow me to desire the desirable, the obvious answer is that I know that conditions are ideal because I know that cycling is desirable and that I want to go cycling. But then the epistemological direction is again from left to right, rather than – as the objector would have it – from right to left. If I know that cycling is desirable prior to knowing that conditions are ideal, then (granted the equivalence) I can infer the counterfactual from the fact that cycling is desirable.

[20] For a more sophisticated attempt see Smith (1994, ch. 5). It is worth noting that Smith's conception of an act's being desirable, namely the agent's having "normative reason to do [it]" (132), is broader than the conception in play here.

The circularity objection is, at the very least, hard to make stick. Let us now turn to some complications.

4.2 *Des and Defeasibility*

To say that we typically follow (or try to follow) rule R is not to say that we always do. The rule WEATHER ("If the skies are dark gray, believe that it will rain soon") is a good enough rule of thumb, but it is *defeasible* – additional evidence (or apparent evidence) can block the inference from the premise about the skies to the conclusion about rain. For example, if one knows (or believes) that the trusted weather forecaster has confidently predicted a dry but overcast day, one might not believe that it will rain soon despite knowing (or believing) that the skies are dark gray.

Given that DES is only *practically* (strongly) self-verifying, one might expect that rule to be defeasible too. And indeed the example of accidie, used earlier to show that DES is only practically self-verifying, also shows that it is defeasible.

In that example, I am lying miserably on the sofa, contemplating the pleasures of a bike ride in the sunshine. This is not just a situation in which I know that cycling is a desirable option but nevertheless do not want to go cycling. It is also a situation in which I do not *believe* that I want to go cycling. Yet if I slavishly followed DES, I would believe that I wanted to go cycling. So why don't I?

I believe that I am not going to go cycling, but that is not why I do not think I want to go: I sometimes take myself to want to φ when I believe that I am not going to. For example, I really want to read *Mind and World* this evening, but that is not going to happen because I do not have the book with me.

A better suggestion is that I believe I do not want to go cycling because I believe I *intend* to remain on the sofa. I do *not* believe I intend to avoid reading *Mind and World* this evening, so at least the suggestion does not falsely predict that I will take myself to lack the desire to read *Mind and World*. However, it is obviously not right as it stands. Suppose, to return to the earlier restaurant example, I want to go both to the Indian restaurant and to the sushi bar, and I then form the intention to go to the Indian restaurant, on the grounds that this option is slightly more desirable. When I realize that I have this intention, I will not thereby refuse to ascribe a desire to go to the sushi bar: if the Indian restaurant turns out to be closed, I might say to my companion "No worries, I also wanted to eat Japanese."

This highlights a crucial difference between the cycling and restaurant examples: in the cycling case I do not think that remaining on the sofa is a desirable option – I intend to stay there despite realizing that there is little to be said for doing so. I do not think I want to go cycling because, if I did, why on earth don't I go? The means to go cycling are ready to hand, and the alternative is quite undesirable.

In general, then, this is one way in which DES can be defeated. Suppose one knows that ϕing is a desirable option, and considers the question of whether one wants to ϕ. One will not follow DES and conclude one wants to ϕ, if one believes (a) that one intends to ψ, (b) that ψing is incompatible with ϕing, and (c) that ψing is neither desirable nor better overall than ϕing.

That explains why I do not follow DES in the cycling case, and so do not take myself to want to go cycling. Here the action I intend is not the one I think desirable, and neither is it the one I think best, all things considered. More common cases of action without desire are when the intended action *is* taken to be the best, as in the earlier restaurant example with the tedious dinner companion. Dinner at the Indian restaurant will be terribly boring and I will not have a good time; nonetheless, it is the best course of action available, perhaps even beating out other options (like staying at home with a good book) that are actually desirable. I intend to go, but I really do not want to.

Something else needs explaining, though. It is not just that I fail to believe that I want to go cycling – I also know that I lack this desire. I also know that I lack the desire to go to the Indian restaurant. So how do I know that I *do not* want to go cycling, or do not want to go to the Indian restaurant? (Read these with the negation taking wide scope: not wanting to go, as opposed to wanting not to go.)

In the boring dinner example, I know that going to the Indian restaurant is not desirable – indeed, it is positively undesirable. An obvious explanation of how I know that I do not want to go is that I follow this rule:

NODES If ϕing is an undesirable option, believe that you do not want to ϕ.[21]

NODES does not apply in the accidie example, of course, because I know that cycling is desirable. But the earlier discussion of that case already shows how I know that I lack the desire to cycle: if I really have that desire, what is to stop me getting on my bike? The gleaming marvel of Italian engineering is right there, and staying on the sofa has nothing to be said for it.

---

[21] A similar explanation can be given of the truth of the narrow scope reading – why I also know that I want not to go to the Indian restaurant.

CONCLUSION

As the discussion of the last section brings out, the epistemology of desire is not self-contained, in at least two ways.

First, although one's own desires are not among the features that make for the desirability of an option, one's other mental states sometimes are. For instance, I might well conclude that I want to go to the Indian restaurant partly on the basis of the fact that I *like* Indian food: I like, say, andar palak and plain naans. Liking andar palak (in the usual sense in which one likes a kind of food) is not to be equated with wanting to eat it. One may want to eat broccoli for health reasons without liking it; conversely, one may like double bacon cheeseburgers but not want to eat one. Liking andar palak is doubtfully any kind of desire at all. There is no clear circularity worry here, but the considerations of section 3 indicate that the epistemology of likings should be in the same world-to-mind style. And initially, that is not at all implausible: if I sample andar palak for the first time, and someone asks me if I like it, I turn my attention to its flavor. Does it taste good or bad? There is little reason to think that this involves investigating my own mind, as opposed to the andar palak itself: a lowly rat, who is presumably short on self-knowledge, can easily detect good and bad tastes.[22]

Second, the last section suggested that the complete epistemology of desire partly depends on the epistemology of intention. And in any event, given the case for a unified theory of self-knowledge, if intention cannot be squeezed into the world-to-mind format, that casts doubt on the account defended here. At least that is an excuse for another paper.[23]

---

[22] See, e.g., Berridge and Robinson (2003, 509).   [23] Namely Byrne (2011).

CHAPTER 8

Self-ignorance

Eric Schwitzgebel

I. A BRIEF HISTORICAL POLEMIC

Philosophers tend to be impressed by human self-knowledge. Descartes ([1641] 1984) thought our knowledge of our own stream of experience was the secure and indubitable foundation upon which to build our knowledge of the rest of the world. Hume – who was capable of being skeptical about almost anything – said that the only existences we can be certain of are our own sensory and imagistic experiences ([1739] 1978, 212). Perhaps the most prominent writer on self-knowledge in contemporary philosophy is Sydney Shoemaker. The central aim of much of his work has been to show that certain sorts of error are impossible (1963, 1988, 1994). David Chalmers has likewise attempted to show that, for a suitably constrained class of beliefs about one's own consciousness, error is impossible (2010). Even philosophers most of the community regard as pessimistic about self-knowledge of consciousness seem to me, really, to be fairly optimistic. Paul Churchland, famous for his relative disdain of ordinary people's knowledge about the mind, nonetheless compares the accuracy of introspection to the accuracy of sense perception – pretty good, presumably, about ordinary, medium-sized matters (1985, 1988). Daniel Dennett, often cited as a pessimist about introspective report, actually says that we can come close to infallibility when charitably interpreted (2002).

The above references concern knowledge of the stream of conscious experience, but philosophers have also tended to be impressed with our self-knowledge of our attitudes, such as our beliefs and desires. Consider this: although I can be wrong about its being sunny outside, I cannot in the same way be wrong, it seems, about the fact that I *think* it is sunny outside. Some philosophers have argued that this accuracy is due to the operation of a fairly simple and straightforward self-detection mechanism that takes our attitudes as inputs and produces beliefs about those attitudes as outputs, a mechanism so simple that it rarely errs (e.g. Nichols and Stich 2003;

Goldman 2006). Others have argued that our attitudes, at least some of them, can contain each other in a self-fulfilling way, so that my thought or belief that I think that it is sunny in some sense literally contains as a part the thought or belief that it is sunny.[1] Alex Byrne (this volume) argues that we typically ascribe beliefs by following a rule ("if *p*, believe that you believe that *p*") that is, he says, "strongly self-verifying": merely attempting to follow the rule renders the self-ascription true.

From Descartes to the present, the philosophical literature on self-knowledge of consciousness and attitudes has focused, with a few exceptions, on statements of or attempted explanations of the fact that we know ourselves remarkably well. Even those philosophers who portray themselves as at variance with this tradition have mostly been exercised to concoct bizarre or pathological scenarios designed to show that although our self-knowledge about our attitudes or current conscious experience may be excellent, it is not *wholly* infallible (e.g. Armstrong 1963; Churchland 1988). The debate, that is, has been between the infallibilists and the not-quite-infallibilists. I, however, am inclined to think we do not know our stream of consciousness or our own attitudes very well at all.

II. OF CONSCIOUS EXPERIENCE

First, consider currently ongoing conscious experience. Suppose you are looking directly at a sizeable red object in good light and normal conditions. You judge that you are having the visual experience of red. How could you possibly be wrong about that? Or suppose someone has just dropped a sixty-pound barbell on your toe. You judge that you are feeling pain. How could you possibly be wrong about that either?

Well, in such cases I am inclined to think it *is* highly unlikely that one would go wrong. But the question is this: How *representative* are such cases? Does the apparent difficulty of going wrong in simple judgments about color and pain experiences in canonical conditions reflect the *general* security of our judgments about our ongoing stream of conscious experience, or are those cases exceptional, best cases? Optimists about our self-knowledge of our conscious experience tend to focus on *exactly* the cases of seeing red and feeling pain, generalizing from there, thus implicitly treating those cases as typical.

---

[1] The characterization is a bit simplified, but Burge (1988, 1996), Heil (1988), Dretske (1995), and Shoemaker (1995) have said things along roughly these lines.

Why not start somewhere else for a change? Close your eyes and form a visual image. (Go ahead and do it now if you want.) Imagine, for example, the front of your house as viewed from the street. Assuming that you can in fact form such imagery, consider this: How well do you know, right now, that imagery experience? You know, I assume, *that* you have an image, and you know some aspects of its content – that it is your house, say, from a particular point of view. But that is not really to say very much yet about your imagery experience. Consider these further questions:

How much of the scene can you vividly visualize at once? Can you keep the image of the chimney vividly in mind at the same time you vividly imagine your front door? Or does the image of the chimney fade as you start to think about the door? How much detail does your image have? How stable is it? Supposing you cannot visually imagine the entire front of your house in rich detail all at once, what happens to the aspects of the image that are relatively less detailed? If the chimney is still experienced as part of your imagery when your image-making energies are focused on the front door, how exactly is it experienced? Does it have determinate shape, determinate color? In general, do the objects in your image have color before you think to assign color to them, or do some of the colors remain indeterminate, at least for a while? If there is indeterminacy of color, how is that indeterminacy experienced? As gray? Does your visual image have depth in the same way your sensory visual experience does, or is your imagery somehow flatter, more sketch-like or picture-like? Is it located in subjective space? Does it seem in some way as though the image is in your head, or in front of your forehead, or before your eyes? Or does it seem wrong to say that the image is experienced as though *located* anywhere at all? How much is your visual imagery like the experience of seeing a picture, or having phosphenes, or afterimages, or dreams, or daydreams?[2]

Now these are pretty substantial questions about your imagery experience. They are not piddling details, but questions about major-to-middle-sized features of the visual imagery that is presumably currently ongoing in you right now. If I asked you questions at that level of detail about an ordinary external object near to hand, you would have no trouble at all – about a

---

[2] Jason Ford (in print: Ford 2008) and others (in conversation) have suggested that earlier versions of this exercise (Schwitzgebel 2002a) depend on illegitimate questions about the periphery of experience – questions only appropriate to more detailed, central experience. I believe that this objection is misguided: While it might be illegitimate to ask exactly what specific colors and shapes inhabit the periphery (if the periphery is indistinct), it does not seem to me in the same way illegitimate to ask *whether* colors and shapes in the periphery are clear or indistinct. However, I have heard this objection so often now that I worry there might be something to it that I stupidly or stubbornly refuse to see. Consequently, I now include more questions that do not concern the periphery.

book, say. How stable is it? Does it flash in and out of existence? Does its cover have a durable color? What happens to its shape (its real shape, not its "apparent shape") when you open it up, spin it around, look at the underside? These questions present no difficulty. And yet most of the people I have talked to find that questions at this level of detail about their conscious experience of imagery are somewhat difficult. In fact, I think people often simply *get it wrong* when they think about their imagery experience. One kind of evidence for this is the failure of psychologists, in more than one hundred years of research, to find any real relationship between people's self-reports about their imagery and their performance on cognitive tasks that would presumably be facilitated by imagery. For example, some people say they have imagery as vivid and detailed as ordinary vision, or even more so. Others claim to have no imagery at all. And yet these self-described high- and low-imagery people do not appear to perform any differently, in general, on psychological tests that have widely been thought to be aided by visual imagery – tasks like mental rotation, or mental folding (where you are asked to guess what something would look like when folded or unfolded), or tests of visual memory, or tests of visual creativity (Schwitzgebel 2002a, 2011).

Now of course people might still be quite accurate in their judgments about their visual imagery, even if the differences in their judgments do not correspond to any sort of performance differences in behavioral tests. Maybe phenomenological differences are irrelevant to behavioral performance, or at least performance on the sorts of tasks that psychologists have so far concocted. But if you share my intuitive sense that it feels somehow difficult to introspect your imagery – if you share my insecurity about your self-knowledge of your own ongoing conscious experience of sustaining a visual image – then maybe you will grant me this: There is no special, remarkable perfection in our knowledge of such things, no elite epistemic status. We probably know normal, outward objects better, in fact.

How about emotional experience? Reflect on your own ongoing emotional experience at this moment. Do you even have any? (If not, try to generate some.) Now let me ask: Is it completely obvious to you what the character of that experience is? Does introspection reveal it to you as clearly as visual observation reveals the presence of the text before your eyes? Can you discern the gross and fine features of your emotional phenomenology as easily and confidently as you can discern the gross and fine features of the desk at which you are sitting? Can you trace its spatiality (or non-spatiality), its viscerality or cognitiveness, its manifestation in conscious imagery, thought, proprioception, or whatever, as sharply and infallibly as you can discern the shape, texture, color, and relative position of your desktop? I cannot, of course, force a particular answer to these questions. I can only invite you to share my intuitive sense of uncertainty. And it does not seem to me that the problem here is merely linguistic, merely a matter of finding the right *words* to describe an experience known in precise detail, or merely the conceptual or theoretical matter of determining which aspects of a well-known phenomenology are properly regarded as aspects of emotion.

How about visual sensory experience? Consider not your visual experience when you are looking directly at a canonical color but rather your visual experience, in an ordinary scene, of the region ten degrees or thirty degrees away from the center point. How clear is that region? How finely delineated is your experience of the shape and color of things that you are *not* looking directly at? People give very different answers to this question – some say they experience distinct shape and color only in a very narrow, rapidly moving foveal area, about one to two degrees of arc (about the size of your thumbnail held at arm's length); others claim to experience shape and color with high precision in thirty or fifty or one hundred degrees of visual arc; still others find *shape* imprecise outside a narrow central area, but find *color* quite distinct even twenty or thirty degrees out. And furthermore, people's opinions about this are not stable over time. In the course of a conversation, they will shift from thinking one thing to thinking another. They change their minds. The phenomenal character of their visual experience is not securely known.[3]

We do not really know so much, then, I think, about our stream of conscious experience, about the phenomenology always transpiring within us. We know *certain* things. I know, perhaps, that I am feeling hungry. But I do not know, as reliably or as well, how that hunger manifests experientially – exactly where, for example, I feel it (if it makes sense to give it an experiential location at all), and what other dimensions of phenomenality it may possess. I know, perhaps, that I am, or just was, thinking about where to go for lunch, and maybe I know, too, whether I experienced that thought verbally or imagistically or in both ways simultaneously and maybe a few of the grossest contours of that thought. But if I experienced the thought verbally, I may not know, any more and perhaps even less than I would in speaking aloud, in what words that thought was expressed (unless, perhaps, I work to create the words I self-attribute in the course of self-attributing them); I may not know whether those words were (or are) experienced as though actively spoken ("inner speech") as opposed to passively received

---

[3] The arguments in the last two paragraphs are adapted from Schwitzgebel (2008, 2011).

("inner hearing"), or whether there was (or is) a motoric aspect to the verbal imagery – or maybe, indeed, whether there really was or is no inner verbalization at all and instead only a non-verbal ("imageless"? "unsymbolized"?) apprehension of that content. Nor, it seems, am I likely to know what the full conscious content of the thought was, or is, assuming that any verbalization only reflects a portion of it:[4] People's reports about such matters are highly variable and unstable, at least before training (Hurlburt and Schwitzgebel 2007, 2011); and after training the stability might often be driven more by theory than by accurate apprehension of the target phenomena.[5] Perhaps I typically know what my sensory experience is *of* – but I know little about its general form and structure, sometimes not even what sensory modality it occurs in (consider the feeling of being stared at, the entanglement of olfactory and gustatory input, the denial of echolocation [Schwitzgebel and Gordon 2000; Schwitzgebel 2011]); and to the extent I seem to know details about my sensory experience, typically that knowledge will be grounded in large part (and often either dubiously or vacuously) on my more secure knowledge of the corresponding details of the external world.[6] I probably typically know, broadly speaking, if I stop to think about one or another of them, the approximate thrust of my emotions, or my pains, or my somatic urges, or my degree of sleepiness, or the sense of an impending hiccup. But such knowledge of the approximate gist of our ongoing or very recently past experience, assuming that we do indeed have such knowledge (and sometimes what used to seem obvious and undeniable becomes problematic on further investigation, e.g. color in the eyes-closed visual field [Schwitzgebel 2011]), is just knowledge of the very basic stuff that ought to just hit one over the head unless the most utterly radical skepticism about self-knowledge is true – a tiny island of (apparent) obviousness, that is, in what is mostly a sea of ignorance about our stream of experience. If someone knew so little about the outside world, it would seem the daftest blindness.

---

[4] Consider incomplete or unspecific or misspoken inner verbalizations: "Why can't I remember about the . . .," "John! [in an exasperated tone]," "That's not an unfair deal" [bitterly, with a single negative rather than a double negative intended]. In such cases, the verbal content does not fully reflect the apparently experienced thought content. So also, I am inclined to think, in many other cases where the mismatch or incompleteness is less obvious.

[5] As in the debate about "imageless thought" in the early twentieth century and its contemporary descendant, the debate about cognitive phenomenology (Kusch 1999; Bayne and Montague forthcoming).

[6] See Schwitzgebel forthcoming for a more detailed discussion of the processes driving introspective judgment.

Furthermore, the island falls quickly undersea: You probably know the rough gist of your current experience, and maybe of the last few seconds of experience, and of some selected and probably unrepresentative experiences from your more distant past. But what generally occupies your thoughts – what you *tend* to have near the center of your experience – about that I doubt you have much knowledge at all. I find Russ Hurlburt's work convincing on this point: A person might very frequently have angry thoughts about his children, as he reports when sampled at random moments, and yet he might sincerely deny that it is so in the general case (Hurlburt and Heavey 2006, 6–7); commonly, people think that a random sampling of their mental lives will reveal lots of abstract or intellectual thought, or lots of thoughts about sex, and yet find upon actual sampling that they report virtually no such thoughts (e.g. Hurlburt and Heavey 2006, 141; Kane 2011); nor do people appear to be very good, by Hurlburt's measures, in their generalizations about structural features of their experience, such as whether they experience lots of inner speech or lots of visual imagery (Hurlburt and Heavey 2006; Hurlburt and Schwitzgebel 2007, 2011; Kane 2011). You may know a few rough things about your current experience, but try to extend your knowledge back more than a few seconds, try to generalize, try to articulate a bit of detail, or try to discern even moderately large structural features of your experience, and soon you will err.[7]

III. OF ATTITUDES

How about our self-knowledge of our attitudes? For some of our attitudes I am inclined toward a version of what is sometimes called a "transparency" view. The rough idea here is that if someone asks me something like "do you believe it will rain tomorrow?" I think about whether it will rain. That is, despite the fact that the question is about what I *believe*, in answering it I do not think about what I believe, I think about external affairs – and then I express my judgment about those external affairs using, if it suits me, either self-attributive language ("Of course I don't think it will rain!") or objective language ("Of course it won't rain!"), with the difference between these two sorts of expression grounded more in conversational pragmatics than in the presence or absence of an introspective act. This expressive procedure delivers accurate self-attributions if there is the right kind of hook-up

---

[7] For further exploration of the ideas in this section, see Schwitzgebel (2011). See also Spener and Bayne (2010).

between my judgment ("it won't rain") and my self-attributive expression of that judgment ("I don't think it will rain").[8]

This sort of procedure works fine, I think, for fairly trivial attitudes or attitudes that connect fairly narrowly to our actions – attitudes like my preference for vanilla ice cream over chocolate when I am asked on a particular occasion or my general belief that it does not rain much in California in April. The vanilla preference and the rain belief do not tangle much with my broad values or self-conception, and their connections to my behavior are fairly straightforward and limited – an evening's ice cream consumption, my springtime habits in picnic planning and umbrella carrying.

But those are not the attitudes I care about most – or at least they are not the ones most critical to my self-knowledge in the morally loaded sense of "self-knowledge," in the sense of the Delphic oracle's recommendation to "know thyself." The oracle was presumably not concerned about whether people knew their attitudes toward the April weather. To the extent the injunction to know oneself pertains to self-knowledge of attitudes, it must be attitudes like your central values and your general background assumptions about the world and about other people. And about such matters, I believe (I think I believe!) our self-knowledge is rather poor.

Consider sexism.[9] Many men in academia sincerely profess that men and women are equally intelligent. Ralph, a philosophy professor let us suppose, is one such man. He is prepared to argue coherently, authentically, and vehemently for equality of intelligence and has argued the point repeatedly in the past. And yet Ralph is systematically sexist in his spontaneous reactions, judgments, and unguarded behavior. When he gazes out on the class the first day of each term, he cannot help but think that some students look brighter than others – and to him, the women rarely look bright. When a woman makes an insightful comment or submits an excellent essay, he feels more surprised than he would were a man to do so, even though his female students make insightful comments and submit excellent essays at the same rate as his male students. When Ralph is on the hiring committee

---

[8] For transparency views of self-knowledge of attitudes, see, e.g., Evans (1982c); Moran (2001); Byrne (2005 and this volume); Gordon (2007); against transparency see Gertler (2011). (Incidentally, I wish that Byrne, in this volume, had suggested that we tend to self-ascribe desires on the basis of a rule like "If X is good, believe that you want X," rather than casting the antecedent in terms of desirability. It seems to me that we much more often think about whether things would be good, and self-ascribe desire partly on that basis, than we think about whether things would be desirable. Such an account might suggest less privilege than an account in terms of desirability, but I regard that as a feature, not a bug.)

[9] This example is adapted from Schwitzgebel (2010).

for a new office manager, it will not seem to him that the women are the most intellectually capable, even if they are; or if he does become convinced of the intelligence of a female applicant, it will have taken more evidence than if the applicant had been male. And so on. Ralph may know this about himself, or he may not. I see no reason to think that Ralph would have any special authority in such matters, compared to other people who have observed substantial portions of his relevant behavior. In fact, he may be disadvantaged by a desire not to see himself as sexist and by the more general desire to see himself as someone whose actions reflect his espoused principles.[10]

Now you might want to say that in a case like Ralph's – and let's assume that Ralph is *not* aware of the pervasive sexism in his behavior – there is no lack of authority about what one *believes*. Ralph believes that men and women are equally intelligent, you might suggest, he just tends not to *act* on that belief. But this seems to me an overly linguistic and intellectualist view of belief. Our beliefs manifest not just in what we say, but in what we do – they animate our limbs, not just our mouths – and they are also manifested in our spontaneous emotional reactions and our implicit assumptions. Now I think it is not quite right to call Ralph an out-and-out sexist who simply believes that women are intellectually inferior. What Ralph says and how he reasons in his most abstract and most thoughtful moments is an important part of how he thinks and acts, even if it is only a part. Ralph's attitude toward the intellectual equality of the sexes is what I would call an in-between state. His dispositions, his patterns of response, his habits of thought, are mixed up and inconsistent. It is neither quite right to say that he believes in the intellectual equality of the sexes nor quite right to say that he fails to believe that.[11] But he has no specially privileged self-knowledge of that fact.

Many people profess to believe in God and Heaven. Here again, I think we have a case where sincere linguistic avowal often diverges from behavioral manifestation and spontaneous response. To believe in God, in the mainstream monotheistic sense, is in part to believe that there is an omniscient agent who is always observing you, with the power to reward you with eternal bliss or condemn you to eternal torment. Many people who sincerely verbally espouse the existence of such a God fail to act and react in their daily lives as though such a God exists: They will do before God what they would not do before any neighbor, even the most forgiving

---

[10] For empirically informed discussion of professional philosophers' apparent ignorance of their own sexism, see Haslanger (2008) and Saul (forthcoming).

[11] I develop this idea further in Schwitzgebel (2002b, 2010).

one; and only *human* eyes and *human* condemnation will give them the pinch of fear and remorse. Such people are, I think, like Ralph the sexist. But rarely do they realize that they are. If you take yourself to believe in such a God, and if your behavior is less than saintly, you should be terrified about the state of your faith.

I say I value family over work. When I stop and think about it, it seems to me vastly more important to be a good father than to write papers like this one. Yet I am off to work early, I come home late. I take family vacations and my mind is wandering in the philosopher's ether. I am more elated by my rising prestige than by my son's successes in school. My wife rightly scolds me: Do I really believe that family is more important? Or: I sincerely say that those lower than me in social status deserve my respect; but do I really believe this, if I don't live that way? (*Do* I live that way? How respectfully do I treat cashiers, students, secretaries? I doubt I really know. Ask them when I am not around.)

If my attitudes – my beliefs and my values, especially – are not so much what I sincerely avow when the question is put to me explicitly but rather what is reflected in my overall patterns of action and reaction, in my implicit assumptions, my spontaneous inclinations, then although I may have pretty good knowledge of the simple and trivial, or the relatively narrow and concrete – what I think of April's weather – the attitudes that are most morally central to my life, the ones crucial to my self-image, I tend to know only poorly, either through a facile assumption of alignment between my avowals and my overall patterns of action and reaction or through empirical generalizations of doubtful accuracy, filtered through the distorting lens of self-flattery.

IV. OF CERTAIN OTHER FEATURES OF MENTALITY

How about other features of my mentality? My personality traits, my moral character, the quality of my philosophical thinking, my overall intelligence?

My own view is that traits of this sort are structurally very similar to attitudes. Personality trait attributions, skill attributions, and attitude attributions can all be seen as shorthand ways of talking about patterns of inward and outward action and reaction (Schwitzgebel 2002b). And our degree of self-knowledge is roughly similar: Our self-knowledge is pretty good about narrow and concrete matters, especially when an attribution is normatively neutral in the sense that it does not tend to cast one in either a good or a bad light, and it is also pretty good when there are straightforward external measures. I know I am good at Scrabble. That is pretty narrow, concrete, and measurable. I know that I am more interested in business news than celebrity gossip. Just look at what parts of the newspaper I read.

Now of course there is a whole industry in psychology based on the self-report of personality traits. It often works by asking people broad or medium-sized questions about their traits or attitudes – asking them, for example, whether they enjoy chatting with people or whether they are assertive – and then looking for patterns in the answers. If you generally say yes to questions like that, you will score as an extravert. There is some stability in people's answers to such questions over time, and some relationship between how people rate themselves in such matters and how their friends rate them. Correlations to outward behavior, though, tend to be at best moderate, and self-evaluations and peer-evaluations tend to break apart when the trait in question is difficult to directly observe and evaluatively loaded (John and Robins 1993; Gosling *et al.* 1998; Vazire 2010). It is okay to be talkative and it is okay not to be talkative, and talkativeness is a fairly straightforwardly observable trait; self-evaluations and peer evaluations tend to line up, and in at least one study (Vazire 2010) both measures were moderately correlated with experimentally observed talking frequency. Self-ratings, peer ratings, and actual behavior tend to align much more poorly, though, for attributions like being flexible, creative, or lazy. In fact John and Robins (1993) found self-attributions and peer-attributions tending to correlate *negatively* for some such traits: People whose peers judged them to be (relatively) ignorant, undependable, stupid, unfair, or lazy were actually a bit *less* likely to describe themselves as (relatively) ignorant, undependable, stupid, unfair, or lazy than were people whose peers did *not* attribute them those vices.

One of the most general evaluatively loaded trait attributions is whether one is a morally good person. How well do we know this about ourselves? I would guess that there is approximately a zero correlation between people's actual moral character and their opinions about their moral character. Plenty of angels (but not all) think rather poorly of themselves, and plenty of jerks (but not all) think they are just dandy. If you think pretty well of yourself, it is probably just about as likely that you are actually a relatively good and admirable person as that your overall moral character is below average. It would be nice to have some empirical data on this. Unfortunately, both genuine moral self-opinion and real moral character are hard to measure. People are complex and wily.

I suspect that our habit – the habit of most of us, at least, and certainly me – is to assume that we are pretty decent people, above average overall in moral character (even if some of us are too modest to endorse that attitude explicitly), and then to defensively reinterpret and rationalize any counter-evidence. I have been trying to get out of this habit myself, and it is highly unpleasant. I have been trying to take an icy look at my moral behavior, applying simple objective standards, and I cannot say that I have shown up as well as I hoped. At work, I tend to carry less than the average load of committee duties, suggesting that I am a shirker; too frequently I forget about meetings with students or even qualifying exams, suggesting that I am self-absorbed; I seem to make more requests and ask for more exceptions than average from editors and conference organizers, suggesting that I am difficult and demanding. Now I tend to think of myself as a good department citizen, attentive to my students, and relatively easy-going. But so also, I suspect, do most professors, even those who lack such traits.[12] Attending to simple objective measures like hours in committee meetings, number of forgotten appointments, number of special requests, and the number of undergraduates who appear to be frustrated with me (without, surely, just cause) might help serve as a check against my habitual self-deception. Of course, if I cherry-pick objective measures, I can find some that make me look good; but a self-flattering preference for some measures over others is exactly the sort of defensive rationalization that I seek to avoid.

I can carry this icy look over into my personal life, of course, but I would rather not share that here. Unfortunately, it looks no better. I will tell you one whimsical objective measure I have concocted – whimsical, but I do take it *somewhat* seriously. I call it the jerk–sucker ratio. Suppose there is a line of cars slowed down to make a left turn or to exit the freeway. They are not stopped. Their lane is just slower than your lane, because it is crowded with cars planning to turn. The question is, how far along do you go before you change over into that lane? Cutting in at the last moment, of course, is the jerk option – it puts you in front of everyone else without having waited your turn and furthermore it increases the risk of accident and slows down the cars behind you in your lane who are not turning or exiting. Getting over early and tolerating the jerks is the sucker

---

[12] For example, in one survey study, Joshua Rust and I found that 66 percent of philosophy professor respondents estimated that they responded to 98 percent of the emails they receive from students (49 percent of respondents claimed to respond to 100 percent of student emails) – statistics which, when we have presented them to undergraduates, typically meet with incredulity. And when Josh and I sent to our survey respondents some emails designed to look as if they were from undergraduates, those same philosophers who claimed at least 98 percent email responsiveness responded to just 64 percent of the emails. Philosophers who gave lower estimates of their email responsiveness responded to 57 percent of our emails; and overall, self-described responsiveness predicted 1.1 percent of the variance in measured responsiveness ($r = .11$; $p = .04$; Rust and Schwitzgebel in preparation; Schwitzgebel and Rust in preparation.)

option. Suppose there are forty-eight cars waiting and two who cut in at the last moment. If you are one of those two who cuts in, you are in the 96th percentile for jerks. If there are eighty-five cars waiting and fifteen who cut in, and you cut in, you are in the 85th percentile for jerks. (Of course, this measure breaks down as the ratio of cutters to waiters approaches 1:1.) I might think to myself that I have better reasons to hurry than all the others waiting or that I am a skilled enough driver to cut in at the last second without negative consequences. And maybe for some people that is true, but in my own case I worry that that would just be defensive rationalization. Of course, I do not regard this little test as a valid measure of jerkhood across the board: There may be little if any relationship between one's driving behavior and how one treats one's students or spouse. But this is the *kind* of thing, extended to more serious issues, that constitutes the objectively grounded, icy self-examination I have in mind.

It can also help considerably, I suspect, to have an intimate friend or family member who is ready to – I wish I knew a less crude way of putting this, but the following phrase seems to get the nuance exactly right *call you on your shit*.[13] Need I add details?

Consider intelligence too, and skill in philosophy. What percentage of the people reading this chapter, do you think, substantially misestimate their intellectual or philosophical abilities? Psychologists have repeatedly found that North Americans and Western Europeans – especially men – tend to rate themselves as significantly more intelligent than their peers.[14] Psychologists have also repeatedly found only modest correlations between self-rated intelligence and intelligence as measured by IQ tests (with self-ratings typically accounting for only about 1–9 percent of the variance in test scores).[15] Of course, IQ tests might be poor measures of intelligence: That would explain the poor correlation with self-report. It would also nicely explain the overestimation tendency if people tended self-flatteringly

---

[13] I think of the ancient Confucian Xunzi:

> He who rightly criticizes me is my teacher, and he who rightly supports me is my friend, while he who flatters and toadies to me is someone who would do me villainy. Accordingly, the gentleman exalts his teachers and loves his friends, so as to utterly hate those who would do him villainy ... The petty man is the opposite. He is utterly disorderly, but hates for people to criticize him (third century BCE, 2005, 261)

and Confucius himself:

> How fortunate I am! If I happen to make a mistake, others are sure to inform me. (fifth century BCE 2003, 7.31, 75)

> I wish I could say I shared Xunzi's and Confucius' love of being corrected!

[14] Findings on Asians are mixed. See Furnham (2001) for a review. Some recent studies are Visser, Ashton, and Vernon (2008); Steinmayr and Spinath (2009).

[15] See e.g., Paulus, Lysy, and Yik (1998); Furnham (2001); Visser, Ashton, and Vernon (2008); Vazire (2010).

to regard *real* intelligence to be revealed by just the sorts of things they think themselves good at – whether that be mathematics, verbal fluency, business acumen, or diagnosing automotive troubles. ("Jeez, he doesn't even know what a slipping belt sounds like? What an idiot!") Evidence also suggests that correlations are often quite modest between self-rated ability and measured performance, compared to peers, in various intellectual subdomains such as grammatical ability, spatial ability, and logical reasoning – though to my knowledge philosophical ability in particular has not been tested.[16] Based both on general psychological evidence and on personal experience, I will hazard this guess about you, the reader (and myself too): Your opinion of how your intelligence and philosophical ability compares to the intelligence and philosophical ability of your classmates (if you are a student) or colleagues (if you are a professor) is at best a weak indicator of your actual intelligence and ability. Probably your peers know you better. But don't bother asking; they won't tell you the truth.

V. A DEPRESSING CONCLUSION?

Self-knowledge? Of general features of our stream of conscious experience, of our morally most important attitudes, of our real values and our moral character, of our intelligence, of what really makes us happy and unhappy (see Haybron 2008) – about such matters I doubt we have much knowledge at all. We live in cocoons of ignorance, especially where our self-conception is at stake. The philosophical focus on how impressive our self-knowledge is gets the most important things backwards.

Maybe it is good that way. In a classic article, Shelley Taylor and Jonathon Brown (1988), reviewing a broad range of literature, suggest that positive illusions about oneself are the ordinary concomitant of mental health;[17] and so also, I suspect, is blasé confidence in answering questions about one's attitudes and stream of experience. It is mainly *depressed* people, Taylor and Brown argue, who have a realistic self-image and an adequate appreciation of their limitations. That is a controversial conclusion, of course, but I start to feel the pull of it.[18]

---

[16] See, e.g., Kruger and Dunning (1999); Shynkaruk and Thompson (2006); Visser, Ashton, and Vernon (2008).

[17] More recently, see McKay and Dennett (2009); for caveats see Kwan *et al.* (2008); Moore and Healy (2008).

[18] For helpful discussion and criticism, thanks to audiences at Cal State Fullerton, Monash University, University of Osnabrück, and University of Mainz and especially to Santiago Arango-Muñoz (for calling me on my ****), JeeLoo Liu, and Mimi Vong.

CHAPTER 9

Personhood and consciousness

Sydney Shoemaker

I take as my text John Locke's definition of *person*: "[A] thinking intelligent being, that has reason and reflection, and can consider itself as itself, the same thinking thing, in different times and places, which it does only by that consciousness which is inseparable from thinking, and, as it seems to me, essential to it" (Locke [1689] 1975, 285). One important point about this passage is that it makes being the subject of certain psychological properties essential to persons. This goes well with the view commonly associated with Locke, that personal identity consists in something psychological. I will expand on that connection later on. A second important point is that the properties held to be essential to persons include consciousness – more specifically, self-consciousness. So the two concepts that figure in the title of this book, that of consciousness and that of the self, are linked in Locke's definition.

I think that insofar as "selves" are a kind of entities, they are no different from persons. The term "self" is used to refer to a person as that person conceives and knows itself. Locke's definition asserts a close connection between the nature of selves, or persons, and the access they have to themselves and their identities.

I said that on a natural reading of Locke's definition it makes being the subject of certain psychological properties essential to persons. There is a reading of it on which it does not. If we took his definition to be giving us only the nominal essence of *person*, it could be accepted by those, such as animalists like Eric Olson, who think that the things that are persons are so only contingently, and that they could cease to be thinking beings, and so cease to be persons, without ceasing to exist. One might think that this "nominal essence" reading is recommended by Locke's claims about the unknowability of real essence. But the rest of what Locke says in this chapter goes better with the view that it is necessary *de re* of persons that they are beings that satisfy his definition, i.e. are thinking, intelligent beings, etc. Of course, we want "thinking being" to be understood in such a way that being a thinking being is compatible with undergoing periods of unconsciousness. What is arguably essential to persons is the capacity for rational thought, not the exercise of that capacity.

I think this essentiality claim supports a psychological account of personal identity. This rests on the idea that there is an internal relation between the causal profiles of properties and the identity conditions, or persistence conditions, of their subjects. The causal profiles of properties contribute to determining the synchronic unity of instances of them. So, for example, when a belief and desire are such that they jointly rationalize a certain action, the causal profiles of the properties of having that belief and having that desire determine that if instances of the properties jointly cause that action, they belong to the same subject. But what is more important for present purposes is how the causal profiles of properties determine diachronic unity relations for their instances. The causal profile of a property consists in part in how its instantiation influences the future career of its subject, what successor states its instantiation causes or contributes to causing. The nature of a kind of thing is determined by what properties can be instantiated in the career of a thing of that sort, and collectively the properties that can be instantiated in a thing of that sort determine what series of property instantiations count as the career of a thing of that sort. The fact that the successive property instances in a series are causally related in accordance with the causal profiles of a certain set of properties constitutes that series being the career of a thing having properties in that set. As we might put it, the causal profiles of the properties determine what the diachronic unity relations are for instances of these properties, and these in turn determine the persistence conditions for subjects of these properties. If being the subject of psychological properties is essential to persons, it would suggest that their causal profiles play a central role in determining their persistence conditions.

But of course, its being essential to persons that they are subjects of mental properties is compatible with its also being essential to persons that they are subjects of physical properties. So we need more than essentiality in order to give the mental properties a central role in determining persistence conditions. What we need, I think, is the claim that mental properties are privileged in the sense that persons have the physical properties they do in virtue of relations between the instantiation of these physical properties and instantiations of mental properties.

Assuming physicalism, as I am doing, mental properties are physically realized. A subject of mental properties will at least have physical properties that are realizers of these mental properties. There is of course a good sense in which one has the mental properties because one has their physical realizers. But if we ask what makes a particular physical realizer a property of a particular person, the answer seems to be that it belongs to that person because it realizes a mental property of that person. This gives us a sense in which one has the physical property in virtue of having the mental property. But by itself this doesn't get us very far, for these realizer properties, which will be complex neural properties of whose nature we are largely ignorant, are of course not the physical properties we ascribe to persons in ordinary discourse – properties like height, weight, a certain complexion, etc.

It is natural to speak of these as properties of the person's body, and it might seem that if we can explain what it is for a person to have a certain body we will thereby have explained how it is that the person has the physical properties of that body. And arguably what constitute a body's being the body of a particular person are causal relations between it and psychological states of the person. The perceptual organs of the body are the causal source of the person's perceptual states, and other states of the body are the source of sensations like pains, itches, and feelings of nausea. And the person's volitional states are the source of the bodily movements that constitute the person's actions. Arguably, it is connections of these sorts that make a particular body the body of a particular person.[1]

But it should not go without saying that properties of a person's body are properties of the person. For this will not be true on a Cartesian dualist view. The dualist can allow that the person has a height, a weight, etc. But for the dualist these are relational properties of the person – a person's being six feet tall will be the relational property of having a body that is six feet tall. And these relational properties are not properties of the body – the body's being six feet tall is an intrinsic property of it, not a relational property it has in virtue of being related to something else that is six feet tall. So it is worth inquiring what it is that makes the properties of a person's body properties of the person.

Part of the answer, of course, is the case against Cartesian dualism. But there are non-dualist views, indeed materialist views, on which height, complexion, etc. are relational rather than intrinsic properties of persons. There is, for example, the view, occasionally suggested though not widely held, that persons are brains. My brain does not have as intrinsic properties the height, weight, etc. that are normally assigned to me, although it does have the relational property of animating a body having those as intrinsic properties. The view that persons are brains is no doubt motivated by the

---

[1] See Shoemaker (1976).

intuition that persons are in the first instance subjects of mental properties – for a materialist that might suggest the identification of a person with the organ in which mental properties are thought to be realized. Of course, not all properties of the brain are realizers of mental properties, so the brain-theorist owes us an explanation of what makes the person the subject of these. Perhaps the explanation lies in the fact that instances of these properties stand in relations of synchronic unity to instances of properties that are realizers of mental properties. In any case, if we want to hold that intrinsic properties of bodies of persons can be intrinsic properties of persons, we need a case for rejecting the brain theory as well as Cartesian dualism.

Part of the case comes from considerations about action. One's body is essentially involved in one's actions. Its mass affects the consequences of one's actions, and the performance of actions of a given sort constitutively involves changes in the spatial properties of one's body. If one performs an action, and what performs it must have mass and spatial properties, then one must oneself have mass and spatial properties. And if one has these one must have other bodily properties that are synchronically unified with them – or, more precisely, other bodily properties whose instances are synchronically unified with instances of them.

Perhaps it will be suggested that the property of performing a certain action is a relational property that one has in virtue of having a body that is behaving a certain way as the result of one's volitions, and that likewise any physical predicates one satisfies in virtue of performing an action stand for relational properties rather than physical properties shared with one's body. But if my volitional states, along with my other mental states, are physically realized, then instances of their realizers will stand in relations of synchronic unity to instances of other bodily properties, including the property of having a muscular and nervous system capable of implementing those volitional states, and these in turn will stand in relations of synchronic unity to instances of properties like mass and shape. So given that the volitional states and their realizers belong to me, the bodily states they are synchronically unified with will also belong to me.

But in order to defend the view that persons are in the first instance subjects of mental properties, it is not really necessary to establish that physical predicates that are true of persons ascribe intrinsic physical properties to them rather than relational properties. It is enough to show that physical predicates are true of a person in virtue of the person's being in physical states that are related in certain ways to the mental states of the person, and that will be true whether or not the predicates turn out to be relational. It will be true in virtue of the points I have mentioned: that some physical properties belong to a person in virtue of being realizers of the person's mental states, and that a body belongs to a person, and its states are truth-makers for the application of physical predicates to the person, in virtue of its relations to the person's mental states.

In any case, it is arguable that in one way or another, instances of physical properties belong to a person in virtue of their relations to instances of that person's mental properties (which may be only dispositional properties, as in the case of a person who is asleep). But if mental properties are primary, it is to be expected that features of the causal profiles of mental properties that pertain to diachronic unity will play a central role in determining the persistence conditions, or identity conditions, of persons.

These considerations support the "transplant intuition" that if a brain or cerebrum were transplanted from one body to another, and if this resulted in the recipient having a psychology continuous with that of the donor, the recipient is the donor. Or perhaps I should say that these considerations support and are supported by the transplant intuition. The metaphysical intuition that persons are in the first instance subjects of mental properties and the epistemological intuition that is the transplant intuition mutually reinforce one another.

There is of course a currently popular view that stands in stark opposition to this. This is the animalist view, most forcefully defended by Eric Olson. As I mentioned earlier, on this view Locke's definition of *person* is acceptable only if viewed as giving us merely the nominal essence of persons. Being a person, on this view, is a phase sortal, not a substance sortal, and what is a person is not *essentially* a person. So while it may be analytically true that persons are subjects of mental states, it is not necessary *de re* of a person that he or she is a subject of mental states; what is a person may cease to be one, and will have existed, as a fetus, prior to becoming a person. On this view persons of our sort are in the first instance subjects of biological properties, not mental ones. It is also part of this view that there is no entity numerically distinct from a person that is that person's body, so there is no relation between persons and bodies that is to be explained in terms of causal relations to the person's mental states. I have had my say against this view in other places, and will not repeat it here.

Now let us focus on self-consciousness. It would enhance the unity of this chapter if I could argue that the psychological account of personal identity that I favor falls out from an account of self-consciousness. But unfortunately I cannot argue this. I think that the contents of self-consciousness, which I here take to include both introspective awareness of one's current psychological states and memory awareness of one's past, are neutral with respect to the metaphysical nature of the self. Hume was right, although not for the reason he gives, that one is not in introspection aware of one's self as an object. He was not right in concluding that the self is just a bundle of perceptions.

The Humean denial should not be thought of as itself a deliverance of introspection – that when one looks within for a subject of one's experiences one fails to find one. Looking within would be pointless, for one has no notion of what would count as introspectively observing a self. One obvious point here is that one's perceptual (partly visual and partly proprioceptive) awareness of the flesh and blood person that one is does not count. This is not introspective awareness. And it is plainly not the case that one observes the flesh and blood person perceived in this way to have the mental states of which one has introspective awareness – it is not the case that it is by observing the flesh and blood person in this way that one acquires one's first-person knowledge of these mental states. A further point is that for any candidate for being oneself that one can be aware of as an object, whether it be a flesh and blood person or a supposed Cartesian ego, a question can be raised as to how one knows that it is oneself. In some way or another, such a thing would have to be identified as being oneself. And there being identification opens the door to the possibility of misidentification. But first-person introspective judgments are immune to error through misidentification relative to "I."[2] So it cannot be the case that such judgments are grounded on observing a self, identified as oneself, having whatever state is self-ascribed by the judgment.

If the Humean denial is seen as a purely negative claim about the contents of introspective awareness, it tells us nothing about what sort of thing a self or person is. That is part of what I mean in saying that the contents of self-consciousness are neutral with respect to the metaphysical nature of the self. And a similar point can be made about our memory knowledge of personal identity. If one is impressed by the role facts about what a person can remember play in grounding judgments about his or her identity, one may be tempted by the thought that in making memory-based judgments about one's own past one is using memory itself as a criterion of identity. If this thought were right, it would show that the nature of our awareness of our identity supports a psychological account of its nature. But this thought is obviously wrong. To use, as a ground for saying that I am the person who did something, the fact that I have a memory of doing it, I would have to know independently of that memory that the past thing was

---

[2] See Shoemaker (1968).

done. And this will not be the case when I simply remember doing something in the past, and only in that way know that the thing was done. Memory-based past tense first-person judgments are not themselves identity judgments. But they imply the persistence of their subjects through time, and each of them implies that there are true identity propositions linking the rememberer with someone existing at the past time in question and involved in the past situation that is remembered. These judgments are not grounded on memory as a criterion of identity, but they also are not grounded on any other criterion. They are not grounded on evidence of personal identity of any sort.

Hume's denial has an obvious extension to the case of such memory knowledge. Just as in having introspective knowledge of one's current psychological states one is not introspectively aware of any self as an object, in remembering a past experience or action, and remembering it "from the inside," there is no past self that enters into the content of one's memory as the subject of the remembered experience or action, i.e. as that the memory of which tells one that the past experience or action was one's own. This is not to deny that one can be among the people who enter as objects into the content of one's memory. There are memory demonstratives that enable one to refer to specific things in the past situation remembered; these things can include persons, and these persons can include oneself. And the way one enters into the content of a memory will be somewhat different from the way other persons enter into it – if one remembers seeing oneself, it will have to be a matter of seeing oneself in a mirror or in foreshortened view. But the judgment that the remembered person is oneself will involve an identification, and an identification that could in principle be mistaken. And it will not be the identification of a remembered person as oneself that gives the memory its first-person content. On the contrary, the identification of the remembered person as oneself will rest on first-person judgments that could not themselves rest on a prior identification of a remembered person as oneself. It will be because I remember seeing the remembered person in a certain way, in foreshortened view or in what I take to be a mirror or other reflecting surface, that I take him to be myself. And here my identification is grounded in part on the first-person judgment that I saw such and such. The "I" in that judgment is like the "I" in the present tense perceptual judgment I made at the past time remembered – like that past "I" it does not pick out any observed object the awareness of which grounds the judgment.

I think that the fact that first-person memory judgments are non-inferential, and not grounded on criteria of identity of any sort, is a major source of the view, which found classical expression in the work of Bishop Butler and Thomas Reid, that personal identity is simple and indefinable. The thought may be that the access each person has to facts about his or her own identity is the most direct access to personal identity there can be, and that if there are constitutive criteria of personal identity it is in first-person judgments that we should find these criteria employed. None are employed in the making of memory judgments, and the conclusion drawn is that there are none – that in making such judgments a person has immediate access to facts that others can know only through inference from facts that are contingently evidence for them.

We find such thinking elsewhere in the philosophy of mind – e.g. in the idea that the immediate and non-inferential access we have to our thoughts and sensations shows that the occurrence of these cannot consist in the physical or functional facts that may serve for others as evidence for them. But such thinking does not bear examination. It is certainly not true in general that our most direct way of knowing something is such that in knowing it in that way we are aware of what constitutes its being the sort of thing it is. I suppose that perception is our most direct way of knowing trees and tables, and it is plainly not the case that in perceiving a tree or a table we are immediately aware of what it is that constitutes its being a tree or a table.

Our remembering our pasts in the way we do is of course an instance of the psychological continuity and connectedness that neo-Lockean accounts hold to be constitutive of personal identity. All I have claimed is that in making first-person memory judgments one is not using this psychological continuity and connectedness as a criterion – because one is not using anything as a criterion. Opponents of the neo-Lockean view, such as proponents of the currently fashionable animalism, will of course happily allow that as a matter of contingent fact personal identity is typically accompanied by psychological continuity and connectedness. If one is looking for reasons to oppose their view, one should not look to the first-person epistemology of personal identity. One will do better to look to the considerations mentioned earlier – the case for holding that persons are first and foremost subjects of mental properties, and the transplant intuition about brain and cerebrum transfers.

In the remainder of this chapter I want to address the question of what gives memories their first-person content. I have already rejected one answer to this question – that they get their content from the fact that among objects remembered are ones that the rememberer can identify as himself or herself. But there is a view, of which I myself have been an advocate, that might suggest that some sort of identification of a past self for oneself is involved when one judges on the basis of memory that one did or experienced something in the past. This is the view that there can be quasi-remembering that is not remembering.[3] That is, that there is a possible case in which someone has a seeming memory that corresponds to a past experience or action, and is related to it causally in much the way in which we are related to actions and experiences that we remember, but in which the subject of that past experience or action is someone other than the person having the seeming memory. Remembering will be a special case of quasi-remembering, namely one in which the subject of the past experience or action is the person having the quasi-memory. If one holds this view it may seem that the content of a seeming memory always leaves it an open question whether it is a genuine memory or a mere quasi-memory. And then it will seem that if one can get knowledge of one's own past from memory, one must have some way of answering that question.

It is implicit in what I argued earlier that there is no property of "me-ness" that we remember being instantiated by persons or selves that enters into the contents of our memories, and licenses our use of the first person pronoun in memory judgments. And it goes with this that there is no property of "mine-ness" that we remember being instantiated by experiences or actions occurring in the past. So there are no such remembered properties that distinguish the contents of memories from those of quasi-memories. It might seem to follow that at the most basic level memories do not have first-person content – that first-person content is introduced by some sort of inference. The inference might be based just on the general fact that in the actual world, or at least with creatures of our kind, all quasi-remembering is remembering. So my memory-based knowledge that I ate a banana this morning would have as its basis my awareness that I quasi-remember from the inside the eating of a banana, which given my background knowledge that in creatures of my sort quasi-remembering from the inside is always remembering from the inside, justifies me in thinking that I remember eating a banana this morning, and therefore that I did eat a banana this morning. To have any plausibility at all, the view would have to be that the inference is an unconscious one. But it is surely cause for suspicion that the view makes awareness of what one remembers or quasi-remembers prior to awareness of what one did or experienced in the past – e.g. that my awareness that I remember eating a banana is prior to my awareness that I ate a banana. Intuitively this seems no more plausible than the view that my knowledge that *I see* a chair in front of me is prior to my

---

[3] See Shoemaker (1970).

vision-based knowledge that *there is* a chair in front of me. The natural view, I think, is that the judgment "There is a chair in front of me" is not inferred from anything, and that prefacing it with "I see that" is not providing evidence for it but indicating what kind of knowledge it is. Likewise, the natural view is that the past tense judgment "I ate a banana" is not inferred from anything, and that prefacing it with "I remember that . . ." is not stating evidence for it but indicating what kind of knowledge it is.

So I think that what are rock bottom in memory are judgments with first-person content. But this leaves us with the question of where these judgments get their first-person content. I said earlier that there is no property of me-ness or mine-ness that one remembers being instantiated in things or events one remembers. Part of what I mean by this is that what it is like to remember an action or experience of one's own need be no different from what it is like to quasi-remember an action or experience of another person. This is not the point, which of course also holds, that what it is like to remember an action or experience need be no different from what it is like to have a memory illusion and merely *seem* to remember an action or experience of a certain sort. The point here is that what it is like to have a *veridical* memory need be no different from what it is like to have a *veridical* quasi-memory of an action or experience of someone else. This sharpens the question of how the genuine memory gets its first-person content.

Here it helps to consider some imaginary, perhaps impossible, creatures.[4] The case I am imagining is a version of Derek Parfit's example of creatures who reproduce by fission, and I will call my imaginary creatures Parfit people.[5] In my version of the case, fission occurs only once in the lifespan – what I will call the quareer (for quasi-career) – of one of these creatures. Parfit people are born in the way we are. Around the age of twenty-one each of them undergoes fission, which we can think of as a splitting down the middle somewhat in the manner of amoeba, followed by a rapid regeneration in each of the offshoots of the missing half. But the community of Parfit people does not allow both offshoots to survive – to avoid over-population, and various other complications, they painlessly kill off one of the offshoots shortly after the fission. The remaining offshoot then lives out his or her life in the ordinary way. It is of course part of the example that there is full psychological continuity between the original person and the surviving offshoot. And an important part of this consists in the fact that the surviving offshoot remembers, or quasi-remembers, the past of the original

---

[4] In what follows I draw on my (2009). [5] See Parfit (1971).

person, in just the way that one of us remembers his or her own past. Their memory judgments have quasi-first-person content. But the pronoun that figures in these of course cannot be translated by our first-person pronoun "I." Instead, it should be translated by the "I*" of Carol Rovane and Alan Sidelle.[6] "I* was F," said by one of the Parfit people, is true just in case an episode of being F occurred in the quareer, but not necessarily in the career, of the person saying it. The quareer of a Parfit person is a series of events, exhibiting the sort of psychological continuity and connectedness that characterizes a typical human career, which is made up of two careers conjoined together – the career of the pre-fission person, and the career of a person who is the sole surviving product of that person's fission.

A post-fission Parfit person will have memories, or quasi-memories, that are a mix of memories of her post-fission actions and experiences and of quasi-memories of the pre-fission actions and experiences of her "ancestral self." These can all be equally veridical. And there will be nothing in what it is like to have these memories that will reveal to her that some of them are of her own past while others are of the past of her ancestral self. To have knowledge of that she will need to rely on auxiliary information about how the time of the quasi-remembered event relates to the time when the fission occurred. As I am imagining the Parfit people, they usually will not bother to make this distinction; their intentions and desires, their regrets and feelings of remorse, and their attitudes of special concern, are all indexed to quareers rather than careers. If they have a pronoun that can be translated as our "I," judgments involving it will be for them of only academic interest, except when the truth of the corresponding "I*"-judgments is in question. They will of course know that present tense "I"-judgments are coextensive with the corresponding present tense "I*"-judgments, while this coextensiveness breaks down in the case of past and future judgments involving these pronouns. But the only first-person pronoun they will feel any need for is "I*."

I have used the example of the Parfit people rather than a more realistic, and more often discussed, case of fission, namely that in which it involves transplanting the two hemispheres of someone's brain into two different bodies. The reason the latter is more realistic is that it seems more than just conceptually possible that such transplants could succeed and yield psychological continuity between the original person and the offshoots, whereas the situation in which creatures with human-like mental states could

---

[6] See Rovane (1990) and Sidelle (2002). Rovane cites an unpublished paper of Sidelle's as the source of "I*."

undergo fission in the manner of amoeba is very likely nomologically impossible and may be metaphysically impossible. My reason for using the Parfit people example rather than the double brain-hemisphere transplant example is that while in the latter the offshoots would have quasi-memories of the actions and experiences of the original person, I think that these quasi-memories would be in one respect non-veridical. They would attribute the quasi-remembered action or experience to the person having the quasi-memory. Even if a fission offshoot knows that she is the product of fission, it would still seem to her that she was remembering doing and experiencing things in the pre-fission past. She could learn to correct for this in the judgments she makes. But learning to correct for it would be a matter of learning to override the way things seem – it would be like learning to judge that the lines in the Müller-Lyer diagram are of equal length even while they still look unequal. By contrast, in the case of the Parfit people there would be no illusory impression to be overridden. They would quasi-remember actions and experiences of their ancestral selves from the inside, but this would not involve its seeming to them that they themselves, the very same persons, were involved in those actions and experiences. To be sure, they might say things like "I remember that I myself did that." But here the second "I" should be translated as "I*." The content of the memory is that the action or experience occurred in the past quareer of the subject, not that it occurred in the past career.

What accounts for this difference between the two fission examples? The crucial point is that the double brain-hemisphere transplant is imagined as occurring in one of us – a creature of our kind. It is characteristic of creatures of our kind that memories from the inside of experiences and actions are caused by corresponding events in the past history of the subject of the memories, except when they are memory illusions whose causation involves a malfunctioning of the memory system. This, I think, makes it the case that when a singular term in the content of the memory ostensibly denotes the subject of the past experience or action, the referent of the term is the person having the memory. This will be true even if the person is a fission product, given that he or she is a person of our sort. But the Parfit people are not of our sort. They are in many ways psychologically like us, but their physiology, as well as the mechanisms underlying their psychological processes, is entirely different. In them the standard causes of experiential memories are actions or experiences that occurred in the quareer, but not necessarily the career, of the subject of the memory. So, I think, if a singular term in the content of a quasi-memory of one of these creatures ostensibly designates the subject of a quasi-remembered experience or action, its referent will be the person who at the time of the remembered event occupied the quareer of the person having the quasi-memory. It makes the "first-person content" of Parfit people's quasi-memories properly expressible by "I*" judgments rather than "I" judgments.

This account invokes a causal theory of reference, and applies it to the case of first-person content. The account is, in a certain sense, externalist. In something like the way an Earthian and Twin-Earthian can be exactly alike "inside the head" but mean something different by "water," one of us and a Parfit person can be exactly alike in the phenomenal character of their memories and yet differ in the kind of content their memories have and in the kind of reference possessed by the first-person pronouns used to express those contents.

Of course, the singular term whose past tense reference is fixed in this way by causal facts about the subject of memory states has to be the same as the first-person pronoun that figures in present tense judgments. I think that the best account of what makes an expression the first-person pronoun, and what gives thoughts first-person content, is some combination of points made some time ago by John Perry and Christopher Peacocke.[7] First-person judgments have an intimate relation to action. In Perry's well-known example, it is his realization that *he* is making a mess, what he expresses by saying "I am making a mess," not the realization that the man he sees on the monitor (who is in fact John Perry) is making a mess, that leads to his cleaning-up behavior. And first-person judgments have an intimate relation to sensory input – the immediate cognitive effects of such inputs are judgments with first-person content, such as "I see something red." Presumably other contents get their first-person content due to their inferential connections with contents having these intimate relations to input and action. We might put the view I have offered by saying that my memories and the quasi-memories of a Parfit person can have the same syntax but that they have a different semantics, and a different kind of semantics, owing to differences in the way such memories are caused in the two sorts of creatures. This shared syntax must be such that the contents sharing it have these inferential connections. It should follow from this that the "I*" that figures in the memory contents of the Parfit people should count as a first-person pronoun, despite the fact that it can be correctly used to refer to someone other than the person who uses it, namely when it refers to the "ancestral self" of that person. We can suppose, as I did earlier, that this

---

[7] See Perry (1979) and Peacocke (1983).

pronoun is used to express present tense contents as well as ones concerning the past and the future. When used to express present contents, and also when used in judgments about other times in the subject's career, it will refer just as "I" does – it will refer to the person who uses it. But it can also refer to an ancestral self or a successor self, when it is used in the expression of a judgment about a time in the subject's quareer that is separated from the making of the judgment by an episode of fission. It could also be the case that in addition to having the pronoun with the meaning of "I*" they also have one that behaves just like our "I." In expressing present tense contents it would make no difference whether they use it or "I*." But when used in the past or future tense the use of "I" would involve an implicit inference to the effect that the time referred to is not separated from the time of the judgment by an episode of fission. In such cases it would be their use of "I*," not their use of "I," that would most resemble our use of "I" in memory judgments.

In earlier work I have dithered over whether first-person memory judgments are immune to error through misidentification relative to "I" – over whether the immunity to such error in present tense self-ascriptions of mental states and actions is preserved in memory. Initially I thought that this is so. But when I reflected on the possibility of quasi-remembering that is not remembering, it seemed to me that this implies that such error is possible – one might take a case of quasi-remembering to be a case of remembering when it is not, and so mistakenly take a quasi-remembered experience as one's own, and so misreport the experience by saying "I felt a severe pain," or "I saw an ostrich," or whatever. This could happen to one of the Parfit persons. For them memory-based "I" judgments would be subject to error through misidentification, though memory-based "I*" judgments would not be. This goes with the fact that with them memory-based "I" judgments would be based on a fallible inference. But if what I have said is right, with us the use of "I" in memory judgments is not based on inference, and does not involve an identification of a remembered self as oneself. That inclines me to say that in the case of creatures of our kind, the immunity to error through misidentification relative to "I" of present tense psychological judgments is preserved in memory.

But then what are we to say of the case discussed earlier, in which the two brain hemispheres of one of us are transplanted into different bodies, resulting in two persons with quasi-memories of the original person's past life? If one of the fission products has memories he expresses by saying "I had a severe headache yesterday," won't that judgment be mistaken, not because there was no headache yesterday that is responsible for it, but because the headache was not his? Shouldn't this count as error through misidentification?

If we say that it does, we should at least recognize that it differs importantly from the error through misidentification that could occur in the case of a Parfit person. In the latter there is an identification that goes wrong because of a mistaken, though perhaps justified, inference. In the case that now concerns us there is no such identification. But if there is no identification, how can there be a *mis*identification? I think it is better to say that it is not an error through misidentification, although it resembles one in a certain respect: it involves the use of a term to refer to something other than what it would have to refer to in order for the judgment to be true. And of course we can know things on the basis of memory without having assembled information about the reliability of our memories.

There is another reason, though one I am less confident of, for denying that this case involves error through misidentification. In cases of error through misidentification relative to "I" the subject of the judgment knows that *someone* is F, but mistakenly judges that she herself is F. But suppose that one of the fission products, in the double-hemisphere transplant case, has a veridical quasi-memory "from the inside" of having a banana for breakfast the day before the operation, and says "I had a banana yesterday." Does she on this basis *know* that someone had a banana the previous day? I am inclined to say that she does not. She certainly does not know it in the way I know that someone ate a banana this morning because I remember that I ate one. Later on, when she has learned about the fission and also learned that her quasi-memories of pre-fission events are reliable, she will have knowledge of judgments like "Someone ate a banana that day" on the basis of her quasi-memories plus that auxiliary information. But then, of course, she will no longer make "I"-judgments on the basis of such quasi-memories. By contrast, the quasi-memory based "someone" judgments of the Parfit people would count as knowledge even if they have not assembled information about the reliability of such judgments. And of course we can know things on the basis of memory without having assembled information about the reliability of our memories.

Let me return to the definition of *person* in Locke that I started with. In the first part of this chapter I focused on the implications of this definition for the nature of persons and more particularly the nature of personal identity. I saw it as an expression of the plausible view that persons are in the first instance subjects of psychological properties, and suggested that that view supports a psychological account of personal identity. The last part of the chapter was about the consciousness which is involved in a person's "consider[ing] itself as itself, the same thinking being in different times and places." My focus there was on the way first-person reference to the person enters into the content of that consciousness. And my claim was that this first-person reference is determined, not by the phenomenology of such consciousness or by what property instantiations are represented in it, both of which could be the same in a case in which the reference is strictly speaking not first-personal, but rather by causal facts that do not manifest themselves in consciousness.

CHAPTER 10

My non-narrative, non-forensic Dasein: the first and second self

Owen Flanagan

I. FORENSIC, NARRATIVE PERSONS AND REAL EVERYDAY PERSONS

In (a widely under-discussed paper) "Sexual identities and narratives of self" (2003), Jill Einstein and I proposed that John Locke's conception of persons, Person[Locke], despite its merit as an account of forensic persons, is woefully inadequate as an account of the normal everyday sense of who one is, how one feels, the weather within, personality, and so on, which we argued is better captured by a conception articulated by William James, Person[James]. Our unremarkable conclusion was that the forensic conception, "Locke's resolute cognitive-linguistic view," needed to be supplemented by "James's feeling-of-and-for-the body view." Here I develop our argument further, and in a more provocative direction, arguing that Person[James] is basic and Person[Locke] is, at best, a special case. Person[James] is the first self. Person[Locke] is the – possibly only "a" – second self. Once this much is established, I further argue that in privileging Person[Locke] we open ourselves, even make more likely, a class of projective mistakes in self-understanding. These include first, overrating the constitutive role of autobiographical memories of happenings and doings, and underestimating the constitutive roles of the much larger class of that-which-is-experienced but not remembered; second, projecting normative expectations of self-sameness backwards and forwards over our lives, sometimes in the face of evidence that we do not have (or in the case of the future, evidence we cannot have) that we are, in fact, the same self or person.

Start by granting for the sake of argument that one of the concepts expressed by the polysemous words PERSON or SELF, or, what is different, by one of the homonyms pronounced as PERSON or SELF, can be

I am grateful to JeeLoo Liu, as well as audiences in Cincinnati, NYC, Nashville, and Carbondale, IL. who made helpful comments.

analyzed usefully in terms of relations of a certain kind of psychological connectedness and continuity, specifically, diachronic memory for things I did or that happened to me. This would be the familiar concept of a forensic person championed by Locke as best suited to account for the identity of humans who are legal and moral agents and accountable as such. The key words in the schema are "*a certain kind*" of psychological connectedness and continuity. The schema gives permission to analyze personhood in terms of a subset of the experiences that persons have and a subset of the connections among them, specifically, autobiographical memories. A forensic person is a person who consciously remembers and can report what he or she has done, who distinguishes between things he or she did and things that happened to him or her, and who can do so for others. Call such persons, Person^{Locke}. Forensic persons are called upon to be narrative persons, to self-represent narratively, and to be represented by others as doers of deeds with certain characteristic behavioral dispositions. The two go together like horse and carriage, so I will speak sometimes of one or the other, the forensic or the narrative, but assume the linkage throughout – forensic-narrative persons.

Why anyone ever thought that a forensic person, Person^{Locke}, was a good analysis of personhood as such is puzzling since this conception of person is so obviously exactly what you would get if you asked: What features of persons and their conscious selves do we depend upon to make intelligible our moral and legal practices in the post-Enlightenment North Atlantic? Without that particular interest, a forensic one, at a particular time, it is not remotely plausible that one could have come up with the idea that forensic persons are basic, what we mean really by PERSON or SELF and possibly what in addition grounds personal identity.

Here I propose that we think anew about what makes a PERSON or SELF from the perspective of a principle that is both plausible and widely accepted, which I call the *Experience Principle*:

Experience Principle: Whatever it is (the items and the connections) that makes a person who he or she is first personally, whatever it is that makes for personal identity, subjectively speaking, it involves necessarily the individual's experiences.

The *Experience Principle* is warranted on semantic grounds: Most every, but possibly not all, usages of words such as PERSON or SELF assume a first-personal, subjective, experiential component. It is also warranted on the basis of the empirical evidence from *Geisteswissenschaften*: The proximate cause and constitution of persons but not, for example, plants and minerals, come from experience; and further on general scientific and metaphysical principles such as causal closure and no action at too far a distance, which

naturalists about mind accept. The *Experience Principle* is not analytic or
vacuous since there are both reductionist – a person is just a collection of
bosons and fermions – and inflationist views – a person is whatever God
says he is, his experience of himself be damned, that do not take experience
as necessary. The *Experience Principle* allows an account of personhood that
goes beyond what a person experiences, expresses, or represents himself as
like, but it requires that any account of a person include her experience and
self-understanding.

    The core idea is that experiences make for a person if anything does; non-
experiences, for example, trees and apples might cause tree and apple
experiences, but the trees and apples do not constitute the person, whereas
the tree and apple experiences might. *The Experience Principle* suggests that
experience is necessary for identity; it is silent on whether experience is
sufficient (as I will go on to say, semantics, science, and metaphysics seem to
agree that it is not). Locke actually suggests that experience might be
sufficient, when he writes: "For, it being the same consciousness that
makes a man be himself to himself, personal identity depends on that
only" (Locke [1689] 1975, 286). But he eventually sees that this is too strong
(unless he is just taken here to be telling us what "makes a man be himself to
himself," not what makes a man himself). And in any case, the kinds of
experience Locke thinks constitute a person are very limited; they are pretty
much only the kinds of experience a Puritan (Anglican) God would be
interested in on Judgment Day. Narrative-forensic self-representation is
guided by a normative-metaphysical picture in which God decides and
evaluates lives in accordance with his view of what matters in a human life.
But his view of what matters does not, purely in virtue of his being God,
match up with how my personhood is experienced by me or seems to me.
Or to put the point another way: If we imagine, as many modern people
can, a world without the Lockean normative-metaphysical structure, and if,
in addition, we permit ourselves to take a non-prejudiced phenomenological pose toward how it seems to be the person or self that we are, we will
find that the conviction that we are all essentially or primarily Persons[Locke]
will yield its pride of place. Or, so I say.

2. THE EXPERIENCE PRINCIPLE

There are two points that require clarification so that the *Experience
Principle* is properly understood. First, the core idea that motivates every
naturalistic theory of personhood, although not every soul-based theory, is
that first-personal experience is (a major and necessary part of) what makes a

person himself or herself. There are two senses of "make," make in the sense of *causally contributes*, as in the way "you are what you eat," and *constitutive*, as in the way "I am shy." Second, the schema that is typically used as the motto for the forensic view, and which says that what grounds or constitutes personhood is psychological connectedness and continuity actually says nothing, exactly zero, about: (1) what the psychological *items* are that are experienced, or what is different, expressed or represented that make a person who he or she is.[1] It is commonly assumed that the items are autobiographical memories, but this is taken-for-granted rather than argued. Furthermore, even if we concede that personhood or, more likely, one variety of personhood, can be analyzed in terms of one very specific kind of psychological connectedness and continuity, namely, autobiographical memories for what I did (possibly supplemented by accounts of why I did those things), nothing follows about: (2) the nature of the connectedness and continuity relations among the items of experience, whatever they are, that (also) constitute me as who I am, and that are not, as it were, memorial, or not memorial in the familiar autobiographical way. Call the first question, the ITEMS question; the second the CONNECTIONS question.

To get the concept of forensic person out of the schema that mentions only psychological items and connectedness and continuity relations between these items, one needs to be looking for the items and the connection kinds that are suited primarily for our legal and moral practices.

What are those items? They include episodic memories and intentional action descriptions, but not usually phenomenal experiences or the characteristic weather within each of us. What are those connection kinds? Conscious declarative memory, propositional logic, and a theory of intentional action, but not, for example, the sorts of connections that characterize drinking, eating, walking, exercising, cooking breakfast, having sex, daydreams, REM dreams, sexual fantasizing, fantasies of homicide and suicide, poetic musings, artistic imagination, and so on. Regarding (1) and considered most generally: Are the items that make for a person – sensations,

---

[1] It is a complicated task to distinguish clearly between self-experience, self-expression, and self-representation. Here I have this in mind: An itch is just an itch, a self-experience or just an experience. My itching the itch or grimacing because of the itch is a self-expression of the itch or of the way the itch feels. If I think to myself that I have an itch or say aloud that this is so, then I am self-representing. Experience is inherently private, inside the skin. Expressing is observable. Representation can be for one's eyes only or for public consumption. Self-expression and self-representation involve experience. But self-expression and self-representation need not, often do not, express or represent the experience they seem to express or represent. Self-expression can be misread, whereas self-representation can be manipulated intentionally to disguise or misrepresent.

perceptions, moods, emotions, thoughts, memories, values, beliefs, desires, plans, temperamental traits, personal skills, personal style – a psychological penumbra, a sense of self, a sense of my own phenomenal presence, a sense of myself as agent/author of my life, a sense of myself as owner of my experiences, or something(s) else? If all these things are among the items of experience that constitute the self, is there some ratio among them that is typical or, what is different, expected for being designated a *bona fide* person? Regarding (2): Are the items that constitute a self, experienced, expressed or represented in language, or primarily in gesture, bodily posture and facial expression, conceptually or non-conceptually, first-personally, subjectively, and auto-phenomenologically, or is who and what a person is an objective matter, a matter determined by public heterophenomenology, social consensus, and/or completed neuroscience? Are the items that make a person who he or she is, normally – or, what is different, normatively – connected and continuous experientially, expressively, and representationally in narrative form, or are there myriad ways selves emerge, and that selves are experienced, expressed, and revealed?

The Lockean view, which regiments the polysemous ordinary language terms, SELF and PERSON for forensic purposes, gives insufficient attention to both (1) and (2) even as it endorses the insight, expressed by the motto, that what makes a person that person, who she is, has to do with the items of her experience and how they are connected with each other. If we think that the Lockean picture of forensic persons and forensic selves captures some deep metaphysical features of all persons, or that it captures ordinary self-experience, ordinary self-expression, and ordinary self-representation, we will be mistaken. The view picks out a conception of a certain kind of modern, reflective, public person, but not what a self or person *really*, deep-throat, is.

3. SUBJECTIVE AND OBJECTIVE IDENTITY(IES)

Because Locke's theory is said to be a memory or consciousness criterion it would seem to belong to the consensus which abides the *Experience Principle*, and which analyzes what makes a person who she is in terms of how she experiences herself, and thus how her experiences constitute her experienced being. But this is not quite so.

In Book II, Chapter 27, section 10 of the second edition of his *Essay*, entitled "Consciousness Makes Personal Identity," Locke writes: "For, it being the same consciousness that makes a man be himself to himself, personal identity depends on that only" (Locke [1689] 1975, 286). Call identity, so conceived, "self-experienced identity," *SEI*, or "self-represented identity," *SRI*, where for the present referring to *SEI* or *SRI* is neutral about how, for example, conceptually or non-conceptually, linguistically or non-linguistically, episodically or narratively, or how meta- or non-meta *SEI* or *SRI* are. When speaking about first-order subjective consciousness, it is most natural to speak of self-experienced identity, *SEI*, rather than self-represented identity, *SRI*, which is more naturally suited as a name for some sort of second-order consciousness. But I will not fuss here to distinguish *SEI* from *SRI*. The key is that both *SEI* and *SRI* are entirely subjective. Infants and toddlers, who are pre-linguistic or early in language acquisition and who have not been trained up to know or conform to the normative demands of forensic personhood, are self-experiencers and have an *SEI*, perhaps even an *SRI*, but they do not have it in a meta- or in a linguistic way. No matter what the format of representation is, personal identity conceived as either *SEI* or *SRI* is entirely a first personal matter.[2]

In Book. II, Chapter 27, section 26, "Person is a Forensic Term," Locke states this seeming objection to his own purely subjective account of identity.

Person, as I take it, is the name for this self ... It is a forensic term, appropriating actions and their merit ... The personality extends itself beyond present existence to what is past, only by consciousness, whereby it becomes concerned and accountable, owns and imputes to itself past actions, just upon the same ground and for the same reason that it does the present ... And therefore whatever past actions it cannot reconcile or *appropriate* to that present self by consciousness, it can be no more concerned in it than if they had never been done. (Locke [1689] 1975, 467)

The objection is this: Who a person or self is, is commonly both more and less than what the individual experiences, or, what is different, self-represents. Personhood involves more than what I experience or what self-representation represents because there are things I did (I experienced, I am like), but forget or misremember or fail to see in the first place that I did (I experienced, I am like). And personhood involves less than what I have experienced and less than self-representation represents because familiar self-serving biases lead me to describe my experiences, my character traits, my motives and intentions, and my actions in excessively charitable ways, to puff myself up, and to overestimate my good qualities, good actions, and so on.

Here is Locke's vivid suggestion (also Book. II, Chapter 27, section 26) for solving the problem.

---

[2] What makes *SEI* the identity of a person as opposed to a pig or a frog, who also has its own kind of *SEI*, but not *SRI*, is that the relevant kinds of experience are typed to the species nature of each.

[F]or supposing a man punished now for what he had done in another life, whereof he could be made to have no consciousness at all, what difference is there between that punishment, and being created miserable? And, therefore, conformable to this, the apostle tells us, that, at the great day, when every one shall "receive according to his doings, the secrets of all hearts shall be laid open." The sentence shall be justified by the consciousness all persons shall have, that they themselves, in what bodies soever they appear, or what substances soever that consciousness adheres to, are the same that committed those actions, and deserve that punishment for them. (Locke [1689] 1975, 468)

Call God's description of a person's identity, "actual full identity," *AFI*. *AFI* is the true account of a person's identity, either over a segment or a whole lifetime. God knows and can provide the account of what really happened. *AFI* depicts a person as he or she really is, possibly deep-down-inside, or more plausibly given what Locke says, depicts a person as he really is only in the sense that there is a reunification of consciousness with what actions it, as it were, caused or committed. God knows what you really did, who you really are, even if you misremember, forget, engage in hermeneutic puffery or minimization, and he restores your memory before eternal reward or punishment is doled out in the "soever." If God did not do this he would be unjust, punishing you for something you did not, according to *SEI* or *SRI*, do.

The idea is to introduce a counterfactual test: If it were the case that a person's *SEI* or *SRI* "could be made to have no consciousness at all" of what that person really did, then reward and punishment would make no sense; punishment, in particular, would be absurdly cruel, karmically absurd. But punishment and reward make sense if (*inter alia*) the person could be made conscious of what she really did. The key term is "could." If God is the standard for what could happen, then pretty much everything can or could be done including restoring all true memories, motivation ascriptions, action descriptions, and so on, to any individual. God aside, in the actual world we do hold people accountable and dole out rewards and punishments, based on social assessments of the person's *AFI* even if their *SRI* (or *SEI*) does not own the memory of the action ascribed or, what is different, owns the memory of what happened, but not the description of the action that produced it, as in "I didn't mean to hurt you (by running off with her)." Sometimes we hold folks accountable for what they did, even in cases where, without divine intervention, the agent is incapable of seeing things our way, and thus cannot be brought to be conscious of what he did, who he is, and so on.

This much raises a serious question for the concept of forensic personhood, since it is designed to mark accountable persons, and *SEI* and *SRI* are perfectly compatible with an individual who experiences her life in a way that either because of her unusual memory, an unusual theory of action, or no conscience, is not subjectively accountable. It looks as if the Lockean might need to say that actual consciousness or memory of the individual is neither necessary nor sufficient for personhood. On the memory restoration picture, who I am depends upon how my upgraded (by God) self-consciousness, were it to be restored, matches up (or would match up) with God's comprehension of who I am. God has all the objective facts right, so if he restores my memory on Judgment Day I will experience myself as I really am (was), see what I really did.[3]

4. PERSON^{JAMES}: STREAMS, HALOES, PENUMBRAS, PSYCHIC OVERTONES, FRINGES, AND THE FREE WATER OF CONSCIOUSNESS

How does William James provide an alternative or an amplification of Person^{Locke}? The answer is that he takes all of experience, both the items and the connection types, more seriously than Locke does. The basic insight relevant here is this: If we pay close attention to the phenomenology of experience from a neutral pose, we will see that there are both what James calls "substantive" and "transitive" states of mind. The distinction is not hard and fast, but here are some examples: I experience thirst, I walk to the cabinet, fetch a glass, go to the sink, turn the faucet on, fill the glass with water (all transitive), and drink it (substantive). I leave work and drive home: The road ahead is focal throughout (a "stopping place," "a perch" = substantive state of mind) until I achieve my goal, namely, getting home. But even as the road ahead remains the focus of my attention all the way home, there are numerous other experiences I have while driving that are not focal, namely, everything else that is experienced – sights, sounds,

---

[3] There is something to this idea of *AFI*: For us naturalists, something like our best scientific theory of persons and what makes them tick will play the role of God in fixing facts about personal identity that require more than what the *Experience Principle* provides. Also, suppose that God was interested in more than rewarding and punishing persons in the "soever." Suppose he wanted to let you know who you really are in a deep non-forensic way, akin to the way Socrates and Nietzsche recommend (Freud said of Nietzsche "he had greater self-knowledge than any man who ever lived or ever shall live"). Since God can do anything, he could instead of restoring your memory for everything you did, do that plus make you more sensitively aware of everything you experienced, and better than you are now at seeing the depth and texture of your experiences, and more attuned to the actual causal roles, and constitutive status, of all your experiences. If God did this I could be said to know myself as the person I, OJF, am. In such a case, as perhaps occurs with excellent therapy, I would internalize certain objective truths about persons generally, and about the person I am specifically, and experience myself anew, more clearly, and, as we say, subjectively. Under this scenario, my *SEI/SRI* would approximate my *AFI*.

daydreams, half-hatched musings, listening to the radio, etc. – that are not essential to getting home. All this other stuff is transitive. Or, imagine a class of young students reading an elementary arithmetic problem and then setting to solving it. The problem and its solution involve substantive states, the process of solving it (imagine this is done both in the head and by way of any scribbling that seems useful) is transitive. Each student may fly from perch to perch in a different way. The teacher grades only successful landings on the perch.

From the point of view of experience we are in no position to decide which, the substantive or the transitive parts, are more causally significant or constitutive of who we are overall. Nonetheless, and here James is speaking directly to Locke, among others, "we" – in the traditional faculty psychology of the philosopher and the "brass instrument psychology" of the second half of the nineteenth century – privilege the substantive parts:

We ought to say a feeling of *and,* a feeling of *if,* a feeling of *but,* and a feeling of *by,* quite as readily as we say a feeling of *blue* or a feeling of *cold.* Yet we do not: so inveterate has our habit become of recognizing the existence of the substantive parts alone, that language almost refuses to lend itself to any other use. (James [1890] 2010, 162)

Focusing introspectively or phenomenologically on the underestimated stream, the flow and the transitive, reveals that these parts have depth and texture that extend into a wide horizontal zone that James calls the "fringe." "The object before the mind always has a 'fringe.' There are other *unnamed modifications of consciousness* just as important as the transitive states, and just as cognitive as they" (James [1892] 1984, 149). He then writes about the type(s) of experience constituted by what he calls "the free water of consciousness":

The traditional psychology talks like one who should say a river consists of nothing but pailsful, spoonsful, quartpotsful, barrelsful, and other moulded forms of water. Even were the pails and the pots all actually standing in the stream, still between them the free water would continue to flow. It is just this free water of consciousness that psychologists resolutely overlook. Every definite image in the mind is steeped and dyed in the free water that flows round it. With it goes the sense of its relations, near and remote, the dying echo of whence it came to us, the dawning sense of whither it is to lead. The significance, the value, of the image is all in this halo or penumbra that surrounds and escorts it, – or rather that is fused into one with it and has become bone of its bone and flesh of its flesh; leaving it, it is true, an image of the same thing it was before, but making it an image of that thing newly taken and freshly understood ... *Let us call the consciousness of this halo of relations around the image by the name of "psychic overtone" or "fringe."*[4] (James [1892] 1984, 151, original italics)

The stream is in the first instance a stream of self-experienced identity, *SEI*. James's insight is that it is underestimated in self-representation, in *SRI*, be it intended for first personal or public consumption, as well as in scientific theorizing, possibly for similar reasons. Why are the substantive aspects of experience rated more highly than the transitive aspects? It might be because the substantive parts are objectively more significant than the transitive parts, specifically, that the former are more causally influential or, what is different, constitutive of who I am than the latter. But there is no *a priori* reason to think that all the sights I experienced inattentively biking to work or what I had for breakfast is less important causally or constitutively than this morning's argument with my best friend. Everyone thinks this is so. But one would need a much more advanced science of the mind to actually show this. One possibility, I think it is likely, is that we, especially in our kind of complex and crowded worlds, rate the causal and constitutive role of the latter as greater than the former, because we are more interested in the upstream effects of the latter kind of events, and the reason is that they are probably more consequential to an individual's social behavior, but not necessarily to everything that is true overall about a person, not necessarily more consequential to who the person is. A different and more provocative way to put the point is this: Both the normative-metaphysical structure of the Lockean – really the modern North Atlantic – universe (there is a moral blueprint for doing life the right way and God will judge whether your life was in normative conformity), as well as certain familiar practical features of complex social life cause us to attend disproportionately to happenings and doings (substantive facts) as what makes for a person, when, in fact, these facts (as known first or third personally) are just the main things we are interested in, not necessarily what makes an individual who he or she is.

The *Experience Principle* simply says this: Whatever it is (the items and the connections) that makes a person who he or she is first personally, whatever it is that makes for personal identity, subjectively speaking, it involves necessarily the individual's experiences. The *Experience Principle* is non-committal on which experiences make a person, or on which experiences make the greater contribution to who a person is. Some say dream experiences are both hugely influential to who I am and, what is different, hugely self-expressive. Others say that dreams are largely

---

[4] Christof Koch (2004) deploys the concept of the "penumbra" in his neuroscientific account of qualia.

inconsequential noise. Which is it? Presumably this is an empirical matter, which awaits lots more evidence from mind science than we have at present.[5] Or consider this sort of case: Like many people I read lots of novels and frequently attend concerts. I do both to change myself, to become a more complex and interesting person, mostly in the first instance to myself. I almost always can tell you what books I have read, or more likely you say, "have you read *Freedom* by Jonathan Franzen?" and I say "extremely overrated"; or you ask about David Foster Wallace's *Infinite Jest* and I say "as good as Joyce and Proust." If you ask "What are they about?" I often cannot say (actually in these two cases I can because they are recent reads). It is an empirical question whether and how my novel reading and concert-going affects who I am, but I am betting that they are self-forming and this despite my poor memory for what I have read or heard.

Here one might propose that we ought to distinguish between causal and constitutive claims. The idea would be that the taste experience of even the most wonderful meal is not – cannot be – as significant to who I am as who I had the meal with. The experience of losing a sock is not – cannot be – as significant as losing one's mother. Both might have downstream causal effects but only the latter could ever be thought to be identity constitutive.

This sounds generally right, although there are many exceptions (I once heard an acquaintance say that when he was in the grip of an addiction, a mismatched sock and a family death seemed about equally (un-) important), and the distinction between causes and constituents is an important one. But here it is asked to do too much work. Right now normative views about what counts as constitutive, and what counts as merely causal, are largely determined by our normative views themselves. The sciences of the mind's answers to basic questions about what makes us tick are just emerging. So far, we have largely been dealing with folk theories, pseudo-scientific theories, such as psychoanalysis, and normative views, such as Locke's, about what makes us tick, all of which are designed for a certain kind of complex social commerce in certain types of social worlds.

Experiences make persons. At least experiences are what make a person who he or she is subjectively. But there is also sense to the idea that a person is more than she subjectively experiences herself as being now, certainly more than she expresses or represents herself as being now. Right now there

---

[5] It might be claimed that physicalists must accept that it is more than experiences that play a constitutive role. Say my vitamin D levels are low, this will have an effect on mood. Or if calcium levels are low this will make my bones weak. True. But the idea here is that these differences in the body only make a difference to me, qua person, if they produce experiential effects. I feel low, or ache, say. Are there unconscious experiences? No.

are ever so many experiences, including ones I am having now, that I do not know how to express or represent, and saying so is not a way of expressing or representing those experiences. Part of this, the inability to express or represent what I experience, is a memory problem, but most of it seems to me as due to the fact that most of my experience, conceived in a Jamesian, "free water of consciousness" way, seems first, to have little to do with doings, and second, is not suitable to be narrated, storied, perhaps not even to be spoken about at all.

In *Nausea* (1939), Sartre gestures at this first self, and indicates what attentiveness to it might yield:

[t]here is something new about my hands, a certain way of picking up my pipe or fork which now has a certain way of having itself picked up. I don't know. A little while ago, just as I was coming into my room, I stopped short because I felt in my hand a cold object which held my attention through a sort of personality. I opened my hand, looked: I was simply holding the door-knob ... So a change *has* taken place the last few weeks. But where? It is an abstract change without an object ... I think I'm the one who has changed: that's the simplest solution. Also the most unpleasant. But I must finally realize that I am subject to these sudden transformations. The thing is that I rarely think; a crowd of small metamorphoses accumulate in me without my noticing it, and then, one fine day, a veritable revolution takes place. (Sartre 1939, 4–5)

It seems a perfectly credible hypothesis that who I am is not just some complex summation of all my deeds (plus all the things that have happened to me), but also that who I am involves "a crowd of small metamorphoses [that] accumulate in me." The accumulation involves experiences, but many, possibly most of these are not stored, and do not involve the doings of deeds. They are nonetheless, identity constitutive; at least, it is not remotely incredible to claim that this is so.

Is the "crowd of small metamorphoses [that] accumulate in me" also part of my experience, and thus according to the *Experience Principle* part of what makes me, me? Surely, metamorphoses are based on experiences, some of which may be as inchoate and hard to articulate and remember, as those depicted by Sartre; and some of these metamorphoses are themselves noticed, experienced. Perhaps, there are practices that could make us more attentive to these aspects of our selves.

What I have been calling *AFI* claims to capture the facts about who a person is. But if I am a person constituted not only by what happens to me and by what I do, but in addition, by the transitive flow, the "free water of consciousness," the accumulation of "the crowd of small metamorphoses," then these deserve a place in the story of my *AFI*. *AFI*, conceived as the

God's eye point of view, is clearly a fiction as far as the naturalist is concerned. But it is a useful regulative fiction, and not just for forensic practices. Each of us insofar as we have aspirations for greater self-knowledge distinguishes between how we experience ourselves and how we might experience ourselves if we saw things more clearly and deeply. It is normative for us to wish to remember and to be able to tell our story truthfully. If, however, we conceive experience broadly as involving affect, emotions, moods, the overall way(s) it feels to be me and to go about living, we will realize that there is much more than just autobiographical memory, much more than narrative identity, to be in touch with to get myself for who and what I am. But the *AFI* that derives from Locke's discussion is an exclusively forensic, narrative conception. On Judgment Day, Locke's Puritan God does not restore my phenomenological stream or put me in some sort of deep touch with "the free water of consciousness" that helps constitute me as the person I am. He provides me with a perfect transcript of my deeds and my actual intentions and motives when I did those deeds. God could put me in touch with the "free water" that makes me, me. But the view on offer does not make that "free water" or the "crowd of small metamorphoses [that] accumulate" important.[6]

Earlier I described two extreme views of persons that might deny the *Experience Principle*, a reductive deflationary view that offers a full description of the supervenience base – neurons or lower – that describe this guy OJF, or an inflationary view that says that this guy OJF is whomever God says he is. That is, how OJF is, is however God experiences him as being, which could be nothing like this guy OJF experiences himself. A credible objection to both views is that they are eliminativist. There are persons, so any conclusion that there are no persons at all rests on a mistake, and enacts a *reductio* on itself. I will not develop this reply here, but it seems the right sort of response to give.

The *Experience Principle* favors a more expansive view of personhood than Person[Locke], one that does not privilege the aspects of a person and his or her life that might legitimately be considered most important for forensic purposes and suitable for being depicted in a standard modern narrative. If, descriptively, I am the person constituted by my experiences, and if my experiences have depth, texture, nuance, and display multifarious contents and connections that are not on offer by either the "potsful" and "pailsful" picture and its close forensic and narrative relations, then there are important normative consequences.

---

[6] See note 4 above.

5. THREE THESES OF PSYCHOBIOLOGICAL NATURALISM

The next step to advance the argument for a broader view of personhood than Person[Locke] involves fully embracing scientific naturalism about persons, the sort of view Locke claimed to be neutral about, and James, despite writing in the aftermath of Darwin, was ambivalent about. Consider again the questions: (1) What are the multifarious psychological items that, as it were, bind together to constitute, make, or reflect who a person or self is? – what I called the ITEMS question; and (2) What are the various ways these multifarious items are, can be, and, what is different, should be connected and/or relate to each other in conscious *Homo sapiens* to count as a human person or self? – the CONNECTIONS question.

Start with these credible theses that are widely accepted by naturalists about mind and that form the core of constructive psychobiological naturalism: *Neurophysicalism*; *The Heterogeneity Thesis*; and *Subjective Realism* (Flanagan 1992, 2000, 2002, 2007).

Neurophysicalism is the thesis that in this actual world, experiences supervene only on embodied beings with nervous systems topped off by brains, or that experiences occur only in and to creatures with nervous systems of certain sorts, or some such.

The Heterogeneity Thesis says that any taxonomy of the kinds of states, events, and processes that we call "experiences" will show them to be of multifarious kinds. There are moods, emotions, sensations, perceptions. There are the experiences of 'if,' 'and,' and 'but.' There is taste consciousness, olfactory consciousness, tactile-kinesthetic consciousness, visual consciousness, auditory consciousness. There is time consciousness, the feeling of duration and of the "specious present." There is the experience of orgasm, a tickle, an itch, and the experiences of riding a bike, swimming, doing long division, remembering French vocabulary words or the capitals of the fifty states. There is the memory of the overall feel of our summer cottage on Cape Cod in 1961, and there is the memory that JFK was the president at that time. There is the thrill of victory and the agony of defeat. There is know-how and know-that. There is consciousness while asleep, and there is awake consciousness. And there is probably most of all that "free water of consciousness."

C. S. Peirce expresses one version of *The Heterogeneity Thesis* this way: "The *quale*-consciousness is not confined to simple sensations. There is a particular *quale* to purple, though it be only a mixture of red and blue. There is a distinctive *quale* to every combination of sensations – There is a distinctive *quale* to every work of art – a distinctive *quale* to this moment as it is to me – a peculiar *quale* to every day and every week – a peculiar *quale* to my whole personal consciousness. I appeal to your introspection to bear me out" (Peirce 1898, vol. 6, 223).

The heterogeneous types of mental states are distinguished variously in terms of content, format, and phenomenal feel. Taken together, they are the items of experience – although one might legitimately worry that "items" talk itself favors the forensic, narrative view, by making us prone to commit what A. N. Whitehead called "the fallacy of misplaced concreteness" – making something that is an event or process into a thing or substance. In any case, if consciousness makes a person, then the answer to the first question, the ITEMS question, now interpreting "items" to allow for events and processes (my own metaphysical tendencies are Heraclitean): What are the items that constitute personhood? – is that they are – indeed, they must be – the heterogeneous item types that make up some precise and expanded taxonomy such as this picture provides (Figure 10.1).

Subjective realism says that for creatures that have experiences, that is, creatures with the right kinds of nervous systems, experiences are had,

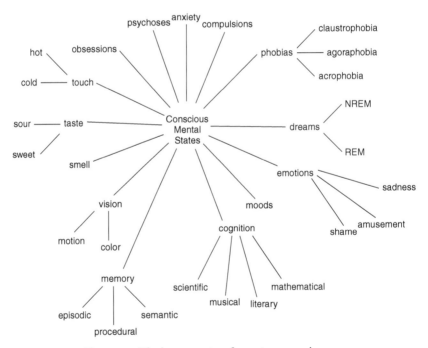

Figure 10.1 The heterogeneity of conscious mental states.

experienced, or possessed only by the creature that has, is constituted by, or is attached to that particular nervous system. Experiencers have their own and only their own experiences. Things or systems that lack nervous systems do not have experiences, and thus there is nothing it is like to be them, nothing at all. For things or systems that are not experiencers, all facts about them are, in principle, accessible from the objective point of view, ergo, *objective realism* for table and chairs, water, gold, bosons and fermions.

In a nutshell, these three theses taken together are the key to under-standing the mind–body problem, or what has been lately dubbed "the hard problem of consciousness," as well as getting a feel for what "experience," in the *Experience Principle*, encompasses. Experiences are (neuro-) physical events, and thus physicalism is safe and secure. But experiences are had only by the creatures, systems, or sentient beings, which are capable of, or positioned to have, them – fish, reptiles, amphibians, birds, and mammals, but not planets, stars, oceans, plants, and dirt. In the portions of the universe for which *subjective realism* obtains, there are opacities that are consequences of evolutionary design. Evolution had no reason to care about making experiences first-personally accessible to all the curious creatures interested in having the experiences of other persons or creatures, bats and the like. If consciousness serves a function, it comes from the fact that passing information phenomenally, rapidly, and accurately, proved a good, satisfactory design solution to the feeding, foraging, dating, and mating problems faced by the very organisms with most need to know what is happening in their own bodies and the immediate surround, namely, each embodied individual. To paraphrase John Dewey: It is amazing that con-sciousness emerged, but given that it did emerge, there is no mystery to its being connected to what it is connected to.

6. THREE CONSEQUENCES OF PSYCHOBIOLOGICAL NATURALISM

This resolutely naturalistic perspective yields immediate insight into several truths about selves, self-experience, self-expression, and self-representation that are occluded by the forensic agenda.

First, regarding our first question, the ITEMS question: (1) What are the items that are connected in consciousness? The answer is that a vast heterogeneity of experiences is normal and expectable, only some of which are propositional memory states, which are privileged on the forensic analysis. Much of the texture of things I did and that happened to me, and that make me who I am, that make my life what it is, seem to fade, sometimes even to evaporate, once the experience is over. Even if the memory remains that such and so happened, or that I did it, or that it seemed a certain way, how it seems often, indeed almost always, passes quickly, as the vivid experience it was. I had a hard-boiled egg and three kinds of berries for breakfast today. When I ate breakfast there was the taste equivalent of a kaleidoscopic visual experience. I am sure of that, but I am not experiencing or re-experiencing it as such now, although I have a fond connection to that experience. But the person I am now is the person who was doing that and having those experiences several hours ago. That breakfast experience is undoubtedly causally relevant to certain things that are happening now, perhaps to some things I am doing now, for example, writing about today's breakfast. On what basis could it be concluded that my breakfast experience is, even if I had not reflected upon it, not also constitutive of this guy OJF? Of course, the better example is the earlier one about novels and concerts that we choose to read or go to in order to change ourselves, but the experience and content of which we cannot conjure up. If the basis is a normative theory about what matters most to those outside me – then it is true that my breakfasts, as well as the novels I have read and concerts I have attended, are largely inconsequential to how the lives of others go and to what makes them, them. But the question of personhood is not about what matters to you about me, but about what makes me, me.

The second consequence of the three theses of psychobiological naturalism involves (2), the CONNECTIONS question. The heterogeneous multiplicity of conscious mental state types that there are, and which form the basis for an answer to the ITEMS question, should make one worry about privileging or highlighting the propositional memory items as the key items that make a person who he or she is, and also about privileging the ways the propositional items are connected in, for example, declarative memory and in a propositional logic that embeds a theory of practical rationality. There is no *a priori* reason to think that the person I am is not both the result of, and constituted by, all the heterogeneous experiences that are part of the stream or flow of experience – including "the free water of consciousness" – as much as they are the result and constituted by the explicitly remembered events and actions that occur in the stream or flow.

It is a plausible general metaphysical thesis that the causal and constitutive relations among *all* a person's experiences make him who he is, whether these experiences involve deeds or memories thereof, and whether memory for these experiences is accurate or not. This plausible metaphysical thesis is the *Experience Principle*. Every cognitive scientific research program seeks to identify the items and connections that are most relevant to the explanation of certain psychological phenomena, certain stable phenomena, domain by domain. But as far as I can tell, what psychological phenomena are studied is driven by interest in a particular type of experience, vision, memory, learning, and no researchers claim that this rather than that kind of experience is most constitutive of personhood, although they often claim that one kind or another is most relevant for negotiating particular aspects of the world. Insofar as mind scientists operate with a general theory of personhood, it is not the forensic conception[7] but something like this:

Experience Principle: Whatever it is (the items and the connections) that makes a person who he or she is first personally, whatever it is that makes for personal identity, subjectively speaking, it involves necessarily the individual's experiences.

The third consequence of the three theses of psychobiological naturalism is epistemic. *Subjective realism* provides the picture given in Figure 10.2.

Subjective realism enables us to quickly gain a picture of the epistemic situations – the facts about, as well as the advantages and disadvantages – of first, second, and third persons trying to understand their own and other minds, themselves and each other. There are three epistemic positions in the actual world marked by the three kinds of pronouns – "I," "you," "he/she/ it/they." Picture each person as represented by a cylinder, a tall 16 oz. drink can, say. What is experienced first personally, as *SEI* or *SRI*, is opaque from the point of view of the second person, from the point of view of those in various kinds of relations, which at the limit are of an I–thou sort, the kind that lovers or true Aristotelian friends have. Think of the "you's" and the "thou's" in one's life as those who stand in various external relations to the long vertical orientation of the cylinder, which represents the outside, the skin of a person – the skin, recall, is the largest bodily organ. Relations who are friends or acquaintances of utility or pleasure see the cylinder as a flat rectangle if they are far away, but start to detect dimensionality and depth as they move closer. True friends are very close and experience me, the cylinder, from all sides, but still only from the outsides – over, under, sideways, down, perhaps; but always from the outside. But no you's and

---

[7] One exception is personality psychology, where psychologists look for characteristic dispositional types – almost always as one would expect in a tradition that privileges forensic-narrative persons – as traits that predict behavior, which is not the only role that such traits play first-personally, where they are also enlisted in the project of self-knowledge, a project that need not reduce to self-prediction and self-control.

The subjective realist picture of mind.
Metaphysically one, epistemically tri-partite.

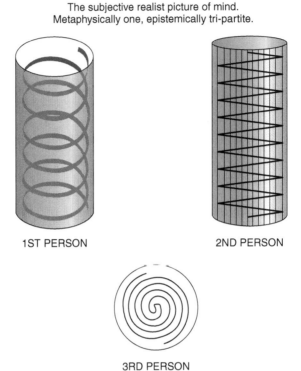

1ST PERSON   2ND PERSON

3RD PERSON

Figure 10.2 The Subjective Realist picture of mind. Metaphysically one, epistemically tri-partite.

thou's, no second persons in my life, no one in the history of interpersonal life in the history of the universe, has ever had one of my experiences, since they are not me.

The third personal perspective – imagine the perspective of the neuroscientist, who gazes into my brain as I eat my hard-boiled egg and berries or as I watch my children running up the driveway to greet me – has yet another, different perspective from me or my loved ones. Whereas friends, acquaintances, and the abundant anonymous souls with whom I interact, read me through my actions, by applying a commonly known theory of intentional action, by reading my self-expressions and listening to my self-representations, the neuroscientist is looking at the supervenience base, and working to link that level with my phenomenological reports (*SEI* and *SRI*) and observations of my behavior.

Each and every perspective of every human individual is, according to the *subjective realist*, a perspective on, of, and by, a living human being who has an inner life comprised of the multifarious items that are the answer to question (1), the ITEMS question, connected in all the different ways these items are connected as provided in the answer to (2), the CONNECTIONS question. These items and the connections among them are better described, more validly depicted, by Person^James than by Person^Locke. If autobiographical memory is the dominant mode of connection for Person^Locke, for the second self, then accumulation of small but significant metamorphoses is the dominant mode of connection for Person^James, for the first self.

One might ask, which perspective, first, second, third, yields the right epistemic position to see the person for who he or she is? Only one perspective, first person, is the perspective of the person himself or herself. But it is not automatic trump. The question of who a person or self is, is not for all purposes, straightforwardly equivalent to the question: How does this individual person experience (*SEI*, *SRI*) himself or herself? Nonetheless, what makes any person, the person he or she is, does according to the view on offer, include essentially experience of himself or herself.

If we think that the second or third person perspective, even as based, in some significant measure, on first personal self-expression and self-representation for social planning purposes, generated in the back and forth of giving and taking instructions/orders, and making commitments for which we hold each other responsible, describe the first person, we will be mistaken. The *Experience Principle* expresses the insight that what makes a person who he is consists first and foremost of experience, not of all this public stuff, but of his experience.

The person or self that I am, is subjectively constituted by whatever things are like or, what might be different, seem like from the inside. This follows from the *Experience Principle*. One question is whether the *Experience Principle* provides direction to capture the necessary and sufficient conditions for personhood. The answer is no. The person I am objectively, according to *AFI*, might be something that the second and third persons in my life see or remember some aspects of more clearly than I do, either because there are facts about me that are not experienced by me at all, or because there are facts about me that are experienced by me, but that I do not see or remember for what they are, or there are certain facts about me that are not amenable to experiencing at all, first, second, or third personally, but that involve surmises (based on mini-theories or big master narratives, psychoanalysis, for example) about patterns that explain who and what I am, and am like.

7. SUBJECTIVE REALISM, ROBINSON CRUSOE, AND THE ORIGINAL PEOPLE

Even the most superficial phenomenology reveals my experiences, both the items and how they are connected, to involve much more than tracking my actions, interpreting them, scoring them for moral quality. Normally I am having my experiences (*SEI*), both substantive and transitive experiences, not mostly evaluating them in terms of some blueprint I may, or may not, have (but the culture almost certainly has) for judging how I am measuring up to some pre-existing and normatively approved game plan for how lives should be and go. It seems obvious that a Robinson Crusoe raised on a tropical island by rabbits would be a person who does things, has experiences, and who self-expresses. Self-expression, which does not always accurately reflect (sometimes on purpose) self-experience is worn often on the face or seen by others who know how to read others' actions in our social world (Darwin 1872; Flanagan 2003, 2007). If rabbits can read human expressions, then Robinson Crusoe is read, understood by rabbits to whatever point that rabbits can get us or him. If rabbits cannot read persons, then Robinson Crusoe is not read even though he is a locus of self-experience (and possesses *SEI*) who is expressing (*SRI*) some of what is going on inside himself. That is, even if Robinson Crusoe is not read by any other sentient being, he is still the person who has and is constituted by his experiences and, what is different, the life he lives. Even though my Crusoe does not have language, he has a memory – episodic, perhaps – of what he has done, and where he has been. He has experiences and he is a person.

Not only is my Crusoe a person, but it is perfectly sensible to say on general naturalistic grounds that cavemen and hunter-gatherers of 200,000 years ago were persons too. Such folk lived lives, had autobiographies, had, but not in the modern linguistic way, their own *lebenswelten*. (If you have ever been on a silent retreat for more than a week, experience can start to be, at least seem, non-conceptual, more holistic.) But cavepersons and hunter-gatherer persons were not forensic persons. They did not in any non-trivial sense conceive their lives as essentially narrative ones. The relevant legal and moral practices that define forensic persons into existence did not yet exist; and the linguistic practices, these involve far more than words, did not exist. There is no doubt that language and other social institutions add complexity, new kinds of texture, and new varieties to all three underlying capacities – for experience, self-expression and self-representation (to self and others) – and thereby allow new efficient vehicles that can do the work of forensic selfhood.[8] The point, however, is that persons pre-exist these practices.[9]

So far, I have tried to make plausible this thesis: All persons are Persons[James]; modern people are also Persons[Locke]. Person[James] is ontogenically and phylogenetically basic, the first self. Person[Locke] is later, derivative, an abstraction, a second self. These two ways of being interpenetrate. In modern times we apply a discount rate to our first selves. But there is as of now no evidence or argument that applying this discount rate is warranted if what we are concerned with is who we are, what makes us tick, and how we are constituted as persons.

8. DIACHRONIC AND EPISODIC SELF-REPRESENTATION

For a long time (Flanagan 1990, 1991, 1996), I have been distinguishing between the descriptive and normative theses about forensic, narrative persons, and suggesting that in its industrial strength forms, as one sees, for example, in the work of Locke, Charles Taylor, and Harry Frankfurt, we are seeing an endorsement of a certain way of being, doing, and representing the self, not a description of normal, everyday self- or person-hood.

Forensic persons may be narrative persons, but that is not because persons are essentially either forensic, called by their nature to be morally or legally accountable, nor called by their nature to think or speak of themselves in terms of narratives that make them suitable objects for prediction and control. To be sure, gregarious social animals such as us

---

[8] Dreaming is a good example of (self-) experience, which is self-expressive. But dreams are not self-represented until put into words in thought or told to others, in which latter case "dreams" are shared. Now whether the experiences that we call "dreams" are self-expressive in the sense that they express deep and significant aspects of one's self is an empirical question. My view is that dreams are the spandrels of sleep (1995, 2000), which means that although dreams are experiences and thus both cause and constitute my self, they are not the best information source about what makes me tick or specifically what I most care about.

[9] Thinking of my Crusoe, as well as cavepersons and hunter-gatherer persons, helps fix attention on three different functions that experience seems to serve, so long as epiphenomenalism is false. First, there is consciousness that works by the familiar five senses, and which at least by the light of day helps me negotiate the immediate environment. Second, there is social consciousness that works to read other animals, including non-human ones, and to help me to negotiate the immediate social environment, to know when opportunities to date and mate are available and when I need to flee or fight. But third, and subserving and subfusing both the latter kinds of focal consciousness, is the "free water of consciousness," the overall experienced state of both my being (my *Dasein*) and the surround. This field, the horizon of consciousness, not only makes my experiences what they are, but also allows quick shifting between figure and ground as necessary. Normally and everywhere, it is experiences which serve these three functions that make a person who he or she is. A forensic person is only possible, when both these functions, but especially the second, are elaborated inside complex modern social practices.

were always held to account by whatever mechanisms were at the disposal of our non-human ancestors and the original people. But no one credibly thinks that those mechanisms involved a theory of moral and legal agency, which Person^{Locke} does involve, nor that keeping score of cooperation or lack thereof in social relations is sufficient for being an essentially narrative being. And if it is, then the concept of narrativity is trivially true and nothing interesting is at stake in discussing the matter. It is incredible to think that we were narrative persons when we evolved say, 200,000 years ago. Forensic persons, persons who are morally and legally accountable, seem to require something like narrative accountability. And clearly, providing narrative accounts is something persons, especially modern persons, know how to do. But it is by no means obvious that this co-occurrence of forensic persons and narrative persons has to do with the naturalness or inevitability of either, but rather more likely with the fact that they are designed to co-occur. Again, I am not doubting that cavepersons and hunter-gatherers held each other accountable for what they did (there is moralistic aggression among non-human primates and there are coalitions of chimps that plot and carry out pay-back for wrongdoing). I am denying that such practices depended in any way on the cognitive-linguistic capacities that underwrite Person^{Locke}.

One possibility that emerges is that the way we self-express and self-represent in modern social worlds, because it depicts persons in forensic and narrative ways, produces the illusion that this is the way most persons always have and always will experience themselves, and that furthermore the actual experiences that makes each of us who we are, are mostly of this form. But if, as I have been arguing, there is a multiplicity, a heterogeneity of experience items types, it is also *prima facie* credible that there is a multiplicity of types of self-experience, and thus that there may be nothing normal and natural about being a modern type of forensic-narrative person. An idea worth seriously entertaining is that *SEI* and *SRI* in the narrative-forensic mode is not the dominant mode of self-experiencing and self-representing because it is so natural, as that it is expected, endorsed, and pulled for by modern social ecologies that are (also) structured by a picture of the universe with the normative, metaphysical structure of the Abrahamic traditions.

Galen Strawson thinks something like this. In "Against narrativity," he distinguishes between "one's experience of oneself when one is considering oneself principally as a human being taken as a whole, and one's experience of oneself when one is considering oneself principally as an inner mental entity or 'self' of some sort" (Strawson 2004, 429). The idea is to first draw attention to the fact that when speaking of one's self, when using first-personal pronouns say, there is often a disconnect between the sense that *phi* happened in my life, that this guy OJF did *phi*, and that the person that I am now, did *phi*. Strawson recommends using self* to mark my (sense of) self now, and self without asterisk to mark the historical being I am.

For example, I, OJF, wrote a desperate, longing love poem to B in my teens. This is something that is part of my experience, of my history, despite the fact that the person I am now, OJF*, is not the same person or self who wrote that desperate, longing love poem. This latter, self as "inner mental entity," is what Strawson calls "self-experience," which is one variety of what I call "experience" or "self-experience" (SEI), and which may or may not involve self-expression and/or self-representation (SRI).[10]

The key point is that the story of my life, even as known and told and lived by me, and my experience of my self, can come apart; it depends on how I am using words like I, MY, and MINE, with or without *. This might not seem surprising given the polysemy of the words PERSON and SELF, but it is consequential for more than the meaning of our words. Indeed, it seems to me that if I do not antecedently ask, expect, or require that my self* now (should) be or feel that I* now am the same self as I was at every other point in my life, if I do require that the actors and owners of past events in my life must be me*, then I can start to think about the multiplicity of ways that experience of myself presents itself to me. It is freeing to not demand that I conform to norms, roughly Lockean, that require that everything that has happened to me and that I have done, has happened to me* or was done by me*. It did not and it was not.

One answer to one of my security questions is "Reggie," the name of my best childhood friend, Reginald J. Sutherland iv. Reggie died in Vietnam in 1969. He was my best friend then, actually not even then, really about ten years earlier, when we were boys, barely in the double digits. But I* am not the same person I was then, not remotely. And thus Reggie is not only not my best friend now, he was not in 1969 when he was killed, and he never ever was the best friend of this guy OJF*, who I* am now. But it is true that Reggie was once the best friend of this guy OJF when I am considering myself "principally as a human being taken as a whole," but he was never even an acquaintance of OJF*, when I am considering myself "principally as an inner mental entity or 'self' of some sort."

---

[10] It would be better, given the way I am using words, to mark the distinction this way: PERSON = SELF and names the historical being I am. PERSON* = SELF* and names the sense I have of my phenomenal occurrent being. But I will not fuss over the matter here.

Strawson uses this disconnect to emphasize this: "One of the most important ways in which people tend to think of themselves . . . is as things whose persistence conditions are not obviously or automatically the same as the persistence conditions of a human being considered as a whole" (Strawson 2004, 430). And he draws attention to one aspect or kind of experience that is underestimated, not properly noticed – perhaps because of the high status of forensic-narrative selfhood:

The basic form of Diachronic self-experience is that
[D] one naturally figures oneself, considered as a self, as something that was there in the (further) past and will be there in the (further) future.
If one is Episodic, by contrast,
[E] one does not figure oneself, considered as a self, as something that was there in the (further) past and will be there in the (further) future. (Strawson 2004, 430)

Strawson describes **D** and **E** as "basic forms of self-experience," as "styles of temporal being," and as "basic dispositions," and proposes that they are based on deep innate individual differences. I will not fuss over these matters, since my main concern is to use the distinction among his varieties of self-experience to create leverage to move forensic-narrative selfhood from the realm of the obvious right way to conceive persons. But I will say this: We ought to consider the old-fashioned historical materialist possibility that the dominant mode of self-experience, self-expression, and self-representation, is **D**-ish, i.e., forensic-narrative, and that this is not because it is the most common innately specified psychobiological configuration of the human mind, but because this way of self-conceiving, expressing, and representing is culturally constructed, endorsed, and pulled for, especially in modern social environments. If the ontogeny and phylogeny of the self is as I have imagined, then cavepersons, hunter-gatherer-persons, like contemporary infants and toddlers were Persons[James] not Persons[Locke]. The linguistic, moral, and legal practices required for Person[Locke] did not exist when the ice melted at the end of the Pleistocene. It seems likely that the forensic, narrative self is normalized by cultural forces, not by human nature as such. And if this is so, it is also possible that being episodic (**E**) is basic, and that being diachronic (**D**) is derivative, later, not necessarily better.

Strawson imagines this challenge from a Diachronic to an Episodic: "Episodics are inherently dysfunctional in the way they relate to their own past. Episodics will reply that the past can be present and alive in the present without being present and alive *as* the past. The past can be alive – arguably more genuinely alive – in the present simply insofar as it has helped to shape the way one is in the present" (Strawson 2004, 432). An emerging jazz composition has a history as it is performed, and what happens at each moment is crucial for what comes next. But the whole thing is improvised, as we say, not composed in advance. The *Experience Principle* says that a person is constituted by his or her experiences. It does not say that a person to be a person must bring, know, articulate, express, or represent her history at each moment to be that person. Strawson gives this gloss on wise remarks from Rilke:

"For the sake of a single poem . . . you must have . . . many memories . . . And yet it is not enough to have memories . . . For the memories themselves are not important." They give rise to a good poem "only when they have changed into our very blood, into glance and gesture, and are nameless, no longer to be distinguished from ourselves." (Strawson 2004, 432)

Normal people are all diachronic in the sense or to the point that they possess memory, a respectable amount of knowledge about what they, considered as a historical being, have done, where they have been, and what has happened in their lives. But diachronicity, in this minimalistic sense, is not sufficient to be a forensic-narrative self, since even my Crusoe, cavepersons, and the other original persons, have such knowledge and such sense of themselves. They are self-experiencers who self-express. What else is necessary to be a narrative-forensic self? Strawson suggests that to make for narrative selves such additional things as form-finding, story-telling, the search for, or the projection of coherence, a fair amount of central planning about how things are supposed to go, to turn out for this guy, and religious beliefs of the sort embedded in the analysis of Person^{Locke}, where the analysis is intended to have personhood conform to an account that takes as basic the reality of God and God's interest in assessing and holding each of us fully accountable for our whole life.

One way of challenging Strawson's nativist interpretation is by claiming that much of pressure to conflate me and me* comes from a normative-cum-metaphysical picture that assigns unity and accountability to a person for his or her whole life, and thus that pressures or directs one to accept that it makes sense to assume that one is the same self* over the course of a life. Experience suggests otherwise, and thus the *Experience Principle* is weighted insufficiently in Person^{Locke}.

I can put the upshot in my terms. The forensic-narrative self that is Person^{Locke} is offered as a deep analysis of what a person is. But a better diagnosis is that Person^{Locke} is an analysis of a certain kind of construct from what a person really is that is not based on experience or self-experience, but is based on an abstraction from experience or self-experience, in particular one that can be offered in the public space where self-representation can traffic so that we can be held mutually accountable for our actions and coordinate our actions. Nothing much follows from how I self-express and self-represent publicly about how I experience myself overall, who I am, and what I seem like to myself, not even with how I self-express and self-represent for first-personal consumption. Thinking carefully about the ways we are all Persons[James] and, more than a few of us also Persons[Strawson], might make us skeptical that Person[Locke] is the right analysis of person-hood. It will realign philosophical analysis of persons with what the *Experience Principle* teaches, and make us more sensitive to the remarkable variety of kinds of persons.

References

Adolphs, Ralph 2002. "Recognizing emotion from facial expressions: Psychological and neurological mechanisms." *Behavioral and Cognitive Neuroscience Reviews* 1: 21–62.

Alston, William P. 1971. "Varieties of privileged access." *American Philosophical Quarterly* 8: 223–41.

Anscombe, G. Elizabeth M. 1975. "The first person." In Samuel Guttenplan (ed.) *Mind and Language*. Oxford University Press, 45–65. Reprinted in Cassam (1994), 140–59.

Aristotle 1907. *De Anima*. Trans. Robert Drew Hicks. Cambridge University Press.

Armstrong, David M. 1963. "Is introspective knowledge incorrigible?" *Philosophical Review* 72: 417–32.

   1968. *A Materialist Theory of the Mind*. London: Routledge & Kegan Paul.

   1980. "What is consciousness?" In David Armstrong, *The Nature of Mind*, St. Lucia, Queensland: University of Queensland Press, 55–67.

Ashwell, Lauren 2009. "Desires and dispositions." Ph.D. Thesis, MIT.

Astington, Janet W. 1993. *The Child's Discovery of the Mind*. Cambridge, MA: Harvard University Press.

Ayer, Alfred J. 1959. "Privacy." *Proceedings of the British Academy* 45: 43–65. Page reference to the reprint in Ayer (1963).

   1963. *The Concept of a Person and Other Essays*. London: Macmillan.

Bar-On, Dorit 2004. *Speaking My Mind: Expression and Self-Knowledge*. Oxford University Press.

Bartsch, Karen and Wellman, Henry M. 1995. *Children Talk About the Mind*. Oxford University Press.

Bayne, Timothy and Montague, Michelle (eds.) (forthcoming). *Cognitive Phenomenology*. Oxford University Press.

Bennett, Jonathan 1991. "How to read minds in behavior: A suggestion from a philosopher." In Andrew Whiten (ed.) *Natural Theories of Mind: Evolution, Development and Simulation of Everyday Mindreading*. Oxford: Basil Blackwell, 97–108.

Berger, Jacob (manuscript). "Intentionalism and representational qualitative character."

Bermúdez, José Luis 1998. *The Paradox of Self-Consciousness*, Cambridge, MA: MIT/Bradford.

Berridge, Kent and Robinson, Terry 2003. "Parsing reward." *Trends in Neurosciences* 26: 507–13.

Biran, Iftah and Chatterjee, Anjan 2004. "Alien hand syndrome." *Archives of Neurology* 61: 292–94.

Blakemore, Sarah-Jayne, Wolpert, Daniel, and Frith, Chris 2000. "Why can't you tickle yourself?" *NeuroReport* 11: R11–R16.

Blanke, Olaf and Metzinger, Thomas 2009. "Full-body illusions and minimal phenomenal selfhood." *Trends in Cognitive Science* 13: 7–13.

Block, Ned 1995. "On a confusion about a function of consciousness." *Behavioral and Brain Sciences* 18, 2 (June): 227–47.

Block, Ned and Stalnaker, Robert 1999. "Conceptual analysis, dualism, and the explanatory gap." *Philosophical Review* 108: 1–46.

Block, Ned, Flanagan, Owen J., and Güzeldere, Güven (eds.) 1997. *The Nature of Consciousness: Philosophical Debates.* Cambridge, MA: MIT Press.

Boër, Steven E. and Lycan, William G. 1980. "Who, me?" *Philosophical Review* 89, 3 (July): 427–66.

Boghossian, Paul 1997. "What the externalist can know a priori." *Proceedings of the Aristotelian Society* 97: 161–75.

Botvinick, Matthew and Cohen, Jonathan 1998. "Rubber hands 'feel' touch that eyes see." *Nature* 391: 756.

Breitmeyer, Bruno G. and Öğmen, Haluk 2006. *Visual Masking: Time Slices through Conscious and Unconscious Vision.* 2nd edition. Oxford University Press.

Brentano, Franz 1874. *Psychology from an Empirical Standpoint.* Ed. Oscar Kraus. English edition Linda L. McAlister. Trans. Anto C. Rancurello, D. B. Terrell, and Linda L. McAlister. London: Routledge & Kegan Paul, 1973.

Buras, Todd 2009. "An argument against causal theories of mental content." *American Philosophical Quarterly* 46: 117–30.

Burge, Tyler. 1979. "Individualism and the mental." *Midwest Studies in Philosophy* 4: 73–121.

  1988. "Individualism and self-knowledge." *Journal of Philosophy* 85: 649–63.

  1996. "Our entitlement to self-knowledge." *Proceedings of the Aristotelian Society* 96: 91–116.

  2003. "Memory and persons." *Philosophical Review* 112: 289–337.

Byrne, Alex 2005. "Introspection." *Philosophical Topics* 33, 1: 79–104.

  2011. "Transparency, belief, intention." *Proceedings of the Aristotelian Society* Supplementary Volume 85: 201–21.

Carpendale, Jeremy and Lewis, Charlie 2006. *How Children Develop Social Understanding.* Malden, MA: Blackwell Publishing.

Cassam, Quassim (ed.) 1994. *Self-Knowledge.* Oxford University Press.

Castañeda, Hector-Neri 1966. "He: A study in the logic of self-consciousness." *Ratio* 8: 130–57.

  1968. "On the logic of attributions of self-knowledge to others." *Journal of Philosophy* 65, 15: 439–56.

  1969. "On the phenomeno-logic of the I." *Proceedings of the 14th International Congress of Philosophy*, III: 200–206. Reprinted in Cassam (1994), 160–66.

Chalmers, David J. 1996. *The Conscious Mind*. Oxford University Press.

2002. "Consciousness and its place in nature." In David J. Chalmers (ed.), *Philosophy of Mind: Classical and Contemporary Readings*. Oxford University Press, 247–72.

2010. *The Character of Consciousness*. Oxford University Press.

Chalmers, David J. and Jackson, Frank C. 2001. "Conceptual analysis and reductive explanation." *Philosophical Review* 110: 315–61.

Chisholm, Roderick 1969. "On the observability of the self." *Philosophy and Phenomenological Research* 30: 7–21. Reprinted in Cassam (1994), 94–108.

1976. *Person and Object: A Metaphysical Study*. La Salle, IL: Open Court Publishing Company.

1981. *The First Person*. Minneapolis, MN: University of Minnesota Press.

Churchland, Paul M. 1985. "Reduction, qualia, and the direct introspection of brain states." *Journal of Philosophy* 82: 8–28.

1988. *Matter and Consciousness*, revised edition. Cambridge, MA: MIT Press.

Cole, Jonathan 1995. *Pride and A Daily Marathon*. Cambridge, MA: MIT Press.

Confucius [5th century BCE] 2003. *Analects*. Trans. Edward Slingerland. Indianapolis, IN: Hackett Publishing.

Critchley, Hugo D., Wiens, Stefan, Rotshtein, Pia, Ohman, Arne, and Dolan, Ray J. 2004. "Neural systems supporting interoceptive awareness." *Nature Neuroscience* 7: 189–95.

Damasio, Antonio 1994. *Descartes's Error: Emotion, Reason, and the Human Brain*. New York: G. P. Putnam's Sons.

1999. *The Feeling of What Happens: Body and Emotion in the Making of Consciousness*. New York: Harcourt.

Dancy, Jonathan 2000. *Practical Reality*. Oxford University Press.

Darwin, Charles [1872] 1965/2002. *The Expression of the Emotions in Man and Animals*. Ed. Paul Ekman. Oxford University Press.

Davidson, Donald 1984. "First person authority." *Dialectica* 38: 101–11. Page reference to the reprint in Davidson (2001).

1991. "Three varieties of knowledge." In A. Phillips Griffiths, (ed.) *A. J. Ayer Memorial Essays*. Cambridge University Press. Page reference to the reprint in Davidson (2001).

2001. *Inquiries into Truth and Interpretation*. 2nd edition. Oxford: Clarendon Press.

Davies, Martin 1998. "Externalism, architecturalism, and epistemic warrant." In Crispin Wright, Barry C. Smith, and Cynthia MacDonald (eds.) *Knowing Our Own Minds*. Oxford University Press, 321–61.

Dennett, Daniel C. 1992. *Consciousness Explained*. Boston, MA: Little, Brown and Company, Back Bay Books.

2002. "How could I be wrong? How wrong could I be?" *Journal of Consciousness Studies* 9, 5–6: 13–16.

De Ridder, Dirk, Van Laere, Koen, Dupont, Patrick, Menovsky, Thomas and Van de Heyning, Paul 2007. "Visualizing out-of-body experience in the brain." *New England Journal of Medicine* 357: 1829–33.

Descartes, René 1984. *The Philosophical Writings of Descartes*. (Eds.) John Cottingham, Robert Stoothoff, and Dugald Murdoch, vol. II. Cambridge University Press.

[1641] 1984. *Meditations on First Philosophy*. In Descartes, René 1984.

Dretske, Fred I. 1981. *Knowledge and the Flow of Information*. Cambridge, MA: MIT Press.

1988. *Explaining Behavior*. Cambridge, MA: MIT Press.

1995. *Naturalizing the Mind*. Cambridge, MA: MIT Press.

2003. "How do you know you are not a zombie?" In Brie Gertler (ed.) *Privileged Access and First-Person Authority*. Burlington, VT: Ashgate Publishing Company, 1–13.

DSM-IV 1994. *Diagnostic and Statistical Manual of Psychiatric Disorders*. 4th edition. Washington, DC: American Psychiatric Association.

du Boisgueheneuc, Foucaud, Levy, Richard, Volle, Emanuelle, Seassau, Magali, Duffau, Hughes, Kinkingnehun, Serge, Samson, Yves, Zhang, Sandy, and Dubois, Bruno 2006. "Functions of the left superior frontal gyrus in humans: A lesion study." *Brain* 129: 3315–28.

Einstein, Gillian and Flanagan, Owen 2003. "Sexual identities and narratives of self." In Gary Fireman, Ted McVay, and Owen Flanagan (eds.) *Narrative and Consciousness*. Oxford University Press, 209–32.

Ekman, Paul 2003. *Emotions Revealed: Recognizing Faces and Feelings to Improve Communication and Emotional Life*. New York and London: Times Books (US), Weidenfeld & Nicolson.

Eliot, George 1985. *Mill on the Floss*. Harmondsworth: Penguin Classics.

Evans, Gareth 1982a. "Demonstrative identification." In Evans (1982c), 142–266.

1982b. "Self-identification." From Evans (1982c). Reprinted in Cassam (1994), 184–209.

1982c. *The Varieties of Reference*. Ed. John McDowell. Oxford University Press.

Farrer, Chlöe, Franck, Nicolas, Georgieff, Nicolas, Frith, Chris D., Decety, Jean, and Jeannerod, Marc 2003. "Modulating the experience of agency." *Neuroimage* 18: 324–33.

Feit, Neil 2008. *Belief About the Self*. Oxford University Press.

Fernández, Jordi 2005. "Self-knowledge, rationality and Moore's paradox." *Philosophy and Phenomenological Research* 71: 533–56.

2007. "Desire and self-knowledge." *Australasian Journal of Philosophy* 85: 517–36.

Fiala, Brian (manuscript) "The phenomenology of explanation and the explanation of phenomenology."

(forthcoming). "Explaining the explanatory gap." Ph.D. Thesis. University of Arizona.

Finkelstein, David H. 2003. *Expression and the Inner*. Cambridge, MA: Harvard University Press.

Fitzgerald, Scott F. 2000. *This Side of Paradise*. Harmondsworth: Penguin Classics.

Flanagan, Owen J. 1990. "Identity and strong and weak evaluation." In Owen Flanagan and Amélic Oksenberg Rorty (eds.) *Identity, Character, and Morality*. Cambridge, MA: MIT Press, 37–65

1991. *Varieties of Moral Personality: Ethics and Psychological Realism*. Cambridge, MA: Harvard University Press.

1992. *Consciousness Reconsidered*. Cambridge, MA: MIT Press.

1995. "Deconstructing dreams: The spandrels of sleep." *Journal of Philosophy* 92: 5–27.

1996. *Self Expressions: Mind, Morals, and the Meaning of Life*. Oxford University Press.

2000. *Dreaming Souls: Sleep, Dreams, and the Evolution of the Conscious Mind*. Oxford University Press.

2002. *The Problem of the Soul: Two Visions of Mind and How to Reconcile Them*. New York: Basic Books.

2003; revised 2009. "Emotional expressions." In Jonathan S. Hodge and Gregory Radick (eds.) *The Cambridge Companion to Darwin*. Cambridge University Press, 413–34.

2007. *The Really Hard Problem: Meaning in a Material World*. Cambridge, MA: MIT Press.

Flavell, John H. 2003. *Development of Children's Knowledge About the Mind: The Heinz Werner Lectures*. Worcester, MA: Clark University Press.

Flavell, John H., Miller, Patricia, and Miller, Scott 1993. *Cognitive Development*. Englewood Cliffs, NJ: Prentice Hall.

Fodor, Jerry A. 1990. *A Theory of Content and Other Essays*. Cambridge MA: MIT Press.

Ford, Jason 2008. "Attention and the new skeptics." *Journal of Consciousness Studies* 15, 3: 59–86.

Frith, Chris D. 2007. *Making up the Mind: How the Brain Creates Our Mental World*. Malden, MA: Blackwell Publishing.

Frith, Chris D., Blakemore, Sarah-J., and Wolpert, Daniel M. 2000. "Abnormalities in the awareness and control of action." *Philosophical Transactions of the Royal Society of London* B355: 1771–88.

Furnham, Adrian 2001. "Self-estimates of intelligence: Culture and gender differences in self and other estimates of both general (g) and multiple intelligences." *Personality and Individual Differences* 31: 1381–1405.

Gallois, André 1996. *The World Without, the Mind Within: An Essay on First-Person Authority*. Cambridge University Press.

Gallup, Gordon 1970. "Chimpanzees: self-recognition." *Science* 167: 86–87.

1979. *Self-Recognition in Chimpanzees and Man: A Developmental and Comparative Perspective*. New York: Plenum Press.

Gazzaniga, Michael 1985. *The Social Brain*. New York: Basic Books.

Geach, Peter T. 1957. "On beliefs about oneself." *Analysis* 18, 1: 23–24. Reprinted in Geach, *Logic Matters*. Oxford: Basil Blackwell, 1972, 128–29.

Gennaro, Rocco J. 2004. "Higher-order thoughts, animal consciousness, and misrepresentation: A reply to Carruthers and Levine." In Rocco J. Gennaro (ed.) *Higher-Order Theories of Consciousness*. Amsterdam and Philadelphia: John Benjamins, 45–66.

2006. "Between pure self-referentialism and the (extrinsic) HOT theory of consciousness." In Uriah Kriegel and Kenneth Williford (eds.) *Self-Representational Approaches to Consciousness*. Cambridge, MA: MIT Press/A Bradford Book, 221–48.

Gertler, Brie 2011. "Self-knowledge and the transparency of belief." In A. Hatzimoysis (ed.) *Self-Knowledge*. Oxford University Press.

Giberman, Dan. 2010. "Glop theory: A new trope ontology." Ph.D. thesis, Stanford.

Goldberg, Ilan I., Harel, Michal, and Malach, Rafael 2006. "When the brain loses itself: Prefrontal inactivation during sensorimotor processing." *Neuron* 50: 329–39.

Goldman, Alvin I. 1993. "The psychology of folk psychology." *Behavioral and Brain Sciences* 16: 15–28.

2000. "Folk psychology and mental concepts." *Protosociology* 14: 4–25.

2006. *Simulating Minds*. Oxford University Press.

Gopnik, Alison 1993. "How we know our minds: The illusion of first person knowledge of intentionality." *Behavioral and Brain Sciences* 16: 1–14.

Gordon, Robert M. 1995. "Simulation without introspection or inference from me to you." In Martin Davies, and Tony Stone (eds.) *Mental Simulation: Evaluations and Applications – Readings in Mind and Language*. Oxford: Blackwell Publishing, 52–67.

1996. "'Radical' simulationism." In Peter Carruthers, and Peter K. Smith (eds.) *Theories of Theories of Mind*. Cambridge University Press, 11–21.

2007. "Ascent routines for propositional attitudes." *Synthese* 159: 151–65.

Gosling, Samuel D., John, Oliver P., Craik, Kenneth H., and Robins, Richard W. 1998. "Do people know how they behave? Self-reported act frequencies compared with on-line codings by observers." *Journal of Personality and Social Psychology* 74: 1337–49.

Hall, Lars, Johansson, Petter, Tärning, Betty, Sikström, Sverker, and Deutgen, Thérèse 2010. "Magic at the marketplace: Choice blindness for the taste of jam and the smell of tea." *Cognition* 117, 1 (October): 54–61.

Haslanger, Sally 2008. "Changing the ideology and culture of philosophy: Not by reason (alone)." *Hypatia* 28, 2: 210–23.

Hatfield, Elaine, Cacioppo, John T., and Rapson, Richard L. 1993. "Emotional contagion." *Current Directions in Psychological Science* 2: 96–99.

Haybron, Daniel 2008. *The Pursuit of Unhappiness*. Oxford University Press.

Heil, John 1988. "Privileged access." *Mind* 97: 238–51.

Hohwy, Jakob 2007. "The sense of self in the phenomenology of agency and perception." *Psyche* 1, 2: 1–20.

Horgan, Terence and Tienson, John 2002. "The intentionality of phenomenology and the phenomenology of intentionality." In David J. Chalmers (ed.) *Philosophy of Mind: Classical and Contemporary Readings*. Oxford University Press. 520–33.

Hume, David [1739] 2000. *A Treatise of Human Nature.* Ed. David Fate Norton and Mary J. Norton. Oxford University Press. Some texts refer to the [1739] 1978 edition: Ed. L. A. Selby-Bigge and P. H. Nidditch. Oxford: Clarendon Press.

Hurlburt, Russell T. and Heavey, Christopher L. 2006. *Exploring Inner Experience.* Amsterdam: John Benjamins.

Hurlburt, Russell T., and Schwitzgebel, Eric 2007. *Describing Inner Experience? Proponent Meets Skeptic.* Cambridge, MA: MIT Press.

   2011. "Presuppositions and background assumptions." *Journal of Consciousness Studies.*

Israel, David J. and Perry, John 1990. "What is information?" In Philip P. Hansonx (ed.) *Information, Language and Cognition.* Vancouver, Canada: University of British Columbia Press, 1–19.

James, William [1890] 2010. *The Principles of Psychology.* Volumes I & II. New York: Cosimo.

   [1892] 1984. "The stream of consciousness." In William James, *Psychology: Briefer Course.* Cambridge, MA: Harvard University Press, 151–75.

Johansson, Petter, Hall, Lars, Sikström, Sverker, and Olsson, Andreas 2005. "Failure to detect mismatches between intention and outcome in a simple decision task." *Science* 310, 5745 (October 7): 116–19.

John, Oliver P. and Robins, Richard W. 1993. "Determinants of inter-judge agreement on personality traits: The Big Five domains, observability, evaluativeness, and the unique perspective of the self." *Journal of Personality* 61: 521–51.

Kane, Michael J. 2011. "Describing, debating, and discovering inner experience: Review of Hurlburt and Schwitzgebel 2007, '*Describing Inner Experience? Proponent Meets Skeptic*'." *Journal of Consciousness Studies.*

Kant, Immanuel [1787]1933/1998. *Critique of Pure Reason.* Trans. and ed. Paul Guyer and Allen W. Wood. Cambridge University Press.

Kaplan, David 1989. "Demonstratives." In Joseph Almog, John Perry, and Howard Wettstein (eds.) *Themes From Kaplan.* Oxford University Press, 481–563.

Karnath, Hans-Otto, Baier, Bau, and Nägele, Thomas 2005. "Awareness of the functioning of one's own limbs mediated by the insular cortex?" *Journal of Neuroscience* 25: 7134–38.

Keysers, Christian, Wicker, Bruno, Gazzola, Valeria, Anton, Jean-Luc, Fogassi, Leonardo and Gallese, Vittorio 2004. "A touching sight: SII/PV activation during the observation and experience of touch." *Neuron* 42: 335–46.

Klein, Stanley B. 2010. "The self: As a construct in psychology and neuropsychological evidence for its multiplicity." *WIREs Cognitive Science* 1, 2 (March/April): 172–83.

Koch, Christof 2004. *The Quest for Consciousness.* New York: Routledge.

Korta, Kepa and Perry, John (forthcoming). *Critical Pragmatics.* Cambridge University Press.

Koyama, Tetsuo, McHaffie, John G., Laurienti, Paul J., and Coghill, Robert C. 2005. "The subjective experience of pain: Where expectations become reality." *PNAS* 102, 36 (September 6): 12950–55.

Kriegel, Uriah 2003. "Consciousness as intransitive self-consciousness: Two views and an argument." *Canadian Journal of Philosophy* 33: 103–32.

2004. "Consciousness and self-consciousness." *The Monist* 87: 182–205.

2005. "Naturalizing subjective character." *Philosophy and Phenomenological Research* 71: 23–57.

2009. *Subjective Consciousness: A Self-Representational Theory*. Oxford University Press.

Kripke, Saul. 1980. *Naming and Necessity*. Cambridge, MA: Harvard University Press.

Kruger, Justin and Dunning, David. 1999. "Unskilled and unaware of it: The difficulties in recognizing one's own incompetence lead to inflated self-assessments." *Journal of Personality and Social Psychology* 77: 1121–34.

Kusch, Martin 1999. *Psychological Knowledge*. London: Routledge.

Kwan, Virginia S. Y., John, Oliver P., Robins, Richard W., and Kuang, Lu L. 2008. "Conceptualizing and assessing self-enhancement bias: A componential approach." *Journal of Personality and Social Psychology* 94: 1062–77.

Levine, Joseph 1983. "Materialism and qualia: The explanatory gap." *Pacific Philosophical Quarterly* 64: 354–61.

1993. "On leaving out what it's like." In M. Davies, and G. Humphreys (eds.) *Consciousness: Psychological and Philosophical Essays*. Oxford: Blackwell Publishing, 121–36.

2001. *Purple Haze: The Puzzle of Consciousness*. Oxford University Press.

2006. "Conscious awareness and (self-)representation." In Uriah Kriegel and Kenneth Williford (eds.) *Self-Representational Approaches to Consciousness*. Cambridge MA: MIT Press, 173–97.

Lewis, David 1972. "Psychophysical and theoretical identifications." *Australasian Journal of Philosophy* 50,3 (December): 249–58.

1979. "Attitudes *de dicto* and *de se*." *Philosophical Review* 88, 4 (October): 513–43.

Lewis, Michael 1993. "Self-conscious emotions: Embarrassment, pride, shame and guilt." In Michael Lewis and Jeannette M. Haviland-Jones (eds.) *Handbook of Emotions*. New York: Guildford Press, 563–73.

1995. "Embarrassment: The emotion of self-exposure and evaluation." In June Price Tangney and Kurt W. Fischer (eds.) *Self-conscious Emotions: The Psychology of Shame, Guilt, Embarrassment and Pride*. New York: Guildford Press, 192–218.

Lewis, Michael and Brooks-Gunn, Jeanne 1979. *Social Cognition and the Acquisition of Self*. New York: Plenum Press.

Libet, Benjamin 2004. *Mind Time: The Temporal Factor in Consciousness*. Cambridge, MA: Harvard University Press.

Libet, Benjamin, Wright, Elwood W. Jr., Feinstein, Bertram, and Pearl, Dennis K. 1979. "Subjective referral of the timing for a conscious sensory experience: A functional role for the somatosensory specific projection system in man." *Brain* 102, 1 (March): 193–224.

Lichtenberg, Georg C. [1765–99]1990. *The Waste Books*. Trans. Reginald. J. Hollingdale. New York Review of Books.

Loar, Brian 1987. "Subjective intentionality." *Philosophical Topics* 15: 89–124.

2003. "Phenomenal intentionality as the basis for mental content." In Martin Hahn and Bjørn Ramberg (eds.) *Reflections and Replies: Essays on the Philosophy of Tyler Burge*. Cambridge, MA: MIT Press, 229–57.

Locke, John [1689/1700]1975. *An Essay Concerning Human Understanding*. Ed. Peter H. Nidditch. Oxford: Clarendon Press.

Lycan, William G. 1987. *Consciousness*. Cambridge, MA: MIT Press.

1996. *Consciousness and Experience*. Cambridge, MA: MIT Press/Bradford Books.

2004. "The superiority of HOP to HOT." In Rocco J. Gennaro (ed.) *Higher-Order Theories of Consciousness*. Amsterdam and Philadelphia: John Benjamins, 93–113.

Marcel, Anthony J. 1983a. "Conscious and unconscious perception: An approach to the relations between phenomenal experience and perceptual processes." *Cognitive Psychology* 15, 2 (April 1983): 238–300.

1983b. "Conscious and unconscious perception: Experiments on visual masking and word recognition." *Cognitive Psychology* 15, 2 (April 1983): 197–237.

McAllister, Margaret M. 2000. "Dissociative identity disorder: A literature review." *Journal of Psychiatric and Mental Health Nursing* 7, 1 (February): 25–33.

McFetridge, Ian 1990. "Explicating 'x knows *a priori* that p'." In John Haldane and Roger Scruton (eds.) *Logical Necessity and Other Essays*. London: Aristotelian Society, 213–32.

McGinn, Colin 1975/6. "*A posteriori* and *a priori* knowledge." *Proceedings of the Aristotelian Society* 76: 195–208.

McKay, Ryan T. and Dennett, Daniel C. (2009). "The evolution of misbelief." *Behavioral and Brain Sciences* 32: 493–561.

McKinsey, Michael 1991. "Anti-individualism and privileged access." *Analysis* 51: 9–16.

Millikan, Ruth G. 1984. *Language, Thought, and Other Biological Categories*. Cambridge, MA: MIT Press.

1990. "The myth of the essential indexical." *Noûs* 24, 5: 723–34.

Moore, Don A. and Healy, Paul J. (2008). "The trouble with overconfidence." *Psychological Review* 115: 502–17.

Moran, Richard 2001. *Authority and Estrangement*. Princeton University Press.

Moro, Valentina, Zampini, Massimiliano, and Aglioti, Salvatore M. 2004. "Changes in spatial position of hands modify tactile extinction but not disownership of contralesional hand in two right brain-damaged patients." *Neurocase*, 10: 437–43.

Nagel, Thomas 1965. "Physicalism." *Philosophical Review* 74, 3 (July): 339–56.

1970. *The Possibility of Altruism*. Oxford University Press.

1979. "What is it like to be a bat?" *Philosophical Review* 83, 4 (October 1974): 435–50. Reprinted in *Mortal Questions*. Cambridge University Press, 1979, 165–79.

1983. "The objective self." In Carl Ginet and Sydney Shoemaker (eds.) *Knowledge and Mind*. Oxford University Press, 211–32.

Ney, Alyssa 2008. "Physicalism as an attitude." *Philosophical Studies* 138: 1–15.

Nichols, Shaun and Stich, Stephen 2003. *Mindreading: An Integrated Account of Pretence, Self-Awareness, and Understanding Other Minds.* Oxford University Press.

Nietzsche, Friedrich [1886]2009. *Beyond Good and Evil.* Trans. Ian Johnson. Arlington, VA: Richer Resources Publications. Ebook edition: http://ebooks. adelaide.edu.au/n/nietzsche/friedrich/n67b/complete.html

   [1901]1968. *The Will to Power.* Trans. Walter Kaufmann and Reginald J. Hollingdale. Ed. Walter Kaufmann. New York: Vintage Books.

   1997. *Daybreak: Thoughts on the Prejudices of Morality.* Trans. Reginald J. Hollingdale. Ed. Maudemarie Clark, and Brian Leiter. Cambridge University Press.

Nisbett, Richard E. and Wilson, Timothy DeCamp 1977. "Telling more than we can know: Verbal reports on mental processes." *Psychological Review 84,* 3 (May): 231–59.

Olson, Eric 1999. *The Human Animal: Personal Identity without Psychology.* Oxford University Press.

Ornstein, Robert 1986. *Multiminds: A New Way to Look at Human Behavior.* Boston: Houghton Mifflin.

Parfit, Derek 1971. "Personal identity." *Philosophical Review* 88: 3–27.

Paulus, Delroy L., Lysy, Daria C., and Yik, Michelle S. M. 1998. "Self-report measures of intelligence: Are they useful as proxy IQ tests?" *Journal of Personality* 66: 525–54.

Peacocke, Christopher 1983. *Sense and Content.* Oxford University Press.

Peirce, Charles S. [1898]1935. *Collected Papers.* Vol. VI. Ed. Charles Hartshorne and Paul Weiss. Cambridge, MA: Harvard University Press.

Perry, John 1979. "The problem of the essential indexical." *Noûs* 13, 1 (March): 3–21. Reprinted in Perry (2000).

   1986. "Thought without representation." *Supplementary Proceedings of the Aristotelian Society* 60: 263–83. Reprinted in Perry (2000).

   1998. "Myself and I." In Marcelo Stamm (ed.), *Philosophie in Synthetischer Absicht.* Stuttgart: Klett-Cotta, 83–103. Reprinted in Perry (2000).

   2000. *The Problem of the Essential Indexical and other Essays.* Oxford University Press, 1993. New, expanded edition, Stanford: CSLI, 2000.

   2001a. *Knowledge, Possibility, and Consciousness.* Cambridge, MA: MIT Press.

   2001b. *Reference and Reflexivity.* Stanford: CSLI Publications. 2nd edition forthcoming, 2011.

   2002. *Identity, Personal Identity and the Self.* Indianapolis, IN: Hackett Publishing.

   2011 (forthcoming). "On knowing one's self."

Pollock, John L. and Cruz, Joseph 1999. *Contemporary Theories of Knowledge.* 2nd edition. Oxford: Rowman & Littlefield.

Prinz, Jesse J. 2004. *Gut Reactions: A Perceptual Theory of Emotion.* Oxford University Press.

Prior, Arthur N. 1967. "On spurious egocentricity." *Philosophy* 42, 162 (October): 326–35.

Putnam, Hilary 1975. "The meaning of 'meaning'." In Hilary Putnam, *Mind, Language and Reality, Philosophical Papers*, vol. ii. Cambridge University Press, 215–71.

Rosenthal, David M. 1990. "A theory of consciousness." ZiF Technical Report 40, Bielfield, Germany. Reprinted in Block *et al.* (1997), 729–54.

    2002. "Explaining consciousness." In David J. Chalmers (ed.) *Philosophy of Mind: Contemporary and Classical Readings*. Oxford University Press, 406–21.

    2004a. "Being conscious of ourselves." *The Monist* 87, 2 (April): 159–81.

    2004b. "Varieties of higher-order theory." In Rocco J. Gennaro (ed.) *Higher-Order Theories of Consciousness*. Amsterdam and Philadelphia: John Benjamins, 17–44.

    2005. *Consciousness and Mind*. Oxford: Clarendon Press.

    2011 (forthcoming). "How to think about mental qualities." *Philosophical Issues* 20.

Ross, Colin A. 1997. *Multiple Personality Disorder: Diagnosis, Clinical Features, and Treatment*. New York: John Wiley and Sons.

Rovane, Carol 1990. "Branching self-consciousness." *Philosophical Review* 99: 355–95.

Ruby, Perrine and Decety, Jean 2001. "Effect of the subjective perspective taking during simulation of action: A PET investigation of agency." *Nature Neuroscience* 4: 546–50.

Rust, Joshua and Schwitzgebel, Eric (in preparation). "Ethicists' and non-ethicists' responsiveness to undergraduate emails."

Ryle, Gilbert 1949. *The Concept of Mind*. London: Hutchinson. Page references to the Penguin Books edition, 1980.

Sartre, Jean Paul 1939 (translation 1962). *Nausea*. Trans. Lloyd Alexander. New York: New Directions.

    1969. *Being and Nothingness*. Trans. Hazel E. Barnes. Oxford: Routledge.

Saul, Jennifer (forthcoming). "Unconscious influences and women in philosophy." In F. Jenkins and K. Hutchison (eds.) *Women in Philosophy*. Newcastle upon Tyne: Cambridge Scholars Publishing.

Saxe, Rebecca and Powell, Lindsey J. 2006. "It is the thought that counts: Specific brain regions for one component of theory of mind." *Psychological Science* 17: 692–99.

Scanlon, Thomas 1998. *What We Owe to Each Other*. Cambridge, MA: Harvard University Press.

Schnider, Armin 2008. *The Confabulating Mind: How the Brain Creates Reality*. Oxford University Press.

Schueler, George F. 1995. *Desire: Its Role in Practical Reason and the Explanation of Action*. Cambridge, MA: MIT Press.

Schwitzgebel, Eric 2002a. "How well do we know our own conscious experience? The case of visual imagery." *Journal of Consciousness Studies* 9, 5–6: 35–53.

    2002b. "A phenomenal, dispositional account of belief." *Noûs* 36: 249–75.

    2008. "The unreliability of naive introspection." *Philosophical Review* 117: 245–73.

    2010. "Acting contrary to our professed beliefs, or the gulf between occurrent judgment and dispositional belief." *Pacific Philosophical Quarterly* 91: 531–53.

2011. *Perplexities of Consciousness*. Cambridge, MA: MIT Press.

(forthcoming). "Introspection, what?" In Declan Smithies and Daniel Stoljar (eds.) *Introspection and Consciousness*. Oxford University Press.

Schwitzgebel, Eric and Gordon, Michael S. 2000. "How well do we know our own experience? The case of human echolocation." *Philosophical Topics* 28: 235–46.

Schwitzgebel, Eric and Rust, Joshua (in preparation). "The self-reported moral behavior of ethics professors."

Shoemaker, Sydney 1963. *Self-knowledge and Self-identity*. Ithaca, NY: Cornell University Press.

1968. "Self-reference and self-awareness." *Journal of Philosophy* 65, 19: 555–67. Reprinted with slight revisions in Shoemaker, *Identity, Cause, and Mind: Philosophical Essays*. Cambridge University Press, 1984; expanded edition, Oxford: Clarendon Press, 2003, 6–18.

1970. "Persons and their pasts." *American Philosophical Quarterly* 7, 4: 269–85.

1976. "Embodiment and behavior." In Amélie Oksenberg Rorty (ed.) *The Identities of Persons*. Berkeley and Los Angeles: University of California Press, 109–38.

1986. "Introspection and the self." In Peter A. French, Theodore E. Vehling and Howard K. Wettstein (eds.) *Studies in the Philosophy of Mind. Midwest Studies in Philosophy* 10. 101–20. Reprinted in Cassam (1994), 118–39.

1988. "On knowing one's own mind." *Philosophical Perspectives* 2: 183–209.

1994. "Self-knowledge and 'inner sense'." *Philosophy and Phenomenological Research* 54: 249–314. Page reference to the reprint in Shoemaker (1996).

1995. "Moore's paradox and self-knowledge." *Philosophical Studies* 77: 211–28.

1996. *The First-Person Perspective and Other Essays*. Cambridge University Press.

2003. "Consciousness and co-consciousness." In Axel Cleeremans (ed.) *The Unity of Consciousness: Binding, Integration, and Dissociation*. Oxford: Clarendon Press, 59–71.

2009. "Careers and quareers: A reply to Burge." *Philosophical Review* 118: 87–102.

Shynkaruk, Jody M. and Thompson, Valerie A. 2006. "Confidence and accuracy in deductive reasoning." *Memory and Cognition* 34: 619–32.

Sidelle, Alan 2002. "Some episodes in the sameness of consciousness." *Philosophical Topics* 30: 269–93.

Smith, Michael 1994. *The Moral Problem*. Oxford: Blackwell.

Spener, Maja and Bayne, Timothy 2010. "Introspective humility." In Ernest Sosa and Enrique Villanueva (eds.) *Philosophical Issues* 20: 1–22.

Spinoza, Benedictus de. 1677. *Ethics*. Trans. Edwin Curley in *The Collected Writings of Spinoza*. Princeton University Press, 1985, volume 1.

Steinmayr, Ricarda and Spinath, Birgit 2009. "What explains boys' stronger confidence in their intelligence?" *Sex Roles* 61: 736–49.

Strawson, Galen 1999. "Self and body: Self, body, and experience." *Proceedings of the Aristotelian Society*, 73, 307–32.

2004. "Against narrativity." *Ratio* 17 (December): 428–52.

2009. *Selves: An Essay in Revisionary Metaphysics*. Oxford: Clarendon Press.

Strawson, Peter F. 1959. *Individuals: An Essay in Descriptive Metaphysics*. London: Methuen & Co. Ltd.

1966. *The Bounds of Sense*. London: Methuen & Co. Ltd.

1994. "The first-person: and others." In Cassam (1994), 210–15.

Taylor, Shelley E. and Brown, Jonathon D. 1988. "Illusion and well-being: A social psychological perspective on mental health." *Psychological Bulletin* 103: 193–210.

Thomson, Judith Jarvis 2008. *Normativity*. Chicago: Open Court.

Tsakiris, Manos 2010. "My body in the brain: A neurocognitive model of body-ownership." *Neuropsychologia* 48: 703–12.

Tsakiris, Manos, Hesse, Maike, Boy, Christian, Haggard, Patrick, and Fink, Gereon R. 2007. "Neural correlates of body-ownership: A sensory network for bodily self-consciousness." *Cerebral Cortex* 17, 10: 2235–44.

Tunik, Eugene, Lo, On-Yee, and Adamovich, Sergei V. 2008. "Transcranial magnetic stimulation to the frontal operculum and supramarginal gyrus disrupts planning of outcome-based hand-object interactions." *Journal of Neuroscience* 28: 14422–27.

Vazire, Simine 2010. "Who knows what about a person? The Self–Other Knowledge Asymmetry (SOKA) model." *Journal of Personality and Social Psychology* 98: 281–300.

Vendler, Zeno 1972. *Res Cogitans: An Essay in Rational Psychology*. Ithaca, NY: Cornell University Press.

Visser, Beth A., Ashton, Michael C., and Vernon, Philip A. 2008. "What makes you think you're so smart? Measured abilities, personality, and sex differences in relation to self-estimates of multiple intelligences." *Journal of Individual Differences* 29: 35–44.

Vosgerau, Gottfried and Newen, Albert 2007. "Thoughts, motor actions, and the self." *Mind & Language* 22: 22–43.

Wegner, Daniel M. 2002. *The Illusion of Conscious Will*. Cambridge, MA: MIT Press.

Wegner, Daniel M. and Wheatley, Thalia P. 1999. "Apparent mental causation: Sources of the experience of will." *American Psychologist* 54: 480–92.

Weisberg, Josh 2008. "Same old, same old: The same-order representation theory of consciousness and the division of phenomenal labor." *Synthese* 160, 2 (January): 161–81.

Wiggins, David 1967. *Identity and Spatio-Temporal Continuity*. Oxford: Basil Blackwell.

Williams, Bernard 1957. "Personal identity and individuation." *Proceedings of the Aristotelian Society*, New Series 57: 229–52. Reprinted in Bernard Williams, *Problems of the Self*. Cambridge University Press, 1999, 1–18.

Williamson, Timothy 1995. "Is knowing a state of mind?" *Mind* 104: 533–65.

2004. "Armchair philosophy, metaphysical modality and counterfactual thinking." *Proceedings of the Aristotelian Society* 105: 1–23.

Wittgenstein, Ludwig [1958] 1969. *The Blue and Brown Books*. 2nd edition. Oxford: Basil Blackwell.

1974. *Tractatus Logico-Philosophicus*. Trans. David F. Pears and Brian F. McGuinness. Revised edition. London and New York: Routledge.

1984. *Notebooks: 1914–1916.* 2nd edition. University of Chicago Press.

Wolpert, Daniel M., Ghahramani, Zoubin, and Jordan, Michael I. 1995. "An internal model for sensorimotor integration." *Science* 269: 1880–82.

Xunzi [3rd century BCE] 2005. "Cultivating oneself." Trans. Eric Hutton. In Philip J. Ivanhoe and Bryan W. Van Norden (eds.) *Readings in Classical Chinese Philosophy*, 2nd edition. Indianapolis: Hackett, 261–67.

Yun, Richard, Krystal, John H., and Mathalon, Daniel H. 2010. "Working memory overload: Fronto-limbic interactions and effects on subsequent working memory function." *Brain Imaging and Behavior* 4: 96–108.

Zahavi, Dan and Parnas, Josef 1998. "Phenomenal consciousness and self-awareness: A phenomenological critique of representational theory." *Journal of Consciousness Studies* 5, 5–6: 687–705.

Index

Italicized numbers refer to footnotes.

21412128R00156

Made in the USA
Middletown, DE
28 June 2015